Operation ANADYR

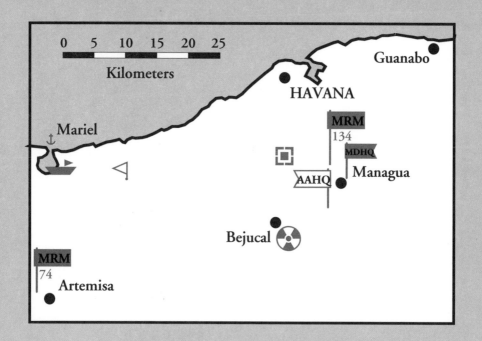

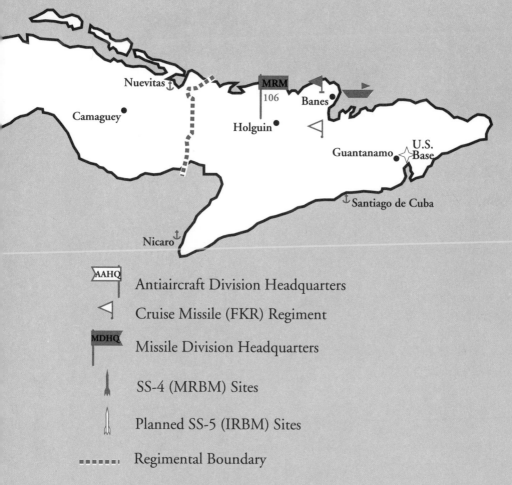

AAHQ	Antiaircraft Division Headquarters
◁	Cruise Missile (FKR) Regiment
MDHQ	Missile Division Headquarters
SS-4 icon	SS-4 (MRBM) Sites
SS-5 icon	Planned SS-5 (IRBM) Sites
▪▪▪▪▪▪▪	Regimental Boundary

Operation ANADYR

U.S. and Soviet Generals Recount the Cuban Missile Crisis

by
General Anatoli I. Gribkov
and
General William Y. Smith

Edited by Alfred Friendly, Jr.

With a Foreword by Michael R. Beschloss

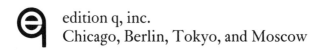
edition q, inc.
Chicago, Berlin, Tokyo, and Moscow

Chapters 1 through 5 are based on *Im Dienste der Sowjetunion*, published by edition q Verlags-GmbH, Berlin.

Excerpts from Robert F. Kennedy, *Thirteen Days: A memoir of the Cuban missile crisis*, W. W. Norton, New York, 1969, reprinted with permission. Copyright © 1971, 1969 by W. W. Norton & Company, Inc. Copyright © 1968 by McCall Corporation. Excerpt from *On the Brink: Americans and Soviets Reexamine the Cuban Missile Crisis*, by James Blight and David Welch, copyright © 1989, 1990 by James Blight and David Welch, reprinted by permission of Hill & Wang, a division of Farrar Straus & Giroux, Inc.

Library of Congress Cataloging-In-Publication Data:

Gribkov, A. I.
    Operation ANADYR: U.S. and Soviet generals recount the Cuban missile crisis / by Anatoli I. Gribkov and William Y. Smith; edited by Alfred Friendly, Jr., with a foreword by Michael R. Beschloss.
      p.   cm.
    Includes bibliographical references and index.
    ISBN 0-86715-266-4
    1. Cuban Missile Crisis, 1962.   2. Cuban Missile Crisis, 1962—
Sources. I. Smith, William Y. II. Friendly, Alfred, 1938- .
III. Title.
E841.G675   1994
909.82'6—dc20   93–35789
                                                            CIP

Manufactured in the United States of America

Contents

Foreword

For nearly three decades after the Cuban Missile Crisis, the history of that most dangerous episode remained largely secret. Since Soviet military doctrine held secrecy to be such a vital part of national security, the diplomatic, political and military archives of the Soviet Union were completely concealed. With the exception of Nikita Khrushchev (in his 1974 memoirs, smuggled out to the West), no Soviet official involved in the crisis would speak of it to westerners. To understand the Cuban perspective on the crisis, we had little more than Fidel Castro's gasconading before audiences large and small, which often owed more to fable than truth.

Despite ancient American boasts about freedom of information, American sources were also surprisingly fragmentary. Cold War sensitivities caused U.S. documents as harmless as the record of John Kennedy's 1961 talks with Khrushchev at Vienna (which had been heavily paraphrased and quoted from in books and public prints since at least the mid-1960s, and which was hardly a secret to the Soviets) to be classifed for twenty-nine years. Veterans of Kennedy's government were delighted to speak of a crisis in which their President's (and their own) performance was viewed as uniformly heroic, but in most cases these reminiscences were unprompted and uncorrected by the classified record, which told a different story.

The result of all of this was that for almost thirty years, the history of the Cuban Missile Crisis was like a needle stuck on a phonograph record. Deprived of the new sources they needed, scholars and citizens were compelled to view the crisis in terms of a passion play pitting a consistently masterful American President against an irrational Soviet dictator and an unstable Cuban. To break through that cliche, we needed exactly the kind of information and interpretation offered in this volume.

Performing simultaneously as memoirists and as scholars, the two authors of *Operation ANADYR* offer an unusual perspective on the events of 1962. Both are senior military men intimately involved—at different levels and on opposing sides—in the missile crisis. They are the first members of their profession who witnessed the confrontation to explore it with the depth that the reader will find in these pages.

A general officer in May 1962, Anatoli I. Gribkov oversaw the deployment of Soviet troops and weapons to Cuba. Then-Major William Y. Smith, an assistant to General Maxwell Taylor in the White House and at the Joint Chiefs of Staff, witnessed the Kennedy government's effort to fathom Soviet intentions in the crisis and fashion a response. In this volume, General Gribkov describes a Soviet military establishment rising with unquestioning obedience and surprising speed to implement Nikita Khrushchev's designs for Cuba. General Smith describes a Pentagon command structure demoralized by previous clashes with its civilian masters and anxious to use overwhelming force against Cuba both to eliminate the external threat and to regain President Kennedy's confidence.

As this book relates, the momentum that nearly brought these two "ignorant armies" into the conflict was potentially more destructive than political leaders understood at the time. General Gribkov, who in recent years was the first to disclose the presence of tactical nuclear weapons in the Soviet arsenal on Cuba, provides the alarming details of their deployment and of Khrushchev's cavalier attitude toward their possible use. Grounded on newly declassified material from Soviet archives, Gribkov's account adds a new dimension of risk to the history of the Cuban Missile Crisis and the Cold War.

General Smith combines his own research into newly opened CIA and Pentagon files with his own recollections to describe in new detail the divisions within the Kennedy administration over Cuba—between avenging the Bay of Pigs humiliation and learning to live with Castro. These mixed signals confused even the canniest observers in 1962. One need not take at face value General Gribkov's description of Operation ANADYR as a Soviet mission to rescue Cuba to understand why both Moscow and Havana thought that a U.S. attack was imminent.

This book takes the reader into the closed rooms of the drama and throws new light on lingering questions. By focusing on the sources of the crisis more than the better-known period of its climax, Generals Gribkov and Smith document how close to the precipice we all came. Both the Soviet and American authors insist in this book that their respective superiors were determined to avoid war. Their separate narratives, ably edited by the longtime student of American-Soviet affairs, Alfred Friendly, Jr., show two great powers stumbling—often through actions and reactions undertaken with little debate or forethought—into confrontation and near-disaster.

Thankfully, as the shadow of global nuclear war recedes, such issues are moving from the realm of current politics into history. Now that the Cold War and the Soviet Union are receding memories, and Cuba is on the way to becoming a very different kind of society, we can begin to see the Cuban Missile Crisis whole and to reach final judgments on these and other basic questions. Scholars and citizens who are crafting those judgments must take account of this book.

—MICHAEL R. BESCHLOSS

Author of *The Crisis Years: Kennedy and Khrushchev, 1960–1963,* 1991.

Preface

This unique book brings together two men who are former adversaries and virtual strangers to provide the first detailed accounts of the 1962 Cuban Missile Crisis by military officers with firsthand knowledge of the episode. As a memoir of the Cold War, it breaks new ground in presenting authoritative U.S. and Soviet military points of view in a single volume. As a work of research, moreover, it has been enriched by its authors' access to long-closed official archives in Washington and Moscow.

The opening of those files has been the slow work of many hands. A key force in the United States has been the persistence of the National Security Archive in Washington, D.C. Its personnel, files and publications made an invaluable contribution to this book. Equally valuable work on clarifying and amplifying the record has come from the Cuban Missile Crisis Project at Brown University's Center for Foreign Policy Development. In the course of five conferences organized by the Project between 1987 and 1992, U.S., Soviet and Cuban experts have been able to draw out both individual judgments and official documents that might otherwise have remained secret. Without such diligent scholarship, this book would not have come into being.

The meeting in Havana organized by the Cuban Missile Crisis Project in January 1992 brought Generals Anatoli I. Gribkov and William Y. Smith together for the first and only time. As authors of this study, they have since worked completely independently of one another. Connecting them was the inspiration and accomplishment of Henno Lohmeyer, the U.S. representative of edition q, which published General Gribkov's memoirs, *Im Dienste der Sowjet-*

union, in German in 1992. That book told the story of the author's military career, of a peasant's son who saw combat as a tank officer in the Russo-Finnish War and World War II and who rose through a number of important command responsibilities in the Soviet Army to serve from 1979 to 1991 as Chief of Staff of the Warsaw Pact Armed Forces. During four years of General Gribkov's last assignment, General Smith, a West Point graduate, a Korean War fighter pilot, holder of a Harvard University doctorate and a veteran of many Pentagon staff assignments, was General Gribkov's almost-opposite number as Chief of Staff, Supreme Headquarters Allied Powers Europe (SHAPE) and Deputy Commander-in-Chief of the United States European Command.

Two chapters from General Gribkov's original memoirs deal with the Cuban Missile Crisis and provide the basis for his portion of *Operation ANADYR.* Translated from Russian by Catherine Fitzpatrick, who also turned the treaty text and Castro-Mikoyan conversation in Appendix 1 into lucid English, the material has been greatly amplified and extensively reorganized in an editing process that included lengthy discussions with General Gribkov in Moscow in January 1993 and both correspondence and telephone conversations since then. Pushing back the barriers of secrecy that limited his first written account of the crisis and his Havana disclosures about the short-range, low-yield atomic arms that Soviet forces on Cuba possessed in 1962, General Gribkov has unearthed important Ministry of Defense documents to confirm his account. Reproduced in English in the text, they are also printed in Russian in Appendix 1 to satisfy questions about their authenticity.

General Smith has also obtained revealing records of the deliberations of the Joint Chiefs of Staff during the missile crisis, and excerpts from those documents are published for the first time in Appendix 2 to enable scholars to consult original sources in addition to the author's careful analysis of them. The end of the Cold War made it possible to gain access to these historic materials and to put them on the public record. If the authors of *Operation ANADYR* had done nothing more, their contribution to an accurate picture of an epochal East-West confrontation would still be of great importance.

The authors and their editor are indebted to a number of individuals for assistance in completing the project—to Brian Bank for research help, to Joseph Foote and Mary Cadette for copy editing, to Margaret Nalle for editorial advice and to Amanda Tate of Middlebury College's Department of Geography for preparing the maps that serve as endpapers for the book. It is also a pleasure to acknowledge the thoughtful comments and measured encouragement received from James Blight, Bruce Allyn, Ray Cline, Adm. Robert T. Hilton, Raymond Garthoff, Robert McNamara and Gen. Andrew Goodpaster.

—ALFRED FRIENDLY, JR.

PART I

The View from Moscow and Havana

by
General Anatoli I. Gribkov

Launching Operation ANADYR

For most of the world, the Cold War's most incendiary confrontation began on 22 October 1962. For President John F. Kennedy, who that evening disclosed the presence of Soviet missiles on Cuba, the crisis was nearly a week old. For me, it had been five months in the making. Reading Kennedy's speech as it was hurriedly translated at Soviet military headquarters in Havana that night, I was surprised only that the Americans had not found us out sooner and relieved that they had not reacted more violently.

In his televised broadcast, President Kennedy revealed that U.S. "surveillance of the Soviet military build-up on the island of Cuba" had uncovered "a series of offensive missile sites . . . now in preparation. . . ." Declaring that "the purposes of these bases can be none other than to provide a nuclear strike capability against the Western Hemisphere," he called for the "prompt dismantling and withdrawal of all offensive weapons" under United Nations supervision. "[T]his secret, swift, and extraordinary build-up of Communist missiles. . . . ," said Kennedy, "this sudden, clandestine decision to station strategic weapons for the first time outside of Soviet soil is a deliberately provocative and unjustified change in the status quo. . . ."[1]

I could understand his anger. He had been tricked, not just misled but lied to by Nikita S. Khrushchev.

In one minor respect Kennedy was mistaken. The Soviet decision only seemed sudden. Actually taken five months earlier, it was both a high-stakes gamble and the logical product of sustained provocation. More importantly, the

President misread Kremlin motives. Gaining "a nuclear strike capability" was not Khrushchev's "only" or main purpose.

In fact, the Soviet leader had persuaded his Politburo colleagues that U.S. aggression against Cuba was all too likely and could only be forestalled by the installation of the medium-range R-12 ballistic missiles and intermediate-range R-14 ballistic missiles that I had come to Cuba to help make operational. Additionally, these MRBMs and IRBMs [SS-4s and SS-5s in U.S. military terminology] positioned so close to North America would help redress the balance of nuclear terror by making up for the backwardness of the Soviet arsenal of intercontinental ballistic missiles (ICBMs.) Even withdrawn, the weapons achieved their first goal.

In his speech, Kennedy announced what he called a naval quarantine "on all offensive military equipment under shipment to Cuba," and warned that "these actions may only be the beginning. We will not prematurely or unnecessarily risk the costs of worldwide nuclear war," he said, "but neither will we shrink from that risk at any time it must be faced."[2]

Would he shrink, I wondered then, if he realized just how great the risk actually was? As he raised the specter of war, Kennedy may have suspected that among the nuclear munitions on Cuba were twelve two-kiloton warheads for the solid-fueled, twenty- to twenty-five-mile range "Luna" missiles—the North Atlantic Treaty Organization (NATO) called them FROGs—that could be fired at invading troops. Soviet weaponry on the island also included six Ilyushin-28 bombers specially fitted to carry atomic bombs and sixteen cruise-missile launchers with five rockets each.

The bombers could deliver their six-kiloton payloads some 200 miles away,* and the eighty cruise missiles—we called them "frontoviye krilatiye raketi" or FKRs—with five- to twelve-kiloton warheads, had a range of about ninety miles. In theory, the planes could have attacked U.S. embarkation ports, while the FKRs, deployed to cover the sea approaches to likely landing sites in western and southeastern Cuba, could have targeted ship clusters in an invasion fleet.

U.S. intelligence might have spotted these armaments, but no one in Washington could have known that Khrushchev had personally given General Issa Pliyev, commander of the Soviet Group of Forces on Cuba, authority to use his battlefield weapons and their atomic charges if, in the heat of combat, he could not contact Moscow. For that matter, only a narrow circle of Soviet leaders was aware either that nuclear arms had been shipped to Cuba for the "Lunas" or that Khrushchev, in delegating the authority to use them *in extremis,* had given Pliyev—7,000 miles from Moscow—a kind of discretion not accorded to any other Soviet commanders.

---

* U.S. intelligence put the bombers' "cruise radius" at 750 nautical miles.[3]

The Loaded Rifle

"Lunas" and other short-range weapons had previously been stationed outside the Soviet Union, but if they were transferred to our Warsaw Pact allies, they carried only conventional warheads, as did twenty-four of the thirty-six on Cuba. If armed with nuclear explosives on the territory of the USSR or outside it, they were kept strictly in Soviet hands and under Moscow's absolute control.

Khrushchev had told Pliyev that only Moscow could decide to fire atomic weapons against targets on the U.S. mainland, an act that would almost certainly provoke Washington into an all-out nuclear response. In line with standard Soviet military doctrine at the time, however, Khrushchev saw tactical atomic weapons, meant for the battlefield, in a different light. With their short ranges and low yields, such arms apparently did not carry, in his mind, much risk of drawing an overwhelming retaliation. Yet any atomic explosion on Cuba in the course of a fight with U.S. troops could have detonated a nuclear response—and not just against Soviets on Cuban battlefields.

The deployment of the intermediate- and medium-range ballistic missiles was a major provocation in itself. Had the Soviet troops on the island been required to defend those MRBMs and IRBMs and themselves against an invasion, it is hard to believe that they would have held back any of their weapons and fought, in effect, with one hand tied behind their backs.

Anton Chekhov, the great Russian playwright, coined a dramatist's dictum: "Do not put a loaded rifle on stage if no one is thinking of firing it." In Act I of the Cuban crisis, the rifle on stage was loaded with nuclear cartridges. No one thought of firing them, but in combat, no one could be certain that they would not be fired.

Marshal Rodion Malinovsky, the Soviet minister of defense, knew of the exception that had been made for our commander on Cuba. He had been present in July when Khrushchev gave Pliyev his instructions, officially but only orally. Significantly, Malinovsky ruled against confirming the order in writing when a message echoing Khrushchev's guidance was drafted on 8 September for transmission to Pliyev on Cuba.

Advising Pliyev that twelve "Luna" missiles with nuclear warheads and six Il-28 bombers with nuclear bombs were being shipped to him ahead of schedule, the draft message also said:

> If, in the course of an enemy landing on the island of Cuba and of the concentration of enemy ships involved in such a landing off the coast of Cuba in its territorial waters, the destruction of the enemy is delayed and there is no possibility of receiving the instructions of the USSR Ministry of Defense, you are permitted to decide on your own to employ the nuclear

means of the "Luna," Il-28 or FKR-1 as instruments of local warfare for the destruction of the enemy on land and along the coast in order to achieve the complete rout of the invaders of Cuban territory and to defend the Republic of Cuba.*

Marshal Matvei Zakharov, Chief of the General Staff of the Soviet Armed Forces and first deputy minister of defense, also knew about Pliyev's discretionary powers. Zakharov signed both the 8 September telegram (which Malinovsky decided not to send) and, along with Malinovsky, an order that same day to the ministry's 12th Main Directorate, which oversaw storage of nuclear arms, to send the twelve "Luna" warheads and the six atomic bombs for the Il-28s to Cuba.

Zakharov's top aide, Col. Gen. Semyon P. Ivanov,** chief of the General Staff's Main Operations Directorate, had witnessed both Zakharov's signature of the telegram and Khrushchev's talk with Pliyev, so he knew. And I knew because, as head of the Operations Directorate, I had brought the 8 September telegram to Malinovsky for final clearance. He told me, instead, to file it away. "We don't need any extra pieces of paper," Malinovsky said, "Pliyev knows everything already."

Not even Pliyev's senior aides on Cuba, however, were in on the secret. Kennedy and his military advisors certainly were not. They did not even have an accurate picture of Soviet troop strength on Cuba. And U.S. intelligence (even, it seems, in 1992) thought we numbered around 10,000, when the correct figure was more than 40,000. Yet these Washington planners were mobilizing to launch a series of air strikes against Cuba and to follow that bombardment with a massive airborne and amphibious troop assault.

The air attacks would no doubt have destroyed the R-12 emplacements where, on 22 October, no missile had yet been fueled, targeted or mated with a warhead. The U.S. planes would also have been able to demolish the sites still under feverish construction for the farther-reaching R-14 rockets that had not yet arrived on the island.

Such a strike would have denied us the chance to launch any of those weapons. It probably would have also wrecked all of the Ilyushin bombers, most of which were still in their shipping crates or only partly assembled. The subsequent invasion would have cut the Soviet and Cuban defense forces to pieces, disrupting communications on the island and severing contact with Moscow.

---

* See Appendix I for the Russian-language versions of this message and a related order dispatching atomic weapons to Cuba.
** In descending order, the top Soviet military ranks were Marshal of the Soviet Union (Malinovsky and Zakharov); General of the Army (Pliyev); Marshal of air, armor, artillery, engineering or signal forces; Colonel General (Ivanov); Lieutenant General and Major General (Gribkov).

But would the attackers have found and neutralized the bunkers where the nuclear charges for the "Lunas" and the cruise missiles were stored? Or would a desperate group of Soviet defenders, with or without orders from above, have been able to arm and fire even one "Luna" warhead—with a yield one-tenth the power of the bomb dropped on Hiroshima—or one of the more powerful FKR charges? If such a rocket had hit U.S. troops or ships, if thousands of Americans had died in the atomic blast, would it have been the last shot of the Cuban crisis or the first of global nuclear war?

In the days I spent on Cuba before Kennedy's speech, I asked myself such questions more than once. My fellow officers and I could see the huge fleet assembling in the Caribbean. We knew that U.S. spy planes were crisscrossing the island. We expected an attack any day, and I, at least, feared that as a last resort we might use our atomic weapons to stave off humiliating defeat.

A telegram from Moscow that reached Pliyev's headquarters a few hours before Kennedy's speech was prompted by the same fears. It ordered us "to take immediate steps to increase combat readiness and repulse the enemy together with the Cuban Army and with all the power of the Soviet forces" except nuclear weapons.[4] The order, in effect, withdrew the authority Khrushchev had delegated in July.

But the weapons were already in place. Had U.S. troops forced their way onto Cuba in the anxious days that followed, their beachhead could all too possibly have become the first atomic battlefield of World War III.

A Decision to Decipher

For me, the tension had been building ever since Monday, 21 May 1962. Early that afternoon, Semyon Pavlovich Ivanov rushed into my fourth-floor office in the Ministry of Defense. Just back from what should have been a routine meeting of the Defense Council in the Kremlin, my immediate superior was more agitated than I had ever seen him. Clutching a few sheets of paper in his left hand, he started speaking before he was fully through the doorway.

"Anatoli Ivanovich," he said, waving the pages he held, "this has to be written up immediately. In a clean copy. By hand. No typist. You can work with Yeliseyev and Kotov, but no one else. For this assignment just you three."

What could be so urgent, so hush-hush in the notes Ivanov took as secretary of the Defense Council? The council was the forum in which the Kremlin's top political leaders met with senior military advisors; it convened irregularly, as events warranted. The May 21 session had been called mainly to bring Khrushchev up to date on developments during his recent absence from the capital.

I had prepared the standard situation report that Marshals Malinovsky and

Zakharov presented that day to their colleagues. Writing that summary on the status of the Soviet armed forces was one of my regular duties as chief of the central military planning agency. My most recent briefing had noted nothing alarming in Berlin, or in the disposition of NATO forces or the deployment of U.S. strategic bombers—the prime areas on which Soviet military intelligence kept the closest watch.

Khrushchev and Foreign Minister Andrei Gromyko had returned to Moscow on Sunday 20 May from a week-long visit to Bulgaria. The Soviet leader's speeches there, as reported in our press, had sounded familiar themes and in familiar tones: NATO rocket bases ringing the USSR were a danger to peace; any nuclear first strike by the West would be answered by "shattering" retaliation. Both rhetoric and reality seemed normal. I could not imagine what had so upset my friend and boss or why his concern should be contagious.

As soon as I scanned the papers Ivanov thrust at me, I understood. According to his hasty notes, our top policymakers had decided to install medium- and intermediate-range missiles on Cuba capable of carrying nuclear warheads to targets all across North America and to ship large numbers of Soviet troops to the island to defend it and the rockets against U.S. attack. The operation, without parallel in Soviet history in either size or distance to be covered, was to be carried out in secret and to be completed by early November.

The preliminary decision of the Defense Council was the first step in this breathtaking venture. Headed by Khrushchev, the council also included Frol Kozlov and Leonid Brezhnev, then secretaries of the Communist party's Central Committee; party Presidium members Aleksei Kosygin (first deputy premier) and Anastas Mikoyan; and, from the Ministry of Defense, Marshal Malinovsky, his first deputy, Marshal Andrei Grechko, and General Aleksei Yepishev, who had moved just that April from his post as ambassador to Yugoslavia to the job of heading the Main Political Directorate for the armed forces and the Navy. Colonel General Ivanov, my immediate superior as head of the General Staff's Main Operations Directorate, served as the Defense Council's secretary.

The body was powerful, but its 21 May initiative on Cuba was not conclusive. It would have to be approved in final form by the Defense Council and accepted by the full party Presidium, as the Politburo was then called. My immediate job was to translate Ivanov's notes into an operational plan for presentation to a combined Council and Presidium session, Thursday, 24 May, less than three days off.

All I had to work from were Ivanov's few pages of scrawled lines and abbreviations, question marks and ellipses. To make a clean copy, I had to decipher the fragments. I hastily read the pages myself, then called in my aides, and the three of us got down to work reconstructing the document and then building on it.

My deputy, Maj. Gen. Gennadi Ivanovich Yeliseyev, was a quiet man, deliberate in his judgments and thorough almost to the point of pedantry. Col. Vyacheslav Nikolayevich Kotov, aside from many other strengths, had nice handwriting, so he wrote down the final version of the text we drafted. The work kept us up all night. That week, in fact, I do not remember getting home at all. When I could, I napped on a folding cot kept in a closet in my office, a camp bed used many, many times in the following months.

Our troika's initial job was to convert General Ivanov's notes into a full-blown General Staff proposal to Prime Minister and Communist party chief Nikita Khrushchev as Chairman of the Defense Council. Even though Khrushchev was himself the author of the scheme to establish a Group of Soviet Forces on the island of Cuba, our undertaking was much more than a formality. The plan had to be an initial blueprint for the creation, transportation and supply of a military unit similar in its makeup and mission, if not its size, to the Groups of Forces* stationed in eastern and central Europe.

In May 1962, I had twenty-three years of active military service behind me, with more than four in combat and nearly a year and a half in the top echelon of the General Staff. Still, nothing I had done before had quite prepared me for this new task. No Soviet officer, in fact, had such experience. Except for a few brigade- or regiment-size amphibious assaults during World War II—nothing to match the American and British invasions of North Africa, Sicily and Normandy—our military had moved large numbers of troops only by land. Now we were to ship infantry, aviation, construction, naval and rocket forces more than 7,000 miles from the nearest Soviet port and do so at breakneck speed and in secret.

Every sentence in a document of such importance had to be revised several times over, and I was constantly going into General Ivanov's office across the corridor to clarify a point or get his expert guidance. His long tenure as a senior staff officer made his advice invaluable. It was always sensible and to the point. He counseled against getting bogged down in details at this early stage, but the plan that actually went to the 24 May meeting was hardly short.

Its preamble, however, was. All it said—all the substance that the leaders formally ratified—was:

> To the Chairman of the Defense Council
> Comrade Nikita S. Khrushchev
>
> In accordance with your instructions the Ministry of Defense proposes the following:

---

* A Group of Forces combined units from different branches of the Soviet military, such as infantry, armor, engineering and aviation.

1. To deploy a Group of Soviet Forces on the island of Cuba consisting of all types of Armed Forces, under the unified command of the staff of the group to be headed by the Commander in Chief of Soviet Forces on Cuba.

Behind the Scenes

That short paragraph held the seeds of what Americans call the Cuban missile crisis and Soviets, more accurately, term the Caribbean crisis. The conflict that came into the open five months later was not just about missiles, nor just about Cuba. It was a test of strength that showed the reach of Soviet power—all the way to America's backyard—and the limits of nuclear confrontation. It was also a test of wills among three determined men: Nikita Khrushchev, John Kennedy and Fidel Castro. Their confrontation was anything but sudden. It had been brewing for nearly three years.

At the moment of Castro's revolutionary triumph in January 1959, the clash that reached its climax in October 1962 became a possibility. U.S. policy in the following years made it a probability. Reducing purchases of sugar, Cuba's main cash crop; breaking diplomatic relations; sponsoring the failed Bay of Pigs invasion and plotting a second attempt while orchestrating an economic blockade of the island, U.S. leaders pushed Castro (not necessarily against his will) to enlist in the Soviet camp and the Communist cause. Khrushchev's response to this opportunity for political expansion was the factor that turned a competition for influence into a crisis that threatened all the contenders with nuclear annihilation.

Many elements went into the making of the crisis, and many thoughtful historians have worked to sort out the underlying facts and forces. I cannot add to their judgments on Cuban and U.S. actions nor explain all the intricacies of Soviet political and diplomatic conduct before May 1962. On the military considerations that led to the crisis, however, I can expand the record, and I believe it is important to do so.

Many analysts see the Soviet decision as primarily an outgrowth of Khrushchev's double miscalculation of Kennedy's fortitude and America's vital interests. For my part, I believe that the Kremlin leader's action sprang from both his heart and his head. It was both an old Bolshevik's romantic response to Castro and to the Cuban revolution and an old soldier's stratagem for deploying Soviet force to defend an endangered outpost and ally.

Of the two influences, the military may even have been the stronger. Like many other Soviets of his generation, Khrushchev saw nuclear arms as something to be used in battle or diplomacy, not as weapons too destructive ever to be fired. He knew, as did his senior military advisors, that U.S. strategic nuclear forces outnumbered ours by approximately 17 to 1 in 1962 and that the USSR would need years of strenuous activity to pull even. And he interpreted the presence of U.S. rockets in Turkey along with mounting reports of U.S. threats to Cuba as evidence that Kennedy intended to use America's nuclear advantage to force Moscow to desert our new partner in the Caribbean.

Stationing Soviet missiles and the troops to defend them on Cuba was, of course, an enormous gamble; but in the face of a perceived threat to Castro's regime and to Soviet credibility as a superpower, so was inaction. Some leading Cuban politicians were already flirting with China's leader, Mao Tse-tung, Khrushchev's rival for supremacy in the international Communist movement. Had America succeeded in toppling Castro because Soviet support was less than steadfast, Chinese rulers would have crowed over the Kremlin's lack of resolve.

Khrushchev's memoirs are convincing on this point. "While I was on an official visit to Bulgaria," he recalled,

> one thought kept hammering away at my brain: what will happen if we lose Cuba? I knew it would be a terrible blow to Marxism-Leninism. It would gravely diminish our stature throughout the world, but especially in Latin America. If Cuba fell, other Latin American countries would reject us, claiming that for all our might the Soviet Union hadn't been able to do anything for Cuba except to make empty protests to the United Nations. We had to think up some way of confronting America with more than words.[5]

The scheme he devised fit precisely with Khrushchev's fundamental belief that Soviet military power rested on our rockets, our submarines and our civil defense measures. That conviction had justified his massive cuts in ground forces and surface navy two years before. Starting in January 1960, Khrushchev engineered the demobilization of nearly a million enlisted men and a quarter-million Soviet Army and Navy officers. In addition to demolishing hundreds of battle tanks, Khrushchev scrapped scores of ships and planes that could as easily have been mothballed, as the more foresighted Americans did on several occasions.

I recall not only the old soldiers who were discharged with less than full pensions but, just as painfully, the young military academy graduates who were required to go straight from school into the reserves. And I remember the forced retirement of leaders like Marshal V. D. Sokolovsky, Zakharov's immediate predecessor as General Staff chief, who had strongly resisted Khrushchev's force reductions. Sokolovsky's dismissal meant, in effect, that the title of defense minister or chief of staff was a hollow honor. Nikita Khrushchev held all power in his hands and brooked no opposition.

Thus, when he decided on the Cuban operation, none of his uniformed advisors tried to talk him out of it. According to later accounts, only Gromyko and Deputy Premier Mikoyan initially opposed the idea; Malinovsky, among others, backed it from the start.[6] Neither I nor any of my colleagues at the top of the General Staff would have dared to question the initiative, and by the time it was put to a formal Politburo vote, Mikoyan and Gromyko were in accord as well.

Strategy for Deterrence

Mikoyan, Khrushchev's intimate friend and oldest political ally, had traveled to Cuba in 1960 to initiate the relationship with Fidel Castro. He returned from the trip filled with a deep sympathy for the Cuban leaders and their revolutionary aspirations. Once he even told U.S. Secretary of State Dean Rusk that "old Bolsheviks," such as he and Khrushchev, had "been waiting all our lives for a country to go Communist without the Red Army. It has happened in Cuba, and it makes us feel like boys."[7]

Khrushchev himself had told Kennedy at their Vienna meeting in June 1961 that Castro was no Communist, but "you are well on the way to making him a good one."[8] In the same conversation, the Kremlin leader also said that Cuba posed nothing like the threat to the United States that U.S. missiles in Turkey and Italy posed to the Soviet Union. In April 1962 the risk to Cuba and the risk to the Soviet Union from their respective neighbors were still very much on Khrushchev's mind.

The latter concern surfaced first. During a vacation stroll that month along a beach in the Crimea, Khrushchev and Marshal Malinovsky talked about the U.S. missiles across the Black Sea in Turkey. Accenting our vulnerability in a way Khrushchev had done many times himself, the defense minister noted that the Jupiter rockets could reach and destroy vital centers of the Soviet Union in just ten minutes.

Some days after that talk, Ivanov confided to me, Khrushchev raised the matter of Cuba's security with Mikoyan. During the visit to Bulgaria, he pursued the issue with Gromyko, and by the time the two men flew back to Moscow together on 20 May, the need to mount a missile-based defense of Cuba *on* Cuba was firmly lodged in Khrushchev's mind.

Distressed by a spate of intelligence reports of U.S. plans for a second invasion, Khrushchev felt that Cuba could not possibly be defended by conventional weapons. Only missiles with nuclear warheads, he believed, would provide an effective deterrent. To bolster his case for action at the 21 May Defense Council, he asked Malinovsky how long it would take our armed forces to seize a hypothetical island ninety miles off the Soviet coast in the face of desperate resistance.

"Three to five days," Malinovsky replied. "No more than a week."

Cuba, Khrushchev remarked, would be just as vulnerable to U.S. aggression. Emplacing Soviet missiles on the island was the only way, he maintained, to deter attack.

When I learned of the idea that afternoon, it was like a roll of thunder in a clear sky. Until then, the only General Staff-level discussion of Cuba's security needs had concerned the flow of military advisors and conventional arms begun in summer 1960, shortly after Moscow and Havana formally opened diplomatic relations. Even Aleksandr Alekseyev, a KGB expert on Cuba, was caught by surprise when Khrushchev summoned him to the Kremlin and told him of the decision to ask Fidel Castro to accept nuclear-armed Soviet missiles as shields against U.S. attack.

Alekseyev, who had worked for many years in Havana, ostensibly as a TASS correspondent, and whom Gromyko and Khrushchev had decided to name as our ambassador there, predicted that the Cuban leader would resist the idea at first. Stationing Soviet rocket forces on the island, he forecast, would undercut Castro's long-term strategy of building political and diplomatic support among neutral and non-aligned Third World countries and public opinion.[9]

What Castro thought, however, was nearly irrelevant; Khrushchev had made up his mind. Using the document prepared for the 24 May joint Defense Council and party Presidium session, he had compelled all his colleagues to accept his plan as the soundest means of protecting Cuba from its giant neighbor and cementing Soviet influence in the Caribbean.

Installing thirty-six R-12 and twenty-four R-14 missiles, including one back-up rocket for every two deployed on launch pads, had a third compelling attraction for Khrushchev. In one stroke he could redress the imbalance in strategic nuclear forces, putting U.S. targets 1,400 miles from Cuba within reach of the R-12s and the rest of the country east of the Rocky Mountains under threat from the 2,800-mile-range R-14s.

In 1962 the Soviet intercontinental ballistic missile program lagged far behind analogous U.S. systems in rocket numbers and reliability. Basing the R-12s and R-14s on forty launch pads in Cuba would leapfrog the Atlantic as our ICBMs could not. It would also put the United States under the same threat that the U.S. missiles in Turkey and Italy posed to the USSR: a nuclear attack with little or no warning.

Some historians believe that Khrushchev intended to use the rockets on Cuba as bargaining counters to win a tit-for-tat withdrawal of comparable U.S. weapons from the Soviet periphery. If that was his thinking, it was not recorded either in conversations held in 1962 or his later memoirs.

My own view is that his strategic goal was to win status for the USSR in the global superpower rivalry by showing that it could extend its strength to shield a far-away friend. He would be ready to reap whatever negotiating advantages in the continuing disputes over Berlin, Laos and the arms race would flow from such a demonstration of might and ingenuity. By putting Castro's revolution under a powerful Soviet shield, he thought he could also put the USSR itself a step ahead of U.S. nuclear power.

Green Light for Action

Khrushchev's colleagues in the Kremlin either shared his assessment or feared to voice their doubts. Gromyko had privately told Khrushchev that he thought the risks high and the chances of success poor,[10] but the foreign minister was not a Politburo member. With Gromyko absent, there was discussion but minimal open disagreement at the expanded Defense Council session on 24 May. According to the minutes taken by General Ivanov (and until recently kept under a seal of secrecy in military archives), Malinovsky presented the plan, and Khrushchev followed with a commentary. "All other members of the Presidium and those who spoke [including Mikoyan, Kozlov, Brezhnev, Kosygin and three others]," Ivanov recorded, "agreed and were in favor of the decision.

"It was resolved to approve the ANADYR action wholly and unanimously.

"The document [outlining the plan] is to be kept in the Ministry of Defense. It is to be confirmed after obtaining consent from F. Castro.

"A commission is to be sent to F. Castro for negotiations: Sh[araf] R. Rashidov, S[ergei] S. Biryuzov, S[emyon] P. Ivanov and a group of comrades with them. They should fly on Monday-Tuesday, May 28-29."[11]

The official minutes of this crucial meeting suggest that the leaders' professed unanimity was tinged with unease. Although all those present signed their names to Ivanov's minutes, only Khrushchev and Kosygin wrote *za* (for) in front of their signatures as was the usual practice. As record-keeper, Ivanov told me, he had even gone to Khrushchev to report that the party secretaries—not themselves Presidium members—had not signed the minutes. "*Nichevo* [not to worry]," said Khrushchev, "go around to their dachas. They'll sign."

Khrushchev was correct. They did, and Operation ANADYR was under way.

From the start, the undertaking held the seeds of its own failure, partly in the haste in which it was considered and launched, but above all in the compulsive secrecy that cloaked the entire action in deception. In typical style, Khrushchev gambled that the missiles could be successfully transported and installed without America's learning about them until after the fact. Considering the risks, it is surprising that the plan came so close to success. Its collapse brought bitter consequences. The strategy required Khrushchev and Gromyko to lie to President Kennedy and the world, as well as to conceal their true intentions from all but a few associates. The scheme and its unmasking ensured Kennedy's angry feeling of personal betrayal and blocked the path to any superpower relationship built on mutual trust.

ANADYR, the code name for the operation, was an early sign of how far the deception was meant to reach. It is the name of a river in the far northeast of the Soviet Union that flows into the Bering Sea. On all the plans that lower-level Soviet commanders were allowed to see, ANADYR was meant to indicate to them (and to any watching espionage agents) that the action was a strategic exercise involving the movement of troops and equipment to the far north of our country. To preserve that pretense, many units were even outfitted with skis, felt boots, fleece-lined parkas and other winter equipment.

The camouflage worked so well that it even fooled our own people. On Cuba in October, for instance, Maj. Gen. Pavel Petrenko, the top political officer in Pliyev's headquarters, greeted me with an ironic smile. "You know-it-alls in the General Staff," he sneered, "why did you saddle us with all this winter gear? If you'd done the job right, you would have sent us shorts and bathing suits."

"Try to think like an adult," I retorted. "Remember the secrecy of this operation. It's called ANADYR for a reason. We could have given away the game if we had put any tropical clothing in your kits."

In Moscow that May, such details as light- or heavy-weight apparel were far down the list of our priorities. The first order of business was to decide whom to send to Cuba with Rashidov, a Presidium member, and Marshal Biryuzov, a deputy defense minister in command of strategic rocket forces. Alekseyev, whose close relations with Fidel Castro made him a natural choice for ambassador, was one of the few civilians in the group.

On the military side, Lt. Gen. Sergei F. Ushakov, the deputy head of the Air Force's central staff, and Maj. Gen. Pyotr V. Ageyev, a colleague of mine in the Operations Directorate, were assigned to conduct a preliminary reconnaissance of Cuba. Ageyev, in effect, took the place of General Ivanov, who was too busy to leave Moscow, as the eyes and ears of the General Staff. The officers' job was to decide which port facilities could handle our troops and freight, which airfields our planes, and what sites could hold and hide our missile installations.

Theirs was a crucial responsibility, as important as the political effort to persuade Fidel Castro to accept Soviet nuclear weapons on his island. In most respects, the job was well done, but the group accepted what proved to be a myth:

the possibility of concealing the missiles on Cuba's terrain until they could be ready to fire. The reconnaissance team correctly assessed the island's potential to receive our men and equipment, but its members were over-optimistic about camouflaging rocket bases under construction.

That problem lay in the future. As the mission flew off to Cuba, I plunged ahead with the task I had been set—organizing the deployment—in some ways the heaviest responsibility I had ever carried. It was a huge task, and I was not sure that I, or anyone, could see it to success.

Under Way

The Moscow summer of 1962 passed in a blur of work. Detailed plans had to be formulated and, in several cases, revised. Orders had to be drafted. Colleagues had to be briefed. Tasks had to be assigned and their execution checked. All of this activity, moreover, had to be shrouded in a secrecy so thick that the real purpose of Operation ANADYR remained hidden even from most of the men sent to Cuba to carry it out and from those who equipped them, loaded them and their gear onto ships and moved them to the Caribbean.

Considering how much had to be done in how short a time, behind a heavy screen of camouflage and subterfuge, it is remarkable how effectively the Soviet armed forces carried out their mission. Unpracticed in mounting major troop-transport operations by sea and unfamiliar, to put it mildly, with tropical conditions, officers and enlisted men from all the branches of the service were severely tested. They passed with high marks.

The Caribbean crisis should have taught the world about the responsiveness, toughness and adaptability of the Soviet military. However else the events of 1962 are judged, they gave conclusive proof that the USSR could, in the jargon of strategists, project its power farther and faster than its friends or rivals had imagined.

Measured against its primary goal—the defense of Cuba and the Castro regime—Operation ANADYR was a success. President Kennedy kept his October promise to leave the island alone. Although they tightened a cruel economic embargo and periodically escalated a crude propaganda offensive, neither he nor any of his successors ever again set plans in motion either for an armed assault on the island or for organized subversion of the socialist revolution there.

Seen as an attempt to increase Soviet security by redressing the strategic nuclear balance—a secondary purpose in Khrushchev's avowed calculations, but a bonus he surely hoped to win—the 1962 deployment was a short-term disaster that brought longer-term benefits. The confrontation forced both Khrushchev and Kennedy to look annihilation in the face and to recoil from the danger. Having shattered the few, weak bonds of trust between Washington and Moscow, the crisis also prompted both superpowers to begin building new safety measures into their relationship.

The first such step, in June 1963, was an agreement to establish a "hot line" for rapid, direct communications between the White House and the Kremlin. A month later came a tripartite treaty to end American, Soviet and British nuclear testing in the atmosphere and under the sea. Finally, by spring 1972, Moscow and Washington agreed on the Strategic Arms Limitation Treaty (SALT I), the first accord reached in a twenty-year wrangle over reducing atomic arsenals. At the end of May 1962, however, that future progress was hardly imaginable, much less foreseeable. My duty, in any case, was to carry out the Defense Council's orders, not to second-guess them or speculate on possible consequences.

Within the Soviet military, we could argue with one another, even, in measured terms, challenge the views of our superiors—at least until those views became orders. As a junior officer and representative of the General Staff with a front-line tank corps in 1942 and 1943, I had had my share of run-ins with higher-ranking officers who were wary of me as the "eyes and ears" of Moscow. These wartime lessons—the importance of getting all the facts and of making independent judgments—taught me not to fear the consequences of speaking the truth as I saw it. My frankness did not always make my career path smooth, but I earned enough respect to advance steadily.

Asking a colleague in uniform to explain himself or his ideas was one thing; resisting an order from the Kremlin was another—an all-but inconceivable act for a Soviet soldier of any rank. At best, it would result in forced retirement, as Marshal Sokolovsky had found when he protested Khrushchev's stringent troop and weapons cuts in the early 1960s. Until the disbanding of the Communist Party of the Soviet Union (CPSU) in 1991, Soviet political leaders made the policy decisions; Soviet military men, even if they disagreed, obeyed.

That was the rule under Josef Stalin, under Nikita Khrushchev and under Leonid Brezhnev. Brezhnev's Politburo, for instance, brusquely overrode the judgment of the chief of the General Staff, Marshal Nikolai V. Ogarkov, in sending the first of some 85,000 Soviet troops into Afghanistan in late 1979. Talking at the time with Ogarkov and Marshal Viktor G. Kulikov, then first deputy minister of defense, in Ogarkov's office, I found both men were as disturbed as I by the dangerous military course being planned. They were full members of the Defense Council and I, although chief of staff of the Warsaw Pact forces, was not; I pressed my two colleagues to weigh in decisively at the highest levels against the Afghan venture.

Ogarkov, who favored political, diplomatic and economic measures in Afghanistan over the use of force, said that he had already tried to register his opposition at a Politburo session and been told to hold his tongue. "Comrade Ogarkov," said Yuri Andropov, then head of the KGB, "no one is asking for your opinion." Although Ogarkov was the senior professional in the Soviet armed forces, he could not even get his immediate superior, Defense Minister Dmitri Ustinov, to listen to his advice. Andropov, Ustinov and Foreign Minister Andrei Gromyko, by then a Politburo member, were the ones who talked an old and ailing Leonid Brezhnev into the shameful, adventuristic Afghanistan decision.*

Whatever the era or the leadership, a Politburo decree was final, and on 10 June 1962, the party Presidium, meeting with Defense Council members and with the emissaries who had returned from Cuba, voted to confirm the preliminary decision it had taken three weeks earlier: to dispatch a Group of Soviet Forces to Cuba to defend the island by deploying medium- and intermediate-range ballistic missiles (MRBMs and IRBMS) within ninety miles of the U.S. coast. As recorded in the minutes kept by Col. Gen. Semyon P. Ivanov, Defense Council secretary, the determination was undramatic. "On June 10, 1962 at 10:00 A.M.," he wrote,

> a meeting of the CPSU Central Committee Presidium was convened. Present were all members of the CPSU Central Committee Presidium and candidate members; Comrades (A.A.) Gromyko, (R.Ya.) Malinovsky, (M.V.) Zakharov, (A.A.) Yepishev, (S.S.) Biryuzov, (V.I.) Chuykov** and secretaries of the Central Committee.
>
> After hearing the results of the trip to Cuba by Comrades (Sh.R.) Rashidov and (S.S.) Biryuzov, there was a discussion of the substance of the matter, after which Comrade R. Ya. Malinovsky read a memorandum prepared by the Ministry of Defense and everyone voted in favor.[2]

---

* Almost ten years after Soviet troops entered Afghanistan and seven months after their withdrawal, Soviet Foreign Minister Eduard Shevardnadze claimed that as candidate, rather than full, members of the Politburo in 1979, neither he nor Mikhail Gorbachev knew of the invasion plans in advance. "I found out what had happened from radio and newspaper reports," he said. "A decision that had very serious consequences for our country was made behind the back of the Party and the people. We were confronted with a *fait accompli.*"[1]

** The Soviet foreign and defense ministers—Gromyko and Malinovsky—were not Politburo members at the time. Marshals Zakharov and Yepishev were Defense Council members. Marshal Biryuzov was the leading military figure in the delegation to Cuba, and Marshal Chuykov was commander of Soviet land forces.

Later in private, Ivanov confided to me that whatever skepticism Mikoyan, Gromyko or others in the political leadership had earlier expressed went unvoiced in June. Sharaf Rashidov's account of the delegation's reception by Fidel Castro and Marshal Sergei Biryuzov's companion report on the military feasibility of the proposed missile deployments were both positive. Moreover, the Ministry of Defense plan was already a more comprehensive document than it had been at the 24 May Presidium/Defense Council session.

By 10 June, only some dramatic new development on the world scene could have derailed Khrushchev's strategy or slowed its momentum. No such impediment appeared. Fidel Castro approved the plan, acknowledging the risk it entailed but reportedly saying that Cuba would serve as host for the Soviet missiles if doing so would hasten the worldwide victory of socialism. Marshal Biryuzov, for one, returned from the trip with the impression that Cuba's leaders saw themselves much more as benefactors of the Soviet Union and its socialist cause than as our dependents. Whatever the actual political motivations or unspoken reservations, Operation ANADYR was on its way.

Time Out for Diplomacy

Its momentum slowed only slightly when Fidel's younger brother and armed forces minister, Raul Castro Ruz, arrived in Moscow on 2 July for talks with Khrushchev and Malinovsky that soon became treaty negotiations. As head of a four-man military group in charge of technical preparations, I found myself deeply involved but doubly deprived. Secrecy made it impossible to bring in any international legal expert for consultation. And the pressure of the work prevented me from joining friends on the fishing expeditions we had enjoyed together for many years. That summer they went without me.

What could I tell them? That I was staying up all night, drinking tea or very cold water as though in wartime, leafing through handbooks on maritime law, studying the articles of conventions on navigation and fishing, tracing the borders of territorial waters on maps and doing much else that only the day before I could not have imagined as part of my duties? Even through the tightly closed windows of my office I could hear the bustle of Moscow's streets and imagine the people on them, hurrying to catch commuter trains for the countryside and relaxation.

Much as I wanted to share in such leisure, my work was fascinating and the contact with Raul Castro rewarding. Even at our first meeting, he made a strong impression on me. Despite his youth, this dark, handsome man was distinguished by the maturity of his judgment in military matters and by his capacity to grasp new concepts quickly. Obviously, the school of revolutionary struggle and partisan warfare had not been wasted on him.

Raul was easy to work with, and when I came to his Island of Freedom a few months later, we met with pleasure as old acquaintances. Despite the winds and gusts and even storms of Soviet-Cuban relations, Raul Castro, with whom I have reminisced many times in the years since 1962, never deviated from his course of cooperation with the USSR. Under the guidance of his elder brother and with our help, he was able within a short time to transform the guerrilla warriors of the revolution into a strong, modern army.

That July, however, our urgent task was to write a legal document that would clarify Soviet-Cuban relations and put them on a firm footing, providing not only for the immediate defense of Cuban territory but for longer-term military cooperation and mutual security arrangements. Working with me, as they had since May 21, were my deputies Maj. Gen. Gennadi Yeliseyev and Col. Vyacheslav Kotov, as well as my colleague Maj. Gen. Pyotr Ageyev, who had accompanied the Rashidov-Biryuzov group to Cuba a few weeks earlier. As both an interpreter and an active participant in the talks, Aleksandr Alekseyev, newly designated ambassador to Cuba, provided valuable help. And we acquired an unfamiliar resource: a typist. This welcome advance from the practice we had followed since 21 May of writing everything by hand was a happy consequence of having to produce our documents in Spanish and, therefore, on a typewriter with a Latin keyboard.

After intense work, the draft treaty was ready. To be valid for five years, subject to renewal or, on a year's notice, to termination by either party, it specified the defensive role Soviet military personnel were to play, obliged them to observe Cuban laws and granted them only temporary use of Cuban territory. It also provided that, in the event of annulment, Soviet installations and equipment would become Cuban property. Initialed in early July by Raul Castro and Defense Minister Malinovsky, the pact was not to be publicly released until the visit Khrushchev planned to make to Cuba in November.

The document bore the title, "Treaty Between the Government of the Republic of Cuba and the Government of the Union of Soviet Socialist Republics on the Stationing of Soviet Armed Forces on the Territory of the Republic of Cuba." But this July version was not destined to be the last word. After returning home, the Cubans apparently reviewed the text with a more critical eye and in August Fidel Castro sent Khrushchev a coded letter and an amended draft treaty delivered personally by Ernesto Che Guevara. Maj. Emilio Aragones, who had been in Moscow with Raul the month before, also returned with Guevara.

Again my group of soldiers was called to diplomatic duty. Guevara's indomitable spirit, his aura of revolutionary invincibility and the high culture that made him a popular poet as well as a charismatic political leader impressed me deeply.

I remain profoundly grateful to the Cuban government for awarding me the order it struck in his honor after his death.

His August 1962 mission to Moscow, however, only meant more work for my small task force. Among the suggested changes he brought with him, for example, were three alternative titles: "Treaty . . . on Military Cooperation for the Defense of the National Territory of Cuba in the Event of Aggression"; ". . . on the Participation of the Soviet Armed Forces in the Defense of the National Territory of Cuba in the Event of Aggression"; or ". . . on Military Cooperation and Mutual Defense."

In his letter to Khrushchev, Castro couched the alterations as improvements that would enhance the accord's political effect without changing its legal basis and meaning. Inviting us to make amendments of our own, the Cuban comrades also agreed to accept any Soviet decision on the timing and manner of publicizing the treaty. The Cuban demarche required me and my military colleagues to review the proposed changes with Soviet Foreign Ministry experts. Together, we compared the draft treaties and made a thorough analysis of the three suggested title changes as well as the preamble and all the articles. Along with revisions proposed by the Defense Ministry, our conclusions were submitted to Khrushchev, who accepted the changes and the first Cuban alternative title.

The document that had begun as an agreement ". . . on the Stationing of Soviet Armed Forces on the Territory of the Republic of Cuba" became a less open-ended, more precisely defined treaty ". . . on Military Cooperation for the Defense of the National Territory of Cuba in the Event of Aggression." The best answer to those who doubt Soviet intentions toward Cuba is in the terms of the treaty itself.[*]

The full text (Appendix 1) makes clear, as the preamble says, that the accord was premised on "the urgent necessity to take measures to secure mutual defense in the face of possible aggression against the Republic of Cuba and the USSR." Its central aim was to deploy Soviet troops for "the defense of the national territory of Cuba in the event of aggression." Citing the right to individual or collective defense under Article 51 of the United Nations Charter, the final draft of the treaty also stipulated that "[b]oth sides have determined that the armed forces of each country will remain under the command of their respective governments which will decide the matter of deploying their own country's armed forces in order to repel external aggression and restore peace."

---

[*] In these memoirs, the author does not indicate that the pressure for a formal legal agreement may have come from Cuba, nor that Raul Castro, in the words of a noted American historian, proposed that Khrushchev "make a public announcement that the Soviet Union was shipping missiles to Cuba" so that if their presence were revealed, America would not react violently to the deception. Khrushchev reportedly rejected both the idea of an open declaration and the likelihood of premature discovery.[3]

Reworked into Russian and Spanish versions of equal legal validity, the drafts were placed in ceremonial red folders bound with red ribbons and fastened with gray sealing wax bearing the stamp of the Ministry of Foreign Affairs. By the end of August, they were ready for signing. Fidel Castro and Cuban President Osvaldo Dorticos Torrado had sent a joint letter to Moscow giving Guevara power to formalize the agreement. "Having special trust in the person, tact and skill of Ernesto Che Guevara Serna," they wrote, "we invest in him complete authority and authorize him to sign in the name of and on behalf of the Republic of Cuba the treaty of a military nature."

Our side, however, chose to put off a signing ceremony so that Khrushchev could make it the triumphant centerpiece of his prospective November visit to Cuba. For the time being, the document was only initialed—by Che Guevara for Cuba and Rodion Malinovsky for the Soviet Union. And like everything else about Operation ANADYR, the treaty's existence stayed a secret. Among the many what-ifs of modern history is the question of America's likely reaction had the Soviet-Cuban defense pact been disclosed after the parties had agreed on its final text. Such speculation is best left to experts on American politics and policy at the time, and I am not one. Nevertheless, it is conceivable that an open, legal pledge by the USSR, made in late August, to come to Cuba's aid against attack and to deter such an attack by stationing Soviet forces on the island would have provoked a crisis far less dangerous than the one that did break out seven weeks later.

At the very least, public disclosure would have precluded John Kennedy's feeling in October that he had been victimized by systematic deception. Openness in this aspect of superpower competition might even have accelerated a diplomatic search for mutual accommodation and slowed the tempo of the arms race. One result might have been the reconfiguration of the Soviet deployment on Cuba into a smaller force with a clearly defensive mission. Such a symbolic, unthreatening commitment by Moscow might have helped reconcile the United States to the reality of Castro's successful revolution.

Planning for Action

The order of the day—every day of Operation ANADYR—was secrecy, secrecy and speed. Bound by those two demands, the Soviet military confronted an awesome logistical challenge. The task was for us unprecedented: assemble and outfit nearly 51,000 soldiers, airmen and sailors; calculate the weapons, equipment, supplies and support such a contingent would need for a prolonged stay; find 85 freight ships to transport men and gear; put them to sea and ensure them the right reception and working conditions on their arrival in Cuba. Meanwhile, conceal the entire operation and complete it within five months.

There was work enough for scores of experienced hands. Marshal Zakharov, however, designated just five of us to serve at the center of the General Staff's planning apparatus: Colonel General Ivanov in overall charge; myself; Lt. Gen. Mikhail I. Povaliy, Ivanov's deputy, recently returned from sick leave; Major General Yeliseyev and Colonel Kotov. From 10 June onwards, our circle of contacts and collaborators expanded throughout the various services, but although the most senior officers were at least told that Cuba was involved in the operation, only a very few were informed of the exact nature of the mission.

Merchant Marine Minister Vassili G. Bakayev, for example, received his first briefing only on 11 June. Called to Deputy Prime Minister Aleksei Kosygin's Kremlin office, he found Malinovsky and a group of Army generals leaving, while General Ivanov and Leonid Brezhnev stayed behind. As Bakayev recalled the conversation:

> Without any particular preamble, they told me that a very large operation was in the works in Cuba and would require the Navy. "Is it a military operation?" I asked. Leonid Ilyich Brezhnev nodded affirmatively.
>
> I was warned that I could involve only one of the Ministry employees in the details of the operation.[4]

Fortunately, he chose his very able deputy, Yevgeni V. Karamzin, as liaison, and he proved an invaluable source of advice and help. One day in my office Karamzin proposed a common-sense solution to the problem of matching the merchant fleet's cargo and passenger capacity to our military demands.

"Let's do it this way, Anatoli Ivanovich," he said. "I have here blueprints of all the classes of ships you'll be able to use for troops and materiel. You tell me the number of people, the pieces of equipment and their dimensions, and I will fit them on the ships. I'll tell you how much will fit, where the soldiers and their gear will go and so on."

"OK," I agreed. "Let's start with the antiaircraft units and the radar stations." The job was long and very tedious, but it had to be done, and during days that stretched to 16, even 18 hours, we worked out these and other operational details.

The proposal outlined in the handwritten memorandum that the Defense Council adopted on 10 June grew into a full-fledged plan, still handwritten, that was formally approved by Malinovsky on 4 July and by Khrushchev three days later. At almost the last minute, Khrushchev, overruling the General Staff's recommendation, decided to name Army Gen. Issa Pliyev commander—the order said "commander in chief"—of the Group of Forces.

That important personnel choice was an error, on several counts. Pliyev, an accomplished and much decorated cavalry officer who enjoyed great respect in the armed forces, lacked the gift of diplomacy needed in the complex circumstances in which he soon found himself. Part of the problem arose from the General Staff's error of assigning him a headquarters staff drawn from the rocket army that his immediate deputy had commanded. It would have been better had Pliyev been supported by senior officers from the joint staff of the North Caucasus Military District, which he led. These men had the experience required to manage a large organization made up, as the Group of Forces on Cuba was, of units from all branches of the Soviet military.

Equally important, Pliyev proved unable to establish fruitful working relations with Fidel Castro. The Cuban chief was a strong-willed and cultivated man, an extraordinary leader who could be adamant in the defense of his revolution's principles. Pliyev had proved himself an exemplary tactician at the head of motorized rifle combat troops in the Far East in World War II, but those were not a diplomat's skills. Soldier and emissary at the same time, the commander of the Soviet Group of Forces needed tact more than tactical expertise, and Pliyev was deficient in that quality.

Khrushchev selected him, however, because he saw the naming of a nonspecialist as convincing proof that the Soviet MRBMs and IRBMs on Cuba were meant to deter an attack, not to launch one. It is unclear whose judgment Khrushchev thought would be affected—Pliyev's assignment was kept secret and he was even given, over his vigorous protest, a *nom de guerre*.

On 10 July, just as he was about to board the civilian Tupolev 114 that was ostensibly inaugurating a new Moscow-Havana route via Conakry in Guinea, Pliyev, with complete seriousness, reported that he had been given the wrong passport. It was made out in the name of "Ivan Aleksandrovich Pavlov." As a combat-tested officer, Pliyev said, he did not intend to take on a strange name, much less leave his real identification papers at the General Staff. He did not want to part with them for anything, and Ivanov and I had a hard time convincing him to live and work under a pseudonym from then on.

We should have taken that episode as an early warning of Pliyev's lack of subtlety and the difficulties it would spawn. Within the Group of Forces, for example, there was friction between Pliyev/Pavlov and his first deputy, Lt. Gen. Pavel Borisovich Dankevich, commander of a Soviet rocket army and the General Staff's original choice for the top job on Cuba. Dankevich, a field officer rather than a strategist, clearly thought that the missile deployment was the heart of our Cuban initiative and that a specialist such as himself should have been put in charge. His fellow rocketeers even complained that Pliyev misused military terminology, for example, identifying an element of the missile regiments in cavalryman's jargon as an *eskradilya* (squadron) when *divizyon* (detachment) was the proper term.

Although such criticism was unjustified, it did point up Pliyev's shortcomings in matters of diplomacy. Those flaws became a more serious concern during the October crisis when the temperamental mismatch between Castro and Pliyev exacerbated the misunderstandings that arose between Castro and Khrushchev. Even before international tensions escalated, however, Pliyev's relations with his immediate subordinates were less than ideal.

Once on Cuba, he repeatedly expressed dissatisfaction with the work of his staff, notably with the disgruntled Dankevich, his first deputy, and with Maj. Gen. Pavel Maksimovich Petrenko, head of the Group of Forces' Political Directorate. Both men were members of the military council, the group of senior headquarters and field officers who advised the commander on sensitive policy matters and saw to the execution of his orders. The other top aides were Lt. Gen. P. V. Akindinov, chief of staff; Aviation Lt. Gen. Stepan Naumovich Grechko, deputy commander for antiaircraft defense; Vice Adm. Georgi Semyonovich Abashvili, naval affairs deputy; Maj. Gen. Nikolai Romanovich Pilipenko, deputy for the support units; Maj. Gen. Leonid Stepanovich Garbuz, deputy for combat readiness; and Maj. Gen. Aleksei Alekseyevich Dementyev, a tank officer who was deputy commander after Dankevich and chief of the group of Soviet military advisors, the technical specialists helping to build up Cuba's armed forces.

Of Arms and the Men

These officers had been named to lead an exceptionally diverse contingent of Soviet forces. The centerpiece, of course, was the missile regiments. The thirty-six R-12 MRBMs and their twenty-four launchers were equally divided among three regiments, while two other regiments were to share the twenty-four longer-range R-14s and the sixteen launchers provided for them. The MRBM warheads had explosive yields ranging from 200 to 700 kilotons, ten to thirty-five times the power of the atomic bomb that devastated Hiroshima. IRBM warheads for missiles that, in the end, never reached Cuba, had yields from 200 to 800 kilotons.

Each missile regiment had its own mobile technical-support base, including vans to bring the warheads from underground storage bunkers to the rockets once orders were given to ready them for firing. Such physical separation of weapon and delivery vehicle, including special KGB guards for the stored warheads, were standard features of Soviet nuclear deployment until more sophisticated safeguards against accidental launches were developed.

To defend Cuban territory and Soviet rockets alike, the plan that Malinovsky and Khrushchev approved in early July provided for the following forces:

Air and antiaircraft

The 10th and 11th antiaircraft divisions, both subdivided into three surface-to-air missile (SAM-75) regiments of four launch complexes each. In addition to the 72 missile launchers in each division, the 10th was augmented by a 40-plane regiment of MiG-21 fighter-interceptors;

Two cruise-missile (FKR) regiments with five missiles and an equal number of warheads for each regiment's eight launchers—80 missiles in all, each with 5–12-kiloton warheads;

A regiment of 33 Model-4 Mi helicopters;

A squadron of 11 Il-28 bombers (for conventional weapons) and six other Il-28s specially fitted to carry atomic bombs.

A mixed squadron of 11 planes, Li-2s and An-24s, for intra-island transport and communications.

Infantry

Four motorized rifle regiments drawn from the Leningrad Military District, with each 2500-man regiment assigned 31 regular tanks (T-34s or T-55s) and three amphibious ones (PT-76s.) Each regiment was also equipped with ten self-propelled, 100-millimeter cannon called SAU-100s; ten armored reconnaissance vehicles; nine 120-millimeter mortars; nine anti-tank guided missiles; nine 57-millimeter anti-aircraft machine guns; six 122-millimeter howitzers; 60 armored personnel carriers; 18 motorcycles and 233 cars and trucks.

Separate "Luna" rocket detachments from the Kiev Military District composed of two launchers and four missiles each were also attached to the 74th, 134th and 146th regiments deployed, respectively, near Artemisa, Havana and Santa Clara.

Navy

One squadron of 11 submarines and a second of surface ships—two cruisers, two missile-firing and two regular destroyers, a brigade of 16 torpedo boats, a coastal-defense regiment with six "Sopka" missile launchers; a naval-air regiment of 12 Il-28s and, in support roles, two supply ships, two tankers, two bulk carriers and a repair ship.

The decision to include short-range nuclear weapons in the deployment to Cuba was carefully weighed. Although the "Lunas," FKRs and specially fitted Il-28s were not among the standard armaments then assigned to Soviet forces stationed outside the USSR, it was felt that Pliyev's troops on Cuba, so far from reinforcements, might need the added battlefield strength that such tactical atomic arms could provide.

The presence of the MRBMs and IRBMs, due to be disclosed by Khrushchev in late November, was meant to deter U.S. aggression against Cuba. The battlefield nuclear weapons were put on the island in case deterrence failed. Targeted on the approaches an invading fleet was thought most likely to use and on the beachheads where U.S. troops seemed most likely to come ashore, the low-yield "Luna" and FKR warheads were weapons Soviet planners classed as a kind of extra-powerful artillery shell.

Had the missile deployment gone undiscovered as planned and had Khrushchev been able to unveil the R-12s and R-14s with Castro by his side, it is possible that the presence of the tactical arms would also have been announced, bit by bit in the following weeks. No specific planning for such revelations was made, however. Because the twelve "Lunas," eighty cruise missiles and six nuclear-capable Il-28s were treated as war-fighting—rather than deterrent—weapons, Soviet thinkers did not see much defensive advantage to be gained by announcing that such arms were part of our arsenal on Cuba. Arcane theories of nuclear deterrence mattered less to us than practical questions of assuring our exposed troops the strongest possible armor against attack.

The operations plan approved in July envisaged moving 50,874 men to Cuba. The total included personnel for field hospitals, bakeries, mechanical workshops and other support units, all with a three-month supply of food and fuel. In the course of September, however, the plan was revised to eliminate the submarine and surface-ship naval squadrons, both because of concern about our ability to supply them if fighting broke out and worry that their highly visible presence would sound too loud an alarm bell in Washington. That decision also meant removing from the list of munitions four atomic mines meant to protect the fleet. The torpedo boats and "Sopka" coastal-defense rockets remained in the plan, but were to be delivered to Cuba by civilian freighters rather than the Soviet Navy.

The September changes meant cutting 5,640 naval personnel from the deployment, leaving a planned, full contingent of 45,234. Of that number, 3,332 turned back, as did the ship carrying the twenty-four IRBMs, while at sea in October. Actual Soviet troop strength on Cuba when John Kennedy imposed the naval blockade on 24 October was 41,902.

Another change in the preliminary plan was made in July when Malinovsky decided not to send the rocket forces in the first wave, but to deploy the antiaircraft and motorized rifle divisions first. Although we knew it would take a good deal of time to bring the missiles to full operational readiness once they reached Cuba, we also realized that they should not be defenseless while they were being unloaded and installed at the launch sites.

Even had the rocket regiments been in the first echelon to reach Cuba, I imagine that history would have been little changed. The crisis would have come sooner than October, but the end would have been the same. The missiles would have had to be withdrawn, with the condition that the United States pledge to leave Cuba in peace.

My own mind was not focused on probable outcomes, but on the infinity of details to be coordinated and movements to be synchronized just to carry out our assignment on schedule. With shipping to originate from eight different ports—Kronstadt, Liepaya, Baltiysk and Murmansk in the north and Sevastopol, Feodosia, Nikolayev and Poti on the Black Sea—and troops and equipment to be securely housed during the two or three days normally required to load a single ship, I had time only to concentrate on the minutiae of the logistic challenge, not to speculate on larger issues of global strategy and politics.

In the thirty days between the Presidium decision in June and Pliyev's departure with his senior staff on 10 July, the operational plan not only gelled, but actually moved into action. On 7 July, Malinovsky reported to Khrushchev that the Defense Ministry was ready to launch Operation ANADYR:

> All the troops from the planned list of military personnel have been chosen and outfitted and are ready for transport. Plans are in place for all stages of the deployment of troops to Cuba within four months (July, August, September, October). The first shipment is scheduled for July 12, 1962.[5]

The day after Pliyev's flight left Moscow, two more planes followed him, carrying the advance party of officers to scout the sites for our troops to garrison and to prepare for their arrival. All the passengers were disguised as agricultural specialists, engineers and irrigation and drainage technicians, ostensibly civilians assigned to continue the technical assistance work that Rashidov's mission had been publicized as initiating.

Anchors Aweigh

In mid-July the *Maria Ulyanova* actually sailed for the port of Cabañas, arriving there on 26 July. She was the first of what were to be eighty-five merchant marine passenger and freight ships to make some 150 round trips between the Soviet Union and Cuba over the next three months in the service of Operation ANADYR. Each cargo was loaded and each troop contingent embarked on these vessels under such strict secrecy that couriers, rather than radio or telephone lines, carried all messages between the ports and the Defense Ministry in Moscow.

I was curious to know more details than the dry, written dispatches provided, but not until early August did I receive permission from General Ivanov to go myself to see how the operation we had so painstakingly planned was actually being executed. I flew to the Crimean port of Feodosia on the Black Sea to watch the loading of the antiaircraft unit under the command of Col. Yuri Surkhanovich Guseinov. I found tightly controlled chaos.

The loading regimen was very strict. Once they reached the Feodosia docks, all personnel were prohibited from leaving the area and were put under the guard of special troops who answered only to the port commander. All communication with the outside world was cut off—no letters, telegrams or telephone calls permitted, a rule that applied equally to the ship crews and their officers.

Artillery Marshal Konstantin P. Kazakov headed the General Staff operations group on the scene. "Everyone keeps asking me the same question," he moaned. " 'Where are we going? And why?'

"I explain to them that there are to be major strategic exercises in sending troops over long distances by sea, but I can see that they don't really believe me. They ask why their Party and Komsomol [Communist Youth League] cards as well as their military service booklets are being taken away. How can I answer them?"

I told him and all the others who quizzed me hopefully as a General Staff expert fresh from Moscow to use the only response any of us was authorized to make: training exercises were under way and anything could be expected.

And, indeed, there was training: intensive safety exercises in loading and unloading munitions and supplies, in teaching soldiers how to be freight-handlers and how to secure cargo. On board, the work was fast and furious. Soldiers and crew members had to build bunk beds on the lower decks. The missile mounts and targeting stations had to be boarded up with planks to make them look like ship superstructures. Even on-deck field kitchens had to be disguised.

Guseinov's regiment was loaded on the freight ship *Leninsky Komsomol*, with a displacement of 25,000 tons. In order to fend off a possible air or patrol-boat attack, this ship had several large-caliber, precision, antiaircraft machine guns installed beneath special wooden hatches that the ship's cranes could remove. A special company within the regiment was also equipped with submachine and machine guns in case an emergency forced the ship to land somewhere, or attackers tried to board it at sea.

"Comrade General," an Army captain asked me one day, "are we going far away?" Built like an athlete, he wore the emblems of an artillery man.

"Far away, captain, very far."

"Well, for example, how many days?"

"Well, for example, say I don't know," I tried to make a joke, but, judging by his eyes, it fell flat.

By that evening, I knew, the captain and all his comrades would be issued "civvies"—a suit, shirt, even a hat. Like new draftees who have just put on their uniforms, at first they wouldn't recognize each other. In the cabins of the

Leninsky Komsomol, where the officers' corps was to double up in brutally close quarters, I was again cross-examined.

"What news do you bring from the capital, General?" asked the ship's commanding officer.

"Nothing special, nothing you don't know already."

"But where are we going, anyway?"

"You'll learn all that once you're out at sea."

And only then, I might have added. Before casting off, the troop commander and the ship captain would jointly receive a large sealed envelope tied with brown ribbon. Unfastening it, they would find a smaller envelope to be opened only at such-and-such coordinates in the Atlantic Ocean. For that revealing ceremony, an officer of the KGB's Special Department would join them.

The letter inside would tell them to proceed to a Cuban port and authorize them to inform the ship's company of the destination. Further instructions included these: "Conduct necessary explanatory work among Party and Komsomol members and with all passengers and crew members on implementing this special governmental task. Proceed to study material on Cuba. In conducting meetings, use members of the crew who have been on Cuba before."[6]

Every ship carried thick folders prepared by Defense Ministry staffers who had assembled background information on a number of countries with which the Soviet Union had good relations. Buried in these packets, so that not even the compilers would know the real focus of Operation ANADYR, were the study materials on Cuba. The concern for secrecy carried over even to the last sentence of the letter each captain opened in the Atlantic. "After familiarizing yourself with the contents of this document," read the closing lines, "destroy it."[7]

3

Under Cover

The inspection trip to the Crimea lifted my spirits and renewed my energy. Instead of numbers and unit designations on pieces of paper, Operation ANADYR became people whose names I had learned, whose faces I knew. Seeing our troops and sensing their spirit confirmed my pride in our Soviet armed forces. I went back to work in Moscow with fresh confidence in our plans and the way they were being carried out. Except for relatively minor delays in getting ships into the proper berths and trains to the embarkation points on time, everything appeared to be moving smoothly and on schedule.

Appearances were not enough for Defense Minister Malinovsky. He began to have doubts about the completeness of the daily written briefings that General Ivanov and I presented to him. Our information was based on the reports of troop and freight movements, loadings and sailings, arrivals and unloadings that flowed into a new, special department of the operations directorate headed by Col. Ivan Grigorievich Nikolayev and, as his deputy, Col. Vyacheslav Kotov. Their summaries were good enough for me and Semyon Ivanov, but not for the minister.

One day he read our regular report, took off his glasses, laid our papers aside and said:

"You've written up everything here so smoothly—so much out, so much in. But what shape did it arrive in? What happened to the ships and people en route? They had to pass through the Bosphorus, the Dardanelles, Gibraltar, Skagerrak, Kattegat and the Norwegian Sea. All those places are bristling with NATO ships and submarines. Their airplanes were probably circling like vultures. Did our ships get through OK?

"I, for one, don't know. But I'd like to. . . ."

His criticism was a bitter pill that we swallowed in silence, knowing that the minister was absolutely right. We quickly got in touch with the merchant marine—the only service authorized to communicate with the ships en route and our only channel of communications with the forces already on Cuba—and arranged to receive reports by 7:00 A.M. every day on the progress of the ships, the situation on board and unforeseen incidents at sea. By nine o'clock every morning we were ready to provide the minister with the information he wanted.

Early in September I made another inspection trip to the Crimea, this time to Sevastopol, where the three regiments of the missile division commanded by Maj. Gen. Igor Demyanovich Statsenko were being loaded for shipment to Cuba. I found very much the same situation as in Feodosia: round-the-clock work, with only occasional delays caused by the difficulty of docking each ship precisely as the troop units and cargo assigned to it reached the docks.

Adm. Nikolai M. Kharlamov, who headed up the General Staff's operations group in Sevastopol, knew the port well. Because Sevastopol was the primary base of the Black Sea Fleet, it was a closed city, and maintaining secrecy was somewhat easier than in Feodosia. Not only were foreigners barred from such military areas, but the city's residents were also subject to special controls. Once in the port area, the rocket troops were isolated from the rest of the country.

Unlike the tanks, antiaircraft guns, disassembled airplanes and other heavy equipment that we had shipped in July and August, the twenty-meter-long (sixty-seven-foot) MRBMs sailing with Statsenko's troops could not fit into the holds of ordinary freighters. Fortunately, the *Poltava* was one of a class of ships that had oversize cargo areas able to hold the giant missile containers. I watched the cranes hoist these huge crates from the pier and lower them one by one into the ship, impressed by the skill of the crane operators who manipulated such bulky objects with such speed and care.

After the missiles were loaded, the cranes swung large concrete slabs from flatbed cars into the steel belly of the freighter. Not ballast, I learned, the slabs were actually emergency launch pads for the MRBMs. As a senior officer who knew the purpose of Operation ANADYR explained to me, rocket forces head-quarters staff had ordered the foundation blocks shipped to Cuba, "just in case we are put on alert and have to unload and take our launching positions quickly."

"Smart," I thought. "Very smart. All this will help install the missiles faster at the new location."

Sadly, the accommodations for human beings were not as well thought out as the spaces for their weapons. Troops were packed into the freighters' holds like sardines. With Admiral Kharlamov's support, I tried to rearrange the loads so as to free up more space for the men, but we were not able to make much improvement. I worried how the soldiers, non-coms and officers would tolerate a voyage of eighteen to twenty days while crammed in floating steel boxes under the broiling sun, allowed out only briefly at night in packs of twenty to twenty-five for a few minutes of exercise and a gulp of fresh sea air.

My worries were all too well founded. The daily reports from the merchant marine soon brought news of sickness and even of one death, a sergeant whose tarpaulin-wrapped corpse was buried one night at sea. The heat on board also ruined some supplies. Two months' butter, for instance, was part of the standard ration issued for every unit as it was dispatched. In the warm waters of the Caribbean, however, the butter melted, and the boxes that had held it floated in puddles of rancid oil.

Our inexperience in planning for long voyages under tropical conditions brought other losses. Many lightweight uniforms reached Cuba ruined by mildew. Seasickness plagued at least half of the travelers, and a number of soldiers set foot on the island swearing never to get on a ship again. Somehow, though, the vast majority not only bore the burdens and losses stoically, but came ashore with their fighting spirit and capability intact.

Col. Arkadi Fyodorovich Shorokhov, head of the political department of the motorized rifle regiment, kept and later gave me a journal of the crossing he made on the *Khabarovsk* and its aftermath. "On 20 August we approached the Azores," he wrote. "There was a storm. The ship was pitching heavily. All our soldiers and officers were seasick. That night, some enterprising soldiers opened up two barrels of pickles and ate them. That eased the heaving for them somewhat.

"But as they say, bad luck always comes in a streak. The regiment's senior physician, Maj. A.I. Zhirnov, and the ship's doctor were forced to operate on a sergeant who was suddenly stricken with acute appendicitis. The operation was successful, although we were all terribly worried. . . .

"We have been sailing for weeks. All around is the turquoise ocean. The heat. We strip down to our shorts. At night, everyone tries to find a sheltered spot on the decks.

"During the day, American aircraft fly over our ship. Some military vessel has been tailing our freighter and demanding inspection. We just listen over the radio, but don't reply. In the morning, the drone of an airplane wakes us. An American fighter swoops down on our ship almost getting tangled in the masts. The coast of Cuba is visible now. . . .

"Disembarking after so many torments, the men could be heard cursing: 'You're not going to get me back on that mother _____ barge. Until they build a bridge to Russia, I'm not going over the ocean for anything.' But when it came time to return to the Motherland, you could hear them saying: 'All right, I'm willing to go through seasickness again just so we can get back home quicker.' Their words reflected their longing for the far-away Motherland, for their families and their friends."

Camouflage and Disinformation

The secrecy that was such a key element of Operation ANADYR also increased the physical and psychological hardships our troops had to bear. So that foreign intelligence would not discover the truth of what we pretended was a strategic exercise, we assembled all the men, arms and equipment in the loading areas and moved them by rail only at night and under reinforced guard. The trains' routes and final destinations were kept secret. Mail and telegrams along the way were categorically prohibited.

Once they arrived at their embarkation areas, the troops were quartered at the nearest military bases and not allowed outside until, using their own vehicles or those of the local garrisons, they moved to the docks and to the ships that would carry them to Cuba. The crews of those vessels, many of which made more than one round trip, were also forbidden shore leave and correspondence.

At sea, combat and specialized military equipment was stored below, out of sight; ordinary automobiles, trucks, tractors and harvesters were put on the top deck to make it seem that only agricultural gear was being transported. Distinctively military hardware, such as missiles and launchers, was crated and, to foil infrared photography, shielded with metal sheets.

For most of the voyage, the travelers were allowed on deck only for brief nocturnal exercise periods or meals. Once the ships approached the Bahamas, where U.S. Air Force overflights and Navy surveillance began, even those outings ended. During the torrid days, heavy tarpaulins covered the hatches of the lower decks where the troops were berthed. Only ventilation systems moved the air, and temperatures sometimes climbed to 50 degrees centigrade (122 degrees Fahrenheit). Rations were issued twice a day and only in darkness. On some of the ships, even toilet use had to be scheduled.

Such restrictions often made conditions on board nightmarish, but the cover story held. U.S. intelligence discovered neither the true significance of the surge in Soviet shipping to Cuba nor the mission of our troops on the island until nearly all the men had come ashore and—still moving in large numbers only by night—had been deployed to their assigned positions.

A variety of deceptive measures contributed to our success in maintaining secrecy. For instance, when the luxury liner *Admiral Nakhimov* left the Black Sea carrying 2,000 soldiers, we arranged to have the Georgian newspaper *Zarya Vostoka* print a small news item announcing the first tourist cruise to Cuba. The privileged voyagers, in fact, were mainly young recruits, so newly drafted that their shaved heads had barely sprouted crew cuts. As their ship passed from the Black Sea to the Aegean, the only view they had of the minarets of Istanbul and the cliffs of Gallipoli was from their cabin portholes.

Not only were our soldiers not permitted on deck, the ships' captains were under orders to keep all foreigners off their vessels, even the Turkish pilots who customarily guided civilian vessels through the tricky waters of the Bosphorus and the Dardanelles Straits. Whenever these navigators approached our transports, Soviet crews, instead of providing ladders, would lower bulging parcels of vodka, brandy, caviar, sausages and other delicacies. That transparent bribery worked as well as the on-deck camouflage. Everyone likes to get presents, even pilots.

After mid-September, moreover, the Soviet merchant fleet captains and the commanders of the troops being transported were under new orders, personally approved by Nikita Khrushchev on 17 September, to return fire if any ship was attacked at sea. Such an assault by foreign vessels or aircraft, the revised instructions said, "should be interpreted as an act of aggression against the Soviet Union,"[1] reported immediately to Moscow and resisted with the two twenty-three-millimeter antiaircraft guns added to each freighters' on-deck armament.

The ship captains were given the authority to decide whether or not to return fire if attacked and ordered to broadcast their reports of enemy action in the clear. They were to describe their own response, however, only in coded radio transmissions so that Moscow could try to present any such incident to the world as an act of piracy against a peaceful, unarmed transport. Fortunately, U.S. surveillance activities, though intense to the point of harassment, did not escalate to violence. At least until President Kennedy imposed the formal blockade on 24 October, we were able to preserve the fiction of ordinary Soviet cargo ships carrying ordinary cargo to Cuba.

The requirements of our disinformation strategy, though, created moments of confusion in our own ranks, even among those who were told that their mission involved Cuba. Just before the 12 July departure of sixty-seven members of the second advance operations group—following the contingent that had flown with General Pliyev two days before—the entire reconnaissance party gathered in the large meeting hall at the Soviet Army and Navy Main Political Directorate on B.M. Shaposhnikov Lane in Moscow. After a final, preflight briefing, the officers were given passports valid for foreign travel, already stamped with Guinean visas for the plane's stopover in Conakry.

When I asked if there were any questions, two officers stood up together. Each one's passport contained the right photograph, but their last names, first names and patronymics had gotten scrambled—Ivanov had become Petrov, or vice versa. Because there was no time to fix the mistakes, I simply told them that from then on they should live and work under the names printed in their passports.

That problem—the result of haste rather than purposeful deception—had just been put to rest when another officer rose and announced that his passport listed his profession as "machine operator and irrigation specialist." The trouble, he said, was that he had not been briefed about his cover story ahead of time. If anyone were to question him about his supposed field, he wouldn't have the faintest notion of the answers to give.

His concern prompted several other "agricultural specialists" to raise the same issue. They, too, had been given technical identities in specialties that were complete mysteries to them. It was too late, however, to explain how or even why their false occupations had been assigned. Instead, it was suggested that they use the long flight ahead to find and consult the few genuine specialists traveling with them or military comrades who had at least some rudimentary exposure to the jobs listed and how to do them.

On New Ground

On arrival in Cuba, where officials from the Ministry of Agriculture met them and many later Soviet arrivals, the reconnaissance teams discovered that the military job set for them would give them more than enough to worry about. Based on the very preliminary scouting work done by the advance group in early June, the General Staff had worked from maps to choose bases for different troop units and weapons installations. The reconnaissance group had to inspect those areas, determine precise sites, lay out routes of march from the eleven Cuban ports* selected to receive Soviet ships and organize staging areas and supply depots—and then coordinate all these plans with the Revolutionary Armed Forces of Cuba. Time was short. The advance party had to be ready when the first transport, the *Maria Ulyanova*, sailed into Cabañas on 26 July. Nine more ships docked at other ports in the next four days, including the *Latvia* on 29 July, bringing the rest of the headquarters staff for the Group of Soviet Forces.

In those hectic first days and over the months that followed, secrecy created more than a few snafus. Back in Moscow, the General Staff had neglected to provide passwords for the greeting parties and the arriving transports to use in identifying themselves to one another. As a result, some ship captains and on-board troop commanders had a hard time accepting orders to reroute their ves-

---

* Havana, Mariel, Cabañas, Bahia Honda, Matanzas, La Isabela, Nuevitas, Nicaro, Casilda, Cienfuegos and Santiago de Cuba.

sels away from their originally assigned ports. The captain of the *Khimik Zelinsky* went so far as to head back out to sea rather than let a Cuban patrol boat crew come on board to guide him to his anchorage.

In port, it usually took the same two to three days to unload a single ship that had been needed to bring its cargo aboard. Security concerns inevitably complicated the work. Equipment that bore at least a superficial resemblance to agricultural machinery could be unloaded in daylight, but tanks, guns, rockets and other obviously military freight could only be lifted out of the holds at night to be stored in sheds out of sight or moved along back roads, still in the dark, to designated bases.

Once disembarked, the travel-weary troops, dressed as civilians, were subject to further, unfamiliar demands. Their Soviet escorts from the Group of Forces staff, for instance, were required to wear Cuban military uniforms, and all commands issued along the routes the motorized convoys took from the ports to the bases had to be in Spanish, the language of the Cuban guard detachments that accompanied our columns. Until the end of August, when most of the Soviet transport vehicles had arrived, our forces had to use Cuban tractor trailers and similar transport machinery to move our heavy equipment.

On the march and on bivouac, Soviet units were not only kept in civvies but also forbidden to mention either their military designations or the ranks of their commanders, especially in the presence of outsiders. Additionally, all communication between field units and the Group of Forces headquarters in Havana had to be oral, not written, and made in person, not by radio. Except for very brief tests of their equipment and hook-ups, in fact, our troops maintained total radio silence so that no broadcast would give away identity, locations or troop strength to U.S. electronic eavesdropping devices.

Considering such restrictions and the many unanticipated problems that they encountered, our troops performed their tasks on Cuba with remarkable efficiency. Most of them managed to set up their garrisons—usually in unpopulated areas where roads were few and in poor condition—very nearly on schedule. Their success was a tribute to their discipline and fortitude and to the enthusiasm with which they took up the cause of the Cuban Revolution as their own.

The challenges they overcame were practically numberless. What had looked neat and logical on maps in Moscow frequently turned out to be unworkable on the ground. For example, many of the preselected sites had to be dropped or substantially altered for a number of reasons. In selecting actual troop locations, the advance groups had to give priority to such basic necessities as the availability of water, even if doing so meant overriding theoretical guidelines on tactical maneuverability and other operational considerations.

For purposes of camouflage, of course, standard doctrine gave preference to wooded areas, and Sharaf Rashidov had reported to the Defense Council that Cuba's forests would provide just the needed cover for our missiles. Only someone with absolutely no competence in such technical matters could have reached such a conclusion. A missile-launching complex is not easily disguised. The area is filled not with slim, upright rockets but with multiple command and support buildings, rows of fuel trucks and tanks and hundreds of meters of thick cable—all surrounding the large concrete slabs that anchored the missile launchers. Once the heavy equipment had been moved in, such an installation—but not the roads built to it—could be hidden from ground-level view. From above, however, it could and did stick out like a sore thumb.

Cuba's climate, moreover, made wooded areas unsuitable places to hide Soviet troops and arms. The island's forests were generally sparse, consisting of a few clusters of palm trees or a thick undergrowth of bushes where the air barely moved and the intense, moist heat was unbearable. Instead of providing welcome shade during daylight, the woods acted like a sponge, soaking up atmospheric moisture and raising the humidity to levels debilitating for men and machinery alike. On the eastern part of the island, moreover, the forests held many poisonous guayaco trees. Merely touching their bark raised blisters on the skin.

Even with a number of planned bases relocated to take account of actual conditions on the ground, the advance parties and those who followed them regularly came up against unforeseen problems of terrain and weather. In many places troops could not dig conventional trenches in the thin and rocky soil without hitting water just below the surface. For fortifications around the surface-to-air-missile launchers, the air defense forces had to build up earthen embankments and top them with rolls of barbed wire, performing this heavy labor in ten-to-twelve-hour shifts in terrible heat and fierce rainstorms.

Their work was crucial, because defense was the top priority. The first sites manned and equipped were for the antiaircraft defenses, the cruise missiles and the Navy's "Sopka" coastal defense rockets. Depending on actual conditions in the field, it took eight to fifteen days to construct and fortify each of these crucial launching sites, work that regularly required the combined efforts and supplies of engineering troops and of the soldiers assigned to the antiaircraft and rocket emplacements.

It had been planned to deploy the four motorized rifle regiments separately with each assigned to cover a combat zone up to one hundred and twenty-five miles east-to-west and from twenty to one hundred miles north-to-south. In fact, we concentrated our forces in the west where the 134th and 74th regiments ended up stationed south and west of Havana, respectively. The 146th regiment moved into the center of Cuba near the site for the intermediate-range R-12 missiles, and the 106th—the only one without a "Luna" rocket detachment—

provided defense against attack from the U.S. base at Guantánamo Bay on the eastern end of Cuba. Raul Castro's ground forces flanked the Soviet units along most of the front, but air defense consisted almost entirely of our forty MiG-21 interceptors and our six surface-to-air-missile regiments, which had radar equipment more modern than anything then in Cuban hands.

These installations and their perimeter defenses had to protect our men and their arms against two threats: U.S. invasion and U.S.-sponsored subversion and sabotage. As they spread out into the island's six provinces, our forces had to take both dangers seriously. Even with Cuban troops and, sometimes, patrol boats protecting our ships as they landed and unloaded, and even with the Cuban military units near ours on land, our officers and soldiers had to be on constant guard against bands of counterrevolutionaries infiltrated onto the island and against open attack by U.S. forces. America, after all, was very close, and the Soviet Union, very far away.

Travel Orders

From my vantage point in Moscow, the summer-long deployment to and on Cuba seemed to be proceeding very much according to plan. Of course, the plan had to be revised as it was put into practice. On the island, many actual troop and missile dispositions were different from those the General Staff mapmakers had initially contemplated. The organization charts had also been redrawn by the decision not to send Soviet Navy ships into harm's way, and the timetable had been altered somewhat to speed the shipment of the dozen, nuclear armed "Lunas" and the six Ilyushin-28 bombers that had been specially refitted to carry atomic bombs. But all these modifications, big and small, had been accomplished without apparently slowing or upsetting the course of the operation overall.

Therefore, I was surprised when, early in October, General Ivanov and I were suddenly summoned by the defense minister and, on entering his office, immediately offered seats. That was a rare courtesy. Usually we stood in front of Marshal Malinovsky's desk to deliver our reports. Being directed to chairs meant we were in for a long conversation.

Looking at us very intently, as if he were seeing us for the first time, the minister began to speak. "I was just in Frol Romanovich's office," said Malinovsky. (Frol Romanovich Kozlov was a Central Committee secretary and member of the Presidium.) "It has been decided to send a group of Defense Ministry officials to Cuba to assist our forces and oversee their compliance with government decisions.

"Semyon Pavlovich," Malinovsky turned to Ivanov. "Whom would you recommend be appointed to lead this group, and serve, by the way, as my personally authorized representative there?"

"I think it would be appropriate to entrust this assignment to General Gribkov, Comrade Minister," Ivanov immediately replied. "Anatoli Ivanovich has been briefed on all the developments. He knows all the plans and assignments given to Pliyev's troops."

"All right, I agree," said the minister after a moment's reflection. "This is a difficult assignment. The leader's job will be even harder. You had better choose generals and officers for this group who know their fields well and make sure that all the branches of the armed forces are represented. Give them very thorough instructions. When the group is ready to fly out, Comrade Gribkov should report to me personally. We'll have a special conversation then. . . ."

Marshal Malinovsky was not exaggerating when he called the assignment "difficult." I had participated in many such missions, and because they involved outsiders coming in to oversee the work of a field commander, they were always difficult. Officers almost invariably resented such intrusions. Having representatives of the General Staff look over their shoulders diminished their authority and, if they were less than fully competent, put their jobs and careers at risk. The more experienced, proud and power-loving the commanders were, the more prickly they were about such visitations.

The worst such encounter I recall from the wartime years came when I was working as the General Staff liaison in January 1943 with the 19th tank corps on the Bryansk front. The corps had lost more than 80 percent of its tanks in a series of battles, but its commander kept ordering it forward, using the surviving soldiers as infantrymen. Observing this waste of lives and skills—tank crews require much more training than foot soldiers and are therefore significantly more valuable troops—I reported the situation to the chief of the General Staff and recommended that the corps be withdrawn from the front and put in the reserves to save the remaining tank crews and to build up its manpower again.

In violation of standing orders that should have kept my message from the eyes of all but its addressees, the chief of the communications section of the front-line staff reported what I had written to the front commander, Lt. Gen. M. A. Reiter. Furious that a lowly major was sending back-channel reports on him to Moscow, Reiter sent a message of his own, proposing, as I had, that the 19th corps be put in reserve status and adding: "Order Major Gribkov off the front."

When, in turn, I learned what had happened, I was able to get through by telephone to the offices of the General Staff. That same day a telegram arrived for the front commander ordering the tank corps into the reserve. "Major Gribkov," the message from Moscow added, "is a representative of the General Staff and will be recalled when the General Staff considers it necessary to do so."

Nearly twenty years later that episode came to mind as I contemplated the difficulties I anticipated—correctly, as it turned out—in building good relations with General Pliyev and his staff. I knew that Malinovsky counted on me and my multifaceted background to produce a first-class inspection team and to provide, with its members, the necessary operational support for the far-away Group of Forces. I also knew that the minister would support my judgment, but I did not relish the task ahead.

Two days later, I reported to the minister that a group of eight senior officers was briefed and ready to tackle the assignment. He carefully reviewed the list of the traveling party, approved it and then began our "special talk" by saying:

"As soon as all the [R-12 and R-14] missile units are fully prepared for combat deployment, you should report to me personally—to me only, and to no one else. Your assignment is to supervise the preparedness of the troops to fulfill their assignments, but mainly to ensure that the missiles are ready for action.

"Memorize and repeat to Comrade Pliyev that the orders he personally received from Nikita Sergeyevich about using the R-12, R-14 missiles and the 'Luna' rockets must be obeyed strictly and precisely. That means that the missiles may be launched only—I repeat, only—with the personal permission of the Supreme Commander-in-Chief Nikita Sergeyevich Khrushchev.

"You know very well that we are stationing the missiles in Cuba in order to deter possible aggression on the part of the United States of America and its allies. We do not intend to unleash an atomic war; that is not in our interests.

"If there is no way to communicate with Moscow, Pliyev may use the tactical 'Luna' rockets at his discretion in the event of an American attack and if troops actually land on the coast. But there should be no haste to fire the 'Lunas.'

"Make sure that Pliyev has well-organized, secure communications by direct wire and by radio with each missile unit. Under no circumstances can unauthorized launching of those missiles be permitted. Pay particular attention to the way the missile-launching sites are protected. According to plan, that is the duty of the rocket troops themselves, of the motorized rifle regiments and also of the antiaircraft units that are to provide cover from aerial attack."

The minister stood up from his desk, paced around his office, and stopped in front of me.

"When the [medium- and intermediate-range] missile forces are ready, report to me using this prearranged phrase, the meaning of which only you and I will know. The phrase should be this."

He thought for a while, looked at me, and then very carefully pronounced each word syllable by syllable: " 'To the Director: the sugar cane harvest is coming along successfully.'

"From now on, all correspondence between us and the Group of Forces should be addressed to the 'Director.' Tell that to Pliyev as well."

He forced me to repeat the prearranged phrase twice and then wished me a good trip. To the great relief of all involved, I never had to send this "crop report" to Moscow.

4

Before the Storm

The Kremlin decision to send a high-level military inspection team to Havana signaled some alarm about the situation in the Caribbean. But what most concerned the Soviet leadership as the 1962 summer turned to autumn was not so much the pace of our defensive preparations on Cuba as the bellicose words issuing from Washington, from members of Congress and from President Kennedy himself. Having failed in one attempt to overthrow Fidel Castro and undo the Cuban revolution, the United States—as Nikita Khrushchev feared—seemed to be preparing for a second try.

My team's double assignment was to ensure that our MRBMs and IRBMs were being installed on schedule and that the Soviet Group of Forces was as prepared as possible to join in defending the island if an attack came. The reports reaching Moscow from Pliyev's command showed steady advances, but persistent difficulties as well. By early November, our missiles and their multilayered defenses were supposed to be fully operational, and my group was to help meet that timetable.

Thirty-six medium-range R-12 missiles had arrived in mid-September on board the *Poltava* and its sister ship, the *Omsk*. By mid-October the *Poltava* was bound for Cuba again with twenty-four intermediate-range R-14s on board. The atomic warheads for the MRBMs had arrived in Mariel on 4 October on board the freighter *Indigirka* after an anxious but uneventful eighteen-day voyage from the Barents Sea military port of Severomorsk. The KGB troops on that ship, itself specially armed for the perilous trip, were also guarding eighty cruise-missile (FKR) warheads, six bombs for the Il-28 aircraft and a dozen atomic charges for the short-range "Luna" rockets. Separately, another cargo ship, the *Alexandrovsk*, carried the twenty-four warheads for the R-14 missiles. These stayed in the vessel's hold in the port of La Isabela, waiting for missiles that never arrived.

The R-12 warheads had gone into bunkers in Bejucal, about thirteen miles south of Havana and—by road—not much more than fifty miles from the three MRBM missile regiments deployed near San Cristobal. This central nuclear depot in Bejucal was also the storage site for forty warheads for the FKR detachment about forty miles away, west of Mariel, and for the twelve warheads for the three "Luna" rocket units. One of those was attached to the 134th motorized rifle regiment headquartered in Managua, twelve miles east northeast of Bejucal; another belonged to the 74th regiment based near Artemisa, about thirty miles to the southwest. The third "Luna" detachment was near Remedios close to the sites in central Cuba where the R-14 missiles were to be installed.

Other atomic weapons—the six bombs for the Il-28 squadron and the forty warheads for the second cruise missile detachment—had been placed in well-guarded depots closer to either the bombers' airfield in the central portion of the island or to the cruise-missile unit in the hills above the U.S. base at Guantánamo Bay.

Having sent so many troops and so much weaponry—including nuclear arms—so far from Soviet territory, Marshal Malinovsky and the Kremlin leadership wanted a first-hand report on the deployments from knowledgeable and reliable observers. Accordingly, representatives of all the branches of the armed forces were included in my group. Among its top-ranking members were Gen. Mikhail Ivanovich Naumenko, air defense; Gen. Nikolai Gavrilovich Sytnik, air force; and Col. Aleksandr Pavlovich Saprykin, infantry. Gen. Aleksei Savlich Butsky, representing the strategic rocket forces, flew to Cuba ahead of us and joined our group on the scene.

We left on the evening of 14 October, bound for a stopover in Dakar, the capital of Senegal, but our Aeroflot TU-114 lost power in one of its four engines over the Mediterranean. With the passengers nervously watching the remaining three motors for signs of failure, we limped back into Moscow's Vnukovo airport around dawn on 15 October. My deputy from the General Staff, Major General Yeliseyev, met us there with Malinovsky's orders to take another plane to Cuba at 2300 hours that night. The situation in the Caribbean, he added, was heating up.

We were told not to collect our baggage—it would be transferred to the new airplane. Silently thanking Aeroflot for this attentiveness, we did not suspect that our gratitude would prove misplaced. Over the ocean, however, we began to realize how slipshod some of the airline's practices really were. After the stewardess explained how we were to use life jackets in case of a forced landing on the water, we began to look around for the jackets themselves. They were not under the seats, the stewardess told us, but down below in the baggage compartment. Checking that information, one of our comrades confirmed that all the life jackets and other evacuation supplies were in fact stored in the hold, but packed under so many different things that it was impossible to get at them.

"How are you going to hand out the life-saving equipment in case of an emergency?" I asked Aeroflot's slender, beautiful, young employee.

To the general laughter of the passengers, she replied: "Don't worry. We won't sink right away. You'll have time to get everything you need if that happens."

Joking aside, I couldn't help thinking how much carelessness and disorganization there was in Aeroflot. And not just in Aeroflot.

"Reassured," we rounded the African continent as the sun was rising. Like people in a trance, we admired the unique sight. The sky above Africa was suffused with a rosy fire that seemed to chill gradually into shades of blue as the light climbed from the horizon. On the ground in Dakar, however, the heat was staggering. As a first-time visitor to Africa, I found the temperature and the humidity of Senegal's capital on the Atlantic coast almost overwhelming.

The short-sleeved shirts and lightweight trousers my colleagues and I wore felt stifling while the local authorities spent hours debating first, whether we could leave the airplane, and second, whether we and the crew could leave the airport until—if—our airplane was refueled for the long trans-Atlantic flight. No thanks to the hapless diplomat who, in the absence of formal diplomatic relations, represented Soviet interests in Senegal, we won permission for a transit stop.

Sensing the Western pressure that had closed Conakry in neighboring Guinea to Cuban-bound Soviet air traffic the day before, the Senegalese were obviously very reluctant to have any contact with us. But some sympathetic Frenchmen, whose post-colonial influence remained strong, helped us to find a hotel right on the ocean shore, not far from the center of the completely modern, European-style city. Its tall, newly constructed buildings, its cleanness and order and its mixed population of black and white immediately shook my conception of Africa as a backward part of the world.

Interlude in Africa

Soon my image of the dark-skinned population as poor and oppressed also disappeared. There even turned out to be millionaires among the native population.

Apparently not everything depends on the color of a person's skin; entrepreneurial ability and talents can determine social status as well.

Ours was low. At the hotel, we had to wait a long time for room assignments, because most of the many available rooms were too expensive for us Soviet generals and senior officers. The accountants at the Ministry of Defense had doled out a mere $10.00 per diem in U.S. dollars, enough for each of us either to have one meal in the restaurant or to pay for a modest room. We had to decide whether to eat or have a roof over our heads, and not knowing how long our hosts would tolerate such unwelcome guests, we chose to eat.

In the hotel restaurant, we ordered the least expensive fish plate. Scanning the room, where blacks and whites were sitting together at other tables, drinking whiskey and Smirnoff vodka and sampling all sorts of tasty dishes, we couldn't help noticing one table where two white men—French, we later learned—were receiving excellent service. Soon a tall, dark-skinned, well-built man, dressed to the nines and accompanied by two whites, strutted into the room. From the behavior of the whites, it was immediately obvious that this man held some special status for them. The two Frenchmen jumped up from their places and hastened to greet the important arrival, fawning all over him as they ushered him to a chair.

"There's an example of relations between the 'oppressed' and their 'oppressors,' " I remarked to my comrades.

Another incident happened at the same restaurant. Through our translator, the Senegalese waiter asked, "Are you Soviets? From Moscow?" Convinced that we were, he then wanted to know: "You have Lenin. Where does your leader live?"

We tried to explain briefly, in ways he could understand, who Lenin was and that he was no longer among the living. He asked whether we had a portrait of Lenin or any postcards with his picture. To my great regret, no one in our group had a picture of Lenin with them. By chance, however, I had a copy of *Pravda* in my briefcase, the Communist party newspaper illustrated with a drawing of the Order of Lenin on the front page.

I showed the newspaper to the waiter, telling him about the order and about Lenin. He was very pleased and asked that we write something on the newspaper underneath the emblem. The translator signed, in French, and the Senegalese, seeming overjoyed, ran off to his colleagues pointing to the newspaper and to the people who had given him such a souvenir.

As we discussed this incident among ourselves, we agreed that we propagandize our Motherland very poorly. Many countries have their own outlets abroad, distributing books, journals, newspapers, postcards and various souvenirs—American, British, French, Chinese and others. But there is nothing that is ours, nothing to remind people of the great land of the Soviets.

My impression of this deficiency was strengthened in Cuba, where a well-established Soviet embassy certainly had plenty of opportunities to acquaint Cubans with our country. Yet even on the anniversary of the Great October Revolution, you could not find any Soviet souvenirs in the kiosks, although there were magazines and postcards from many other countries. That is how efficient Soviet representatives are abroad.

In Dakar, more bargaining, waiting and arguing finally produced hotel rooms for our group. After settling in, we headed off to the ocean, itself amazingly clean, and to a wonderful sandy beach, several hundreds yards wide, that was crowded with both blacks and whites. Women vendors patrolled the beach carrying large baskets on their heads full of exotic fruits and coconuts, all for sale, but only for hard currency. Wanting to treat ourselves, we dispatched Col. Alexander Saprykin, a colleague who spoke some French, to buy a coconut and three bottles of Coca-Cola. He returned with a whole fistful of money he had received as change, but we soon figured out that the bills were old franc notes, issued before Senegal's independence and now worthless. Our unfortunate purchasing agent went to return them to the black woman or at least to try to buy something else, but his luck ran out. She refused to accept the money, and Saprykin ended up taking it back to Moscow as a souvenir.

Since we were at the beach, we decided to take a swim. Very warm, the water was also very saline, making it easy to float and relax, but leaving the bather's body so covered in salt that each of us, after swimming a few minutes, looked as if he had been rolling around in the powdery white sand.

Gazing at the greenish-blue expanse of the Atlantic, I remembered my native Don River and my youth as one of ten children. We used to lie like this on the banks of the wide river, in bright, hot, fine sand; then we would crash into the water and race each other, swimming the crawl. In those days, we would go swimming after work in the fields. All of us—seven sons and three daughters—helped our parents with the plowing, mowing, weeding and any other farm work. "Oh, my beloved Don," I thought to myself, "unforgettable friend of my poor but happy childhood, how far away you are!"

In the heat of Africa I remembered how I would go in the winter, with a mail sack over my shoulder, to the post office in the neighboring village of Maslovka five miles away to pick up and deliver letters and newspapers, work for which I earned half a day's pay. In those years it never occurred to me that fate would carry me, a rural mailman, to the shores of the Atlantic, to a Senegal of which I had never heard.

My musing ended when a group of French paratroopers sat down near us, threw their automatic rifles down on the sand, undressed and went in swimming. Some of them, more interested in the opposite sex than the ocean, ran to get acquainted with some nubile and frisky half-naked black women who were tossing a ball back and forth on the beach. As I looked at these carefree young men, I couldn't help thinking: "If they only knew that Soviet generals and officers are lying right next to them getting a tan, waiting for their airplane to be fueled so they can fly across the ocean to help make history or perhaps to end it."

We spent the night without incident, but when I woke the next morning, I saw that my suit, shirt and shoes were missing. Except for the underwear I had slept in, I had only my briefcase and diplomatic passport, and I began to doubt that either would do me much good under the circumstances. Suddenly, though, the door I thought I had locked swung open. A dark young man came in smiling, hung up my pressed suit and shirt in the closet and placed my shoes on the floor. They had been polished to a brilliant shine.

My visitor put a slip of paper on the table, bowed, and left. I jumped out of bed and grabbed the piece of paper. It was a bill for the equivalent of six dollars for services. Once again I could not help thinking of our Central Finance Directorate at the Defense Ministry, so grudgingly forking over such a pitiful amount of foreign currency.

Obviously, we had to get out of Dakar, and quickly, or we would end up owing a fortune. At least, I thought, if you pay for service, you do get it—not as in a Moscow hotel, where the staff, by pretending to be unobtrusive, manages never to be on duty, and, if nominally at work, is usually no help to guests at all. Back at the airport, and after a long wait that the French again helped us resolve, we were able to get our airplane fueled and our westward flight resumed.

We left not a moment too soon. The next day the Dakar airport was closed to Soviet planes, as Conakry already had been, thanks to U.S. diplomatic pressure that reflected rising tension over Cuba. Our flight, fortunately, was smooth until we approached the American continent where U.S. fighter planes began to circle our TU-114, even simulating an attack on us at one point.

In contrast to that unwelcome welcoming party, we were met in Havana with music. Three Cubans in national costume stood at the entrance to the airport playing guitars and singing melodious tunes, dancing in step to the music. I was surprised by such ceremony, but it seemed that the Cubans traditionally greeted all visitors this way, no matter where they came from. I don't know whether the custom remains, but on the morning of 18 October 1962, it seemed very nice to arrive to such a hospitable welcome.

Reveille on Cuba

Along with the cheerful reception, however, some bad news awaited us. Aeroflot in Moscow had promised to transfer our suitcases from our crippled plane to our new flight. Something went wrong. Someone forgot. We reached Cuba with our briefcases and the clothes on our backs, nothing else. Aeroflot did try later to send us our baggage, but workers at the Moscow airport mixed things up so badly that our belongings went to Paris and London and were returned to Moscow without ever reaching Havana.

After several days had passed, I had to send a telegram requesting that the suitcases be delivered back to everyone's homes. I stressed that the reason for the luggage's reappearance without its owners should be explained very carefully to our families. All too predictably, many relatives got no preparatory briefing, and some wives, seeing the familiar suitcases, fainted in the belief that something terrible had happened to their husbands.

Except for the strain of the long trip, we were all in fact in good health and spirits. After a night's rest in the comfortable bungalows of El Chico, a Havana suburb where senior Soviet officers were housed, we were ready to tackle the work we had come to do: evaluate the overall readiness of the Group of Forces to defend Cuba against attack and, in the process, to push for speedier construction work at the MRBM and IRBM launch sites. For me the first order of business was to call on General Pliyev, explain our presence and transmit Malinovsky's instructions verbatim.

The key points in those orders were the prohibition on firing the R-12s or R-14s without explicit sanction from the Moscow leadership and the stern caution against using tactical nuclear weapons except in an extreme situation. I made it clear to Pliyev that my repetition of instructions that he had already received was a way of underlining the concern of the top Soviet civilian and military policymakers that the deployments on Cuba be and be seen to be defensive in nature.

Suffering from a recurrent kidney ailment, Pliyev looked physically ill and seemed decidedly unenthusiastic about receiving representatives from the General Staff. On the positive side, he reported that the Cubans were providing the necessary assistance in quartering our troops and that, at the top level, the Cuban General Staff and senior Soviet officers were cooperating satisfactorily in planning the island's coordinated defense.

Our conversation grew strained when he had to inform me that the missile deployments were not only running behind schedule but also had probably been discovered by U.S. intelligence. Progress at the missile sites had been slowed by shortages of construction equipment, he said. The engineers and soldiers of the three R-12 regiments were having to do much of the work by hand.

What they had already installed, moreover, had been under the flight path of U-2 reconnaissance planes, which had been overflying Cuba with impunity since 14 October. Pliyev's forces were forbidden to fire on these aircraft. Our surface-to-air missiles (SA-75s), already operational at a dozen sites along the north coast were the same SAMs that had brought down Francis Gary Powers' U-2 in the

Soviet Union in 1960, but Moscow had sent them to Cuba to defend against air attack, not aerial espionage. With no invasion thought imminent, the SAM commanders were not even allowed to use their radars to track the spy planes overhead.

As a result of that restraint, Pliyev warned me, the MRBM installations under construction in the San Cristobal area may well have been photographed by U-2 cameras as early as 14 October, or during a second mission on 15 October or by one of the six overflights on 17 October. Both Soviet and Cuban intelligence had observed the spy planes and their routes. The U-2 cameras, he said, would also have captured the airfield in the southwest where most of the Il-28 bombers were still in their crates and, almost certainly, the base in central Cuba where our MiG-21s were being assembled.

Pliyev's report was more like a cold shower than an electric shock. Having been out of touch with the General Staff since I set out for Cuba on 14 October, I had had no inkling of the U-2 flights, but we had worried all along about U.S. reconnaissance potential. Sooner or later, the military planners of Operation ANADYR expected Washington to learn about the presence of rocket troops in Cuba. Now that the Americans knew, new questions arose: What action would they take? How ready were we to respond?

For the time being, all that was certain was that the camouflaging of the operation had broken down somewhere. Pliyev criticized his staff for that and other failings—among them, giving inadequate priority to ground troops and aviation—but the truth, as I later learned, was that the missile sites could never have been hidden for long. The terrain did not provide cover, and eighty-foot-long rocket carriers were just too big to go unnoticed on the back roads of Cuba. When a peasant's shack had to be moved or knocked down to let one of the huge trailers turn a tight corner, the villagers who witnessed the event were bound to talk, and their talk was bound to be heard by socialism's enemies. In retrospect, it is remarkable that the secret stayed a secret for a full month after the MRBMs first reached Cuba.

That calm judgment, however, came only after long reflection. My first reaction to Pliyev's news was to set up as rapid a personal inspection as possible of the actual missile sites. I immediately asked Pliyev if Maj. Gen. Leonid S. Garbuz, his deputy commander for combat preparation, could come with me the next day to Gen. Igor D. Statsenko's rocket division. While those arrangements were being made, my traveling companions were also making contact with the units they were to visit and assess on behalf of Defense Minister Malinovsky. Pliyev said he was pleased that we were getting down to work right away, but although he cooperated with our mission, our presence was awkward evidence that Moscow was concerned about his performance.

At the Cuban Revolutionary Armed Forces Ministry, on the other hand, we were welcome guests. Escorted by Gen. Aleksei Alekseyevich Dementyev, the senior Soviet advisor to the Cuban Army, I went from Pliyev's headquarters to those of Raul Castro and Maj. Sergio del Valle, chief of the Cuban General Staff.

Comrades-in-Arms

Raul and I met like the old acquaintances we were. Both of us recalled our work together as soldier-diplomats in Moscow, and I passed on to him Malinovsky's greetings and best wishes while his staff served coffee and a wide variety of fruits, most of which could rarely be seen or bought in the Soviet capital. Both Raul's office and that of the chief of the General Staff were modestly furnished and, despite the laboring air conditioners, very hot. Not just work spaces, the offices obviously served as living quarters as well.

I informed Raul and Sergio of the purpose of my visit. In Cuba, in most cases the custom is to use only first names, and Raul began calling me Anatoli right away as he got down to business. Taking a document from a folder, Raul said, "Anatoli, we have received a very important communication. On 14 October, an American U-2 reconnaissance plane photographed the area of San Cristobal where your missile sites are being built."

"Raul, Comrade Pavlov [Pliyev] has already told me this unpleasant news," I replied. "Apparently we all have to devote more attention to concealing the work and camouflaging the missile sites—and not only the missile sites, but other heavy military equipment." Both my hosts agreed.

"Comrades Raul and Sergio," I continued, "I would like to ask you to reinforce your troops' perimeter guard of these areas now that U.S. intelligence has discovered the location of our rocket forces. They could try to sabotage the rocket units. For our part, we will also step up security and vigilance."

Raul immediately ordered del Valle to give appropriate instructions to his subordinates, and I went on to ask for permission to spend some time with Cuban units during my trip, to get better acquainted with my comrades-in-arms. Raul not only approved but asked me to stay with the Cuban soldiers for long enough to judge how they were preparing to withstand attack by U.S. forces and by the stooges he predicted Washington would recruit.

The Cuban General Staff, he told me, had designed a plan of resistance that would divide the island, in the event of assault, into three zones—western, central and eastern—with a separate command in each. If the worst came to pass and the invaders were able to isolate parts of the island, each command could fight independently in its sector until the enemy was completely destroyed. As Supreme Commander-in-Chief, Fidel Castro was to take the western zone, which included Havana. Maj. Juan Almeida was to command the center from

Santa Clara, and Raul the eastern zone, with Santiago de Cuba as his base. General Dementyev assured me that Pliyev and his staff were aware of the plan.

On parting, the gracious leaders of the Revolutionary Armed Forces and I wished each other success in turning the island into an invincible fortress that could fend off any possible attack. Raul raised his hand and said: "*Patria o muerte, venceremos*" (my country or death, we will overcome).

This patriotic slogan could be heard and seen all over Cuba, even among our troops. One Cuban company leader, I was told, had added these words when he signed his name to receive his uniform. I took that story as further evidence of what at first surprised and then continuously impressed me: the enormous revolutionary spirit of the people, their profound belief in the victory of the revolution and their faith in Fidel Castro.

As I drove through the streets of Havana, I could not but notice the visual propaganda calling for vigilance, unity, friendship and readiness to defend the revolution. One billboard, about six by nine feet, that caught my eye had a bold line dividing it into two equal parts. On the left, two people were fighting; on the right, two others were walking along arm in arm. There was a caption in Spanish above the two drawings, and I asked the translator to explain it to me. The slogan on the first panel said, "If we will not live in peace, this will play into the hands of imperialism." The second caption said, "If we will live in peace, this will be a blow to imperialism."

I liked this style of propaganda. It didn't use any fancy words, but it delivered a graphic message accessible to any ordinary person. I found that my colleagues shared my enthusiasm and were also moved by the revolutionary energy of the people and by the physical setting in which it was displayed. As we traveled around the country, all of us seeing the subtropics for the first time, our amazement at its beauty grew and grew. I could not help thinking that it was no wonder the Americans were trying to keep Cuba as their estate. Aside from its strategic position and the presence of the Marine base at Guantánamo Bay, the island was a marvel of nature.

On-Site Inspections

The next morning, 20 October, Major General Garbuz and I drove the fifty-odd miles from Havana to the missile division headquarters just outside San Cristobal to meet its commander, Maj. Gen. Igor D. Statsenko. He was young and well built, with a small mustache; like all the soldiers and officers, he was outfitted in civilian clothes—dark gray pants and a short-sleeved, checked shirt carefully tucked into a belt. But even in this mufti you could see he was a line officer, and I immediately remembered having seen him in uniform before he and the other members of the advance group flew to Cuba in mid-July to reconnoiter the proposed missile sites.

General Statsenko reported that the personnel of the three R-12 regiments were working around the clock to complete the assembly and installation of their weapons. Some soldiers and non-commissioned officers had been assigned to build housing and support facilities for the new base, he said, but most were living in tents at sites in the field, preparing the control bunkers between the launch pads, laying connecting cable and readying the fuel storage areas.

From division headquarters, we drove immediately to the regimental headquarters of Col. Yuri Aleksandrovich Solovyov, back along the road to Havana. Work at his encampment was indeed in full swing, but conditions were brutal and progress slow. The reinforced concrete slabs I had seen loaded onto the *Poltava* in Sevastopol were being anchored to the ground to serve as the pads on which the mobile launcher erectors could rest firmly for firing. But in humid heat that reached 35–40 degrees centigrade (95–104 degrees Fahrenheit), the men could work only in short shifts, with teams relieving each other every hour.

The rocky top soil, moreover, stubbornly resisted the bulldozers and earth-moving tractors we had brought from the USSR, and much of the digging had to be done by hand. We had shipped to Cuba some of the most sophisticated military technology of the age—rockets that could come within about a mile of targets a thousand miles away—yet we remained shackled to the old soldier's proverb: "One sapper, one axe, one day, one stump."

Despite everything, we found Solovyov's soldiers and officers in good humor. Some even joked that, with a whole ocean nearby, they had no time to go swimming. Secrecy not only prohibited their taking any leave, it also ruled out using Cuban labor on the fenced-in construction sites. A detailed inspection of the area convinced me that even with the commanders' best efforts, total concealment was next to impossible. The tractor-trailers for the missiles could be covered by canvas, but their mass could not be shrunk, and air surveillance, spotting such large objects and the bulky fuel trucks nearby, would quickly uncover the presence of rocket units.

With some bitterness, I recalled Sharaf Rashidov's report that palm trees would make our missiles undetectable. Only someone with no military background, with no understanding of the paraphernalia that accompanied the rockets themselves, could have reached such a conclusion. But the Politburo had accepted it uncritically and as a result some forty thousand Soviet troops who were seven thousand miles from home were perilously exposed to a strong enemy.

Inside the wire fences at the missile sites, troops from both the rocket division and a nearby motorized rifle regiment stood watch, while Cuban soldiers covered the approaches to the sealed-off areas. Although security seemed tight already, we followed up on our talks with Pliyev and Raul Castro the day before by advising Statsenko to put the internal guard at the missile sites on increased alert. In the wake of the U-2 flights, espionage and sabotage had become all too probable.

Aside from the military menace, the physical surroundings were truly hostile. Statsenko's base camp was a mixture of tents and vehicles with metal trailers, and it was hard to know which shelter was worse. Even when all the tent flaps were rolled up, the air inside was simply stifling. The trailers, on the other hand, heated up so much during the day that they were uninhabitable even at night. As darkness fell, though, it was essential to take refuge somewhere from the swarms of mosquitoes, and our men had to retreat either to the baking ovens of their trailers or to tents made airless by the closing of all the flaps.

Our soldiers and officers uncomplainingly tried to fulfil their military duty, but the odds were against them, and the timetable worked out in Moscow was in trouble on the ground in Cuba. No matter what, the plan required that the R-12 regiments be combat ready by 25–27 October. All Statsenko's resources, however, were either exhausted or on the verge of exhaustion. Without help from the motorized rifle regiments, it was obvious that the rocket divisions could not keep up with the schedule.

I took that conclusion to the Group of Forces headquarters the next day, reporting to Pliyev what I had witnessed and the advice I had given Statsenko and Solovyov on beefing up security. Grateful for the information, he promptly began assigning units from the infantry to reinforce the work crews at the missile sites. Accompanied by Aviation Maj. Gen. Nikolai G. Sytnik, I set off to visit other Soviet units and their Cuban allies.

"Operation Checked Shirt"

Our first stop was Santa Clara, headquarters of the Soviet fighter aviation regiment, outfitted with what were then new MiG-21 planes. Considered the best in the Air Force, the regiment had its permanent base in Kubinka, outside Moscow, where demonstration exercises for top officers could be held. The commander in Cuba was a first-rate pilot, Col. Nikolai Vassilyevich Shabanov, who headed the Air Force units in the Leningrad military district that I commanded many years later.

The chief of the regiment's political department, Lieut. Col. Nikolai Petrovich Shcherbina, a man of strong athletic build and a first-class flyer, happened to be running a Party meeting as we arrived. The assembled aviators showed every sign of enthusiasm for their duty and some evidence of frustration at the restrictions they were under. All top-of-the-line flyers, all young and vigorous like their commander, the pilots were full of youthful passion and pointed questions.

One of them expressed the sentiments of the whole unit. "How come," he asked, "the Americans can keep flying over us so brazenly as if they were in their own home? Why can't we retaliate? Why are we stuck here like sitting ducks?"

I explained that there was an order—"Do not open fire on individual violators"—so as not to aggravate an already tense situation. However, giving in to their persistent requests, the commander of the regiment and I, on our own authority, decided that in the right circumstances we should let a pair of our fighters challenge one of the U.S. planes that were, by then, beginning low-level surveillance flights.

We agreed that a pair of our interceptors would scramble but not open fire as soon as radar spotted a lone U.S. airplane. Our pilots would just try to "squeeze" the violator toward the ground, trying to force him to land. The encounter would give us an opportunity to see, under real, near-combat conditions, whose aircraft had the advantage in tactical and technical capabilities.

Our plan was carried out some days later, although not in full. As Colonel Shabanov, the regiment commander, later told me, our two MiG-21s displayed an advantage over the U.S. F-104 in both maneuverability and technical capacity but did not succeed in forcing it to land. After that, however, no U.S. airplane again approached the air field where our fighters were based.

As I looked at all the assembled pilots, I was struck by the fact that most were wearing checked shirts. I saw the same thing in the other units I visited in those hectic days and later asked Maj. Gen. Nikolai R. Pilipenko, deputy commander of the support units, why so many soldiers and officers were wearing plaid. "Every unit received civvies chosen by support staff in the Defense Ministry," he explained, adding dryly, "they didn't select very fashionable items."

So much, I thought, for the sophisticated foresight of our camouflage experts. Even without uniforms, Soviet troops nonetheless stood out from the Cuban civilian population; their clothes gave them away. Many soldiers joked that the operation they were part of should have been code-named "Checked Shirt."

Blunt Words and Early Warning

At the end of each day in the field, I reported back to Pliyev and, by coded telegram, to "Director" Malinovsky, sometimes informing Pliyev of what I was telling Moscow and sometimes not. Like General Reiter in 1943, Pliyev was upset by my ability to communicate with the Defense Ministry without clearing my messages through him. On one of the first nights of my stay in Cuba, Pliyev lost his temper and cursed the staff officer in charge of the code room for refusing to reveal the contents of one of my telegrams. To have done so, however, would have broken the military rules. The code room officer was in the right; Pliyev, in the wrong.

In fact, my reports usually praised the excellent military spirit I had seen everywhere, only noting that spirit was not always enough to overcome the very real physical obstacles the officers and troops faced. When I criticized the conduct of some of Pliyev's deputies, I did not hide my views from him. One evening I turned our talk to the subject of his headquarters staff. Despite the very critical situation, I said, too many of them were sitting placidly in their offices. Worse, his top deputy (and jealous rival), Lt. Gen. Pavel Dankevich, was often out on the tennis courts with Vice Adm. Georgi Abashvili, both playing as though they had not a care in the world.

Agreeing with my assessment, Pliyev promptly convened a meeting of his senior staff, the Group of Forces' military council, to order all its members to take a more active part in working with the troops, helping them to organize cooperation with Cuban units and to hone their defense. In his instructions, Pliyev referred directly to me, saying that Gribkov had expressed dissatisfaction with the top staff's behavior.

"Issa Aleksandrovich," I instantly objected, "I can't agree with your last sentence. Why is it that only I, as a representative of the General Staff, am unhappy with the work of some of the members of the military council? Are you yourself really pleased with the attitude that Generals Dankevich and Petrenko and Admiral Abashvili have shown toward military service and to the job here?"

Pliyev offered no rebuttal. Instead, he immediately issued a number of very clear and specific assignments, detailing each top officer to join right away in the work in the field. The conversation had been blunt and unpleasant, but it had the necessary effect on the headquarters personnel. Their pace picked up noticeably, and officers who had been desk-bound or goofing off began showing up at line units, looking for ways to accelerate the crucial preparatory defense work.

Their activity came none too soon. Five days after I began making my own rounds, I returned to the Havana headquarters to find a new level of tension in the busy offices. In my absence a very important dispatch from our intelligence and the Cuban General Staff had arrived. The news came from the United States.

This was Monday, 22 October. At 1900 hours Washington time, President John F. Kennedy was to make a radio and television broadcast. It was being heralded as an important announcement, and all our intelligence indicated that it would be about Cuba.

We had a few hours to wait. I used them for a mental review of the five months since General Ivanov had burst into my Moscow office with his sheaf of handwritten notes and recruited me to help set Operation ANADYR in motion. Had I done my best in those one hundred and fifty days? Had the Soviet armed forces performed their duties to the full? Were we ready for whatever was to come?

I felt I could answer positively to all those questions. The troops I had seen were full of vigor, ready to be tested. The Soviet officers and enlisted men had been trained for such a moment. Their Cuban comrades-in-arms had Fidel Castro's passion and his example to motivate them. We were well armed, well organized and as well prepared as possible to defend our position, our socialist ideals and our lives.

Deep inside me, though, I did not think war would come. I did not believe that either Khrushchev or Kennedy, looking foursquare at the prospect of nuclear confrontation, would plunge the world into Armageddon. But accidents could happen, and the presence of nuclear arms on Cuba made the possibility of a single misstep, a misjudgment by either side, truly frightening to contemplate.

Until we heard what the American President had to say, however, we could only do what all soldiers do—hurry up and wait.

5

End Games

Among the senior officers gathered at the El Chico staff quarters, the reaction to President Kennedy's 22 October speech was mixed. To many of us, it seemed that the Americans had been late in uncovering the missiles on Cuba. But if their military intelligence was slow, the speed, size and purpose of their reaction were hardly in doubt. An armada was assembling in the Caribbean, and we were its target. Not knowing how soon or whether Soviet ships would challenge the blockade that Kennedy announced, we presumed that attack was not far off.

We began preparing to repel a possible assault even before Kennedy spoke. Fidel Castro announced a nationwide mobilization and put his army on full alert that day, and General Pliyev's senior staff spent a sleepless night in hurried but calm work to boost the readiness of the Soviet Group of Forces. We had to interpret the U.S. naval blockade as the first step, and perhaps only a feint, before a full-scale assault.

Without waiting to learn what Kennedy would say, Soviet leaders in Moscow made the same assumption. General Ivanov and others later described to me the anxious Politburo meeting of 22 October. It ran so long that Khrushchev advised his colleagues to spend the night in the Kremlin so that Westerners watching from outside the walls would not know that the Soviet leaders had conferred so late or suspect the tension they felt.

Not until after midnight, Moscow time, did the Presidium members receive the text of Kennedy's message. By then, they had reviewed the situation thoroughly and decided on a course that mixed defiance with precaution. The first element was aimed at Washington. Charging the U.S. President with creating "a serious threat to peace," Khrushchev dictated a reply that accused the United States of "gross violations" of international law and "naked interference" in purely Cuban and Soviet affairs. The arms "now on Cuba," the Soviet leader declared, "are destined exclusively for defensive purposes," and the United States has no right to "control" them.[1]

Hours before receiving the translation of Kennedy's address, however, Khrushchev and his colleagues had also agreed on measures to reduce the risk that conflict over Cuba might lead to general war. One such action was a coded telegram sent at 11:30 P.M. Moscow time that reached us in Havana some thirty minutes before the U.S. President began his broadcast. Addressed to "*Trostnik*—Comrade Pavlov"* and signed by Defense Minister Rodion Y. Malinovsky as "Director," the message contained both a call to arms and a prohibition on the use of atomic arms. Instructing Pliyev to prepare to fight, it also hedged his authority to use any part of his nuclear arsenal in the event of fighting.

"In connection with the possible landing on the island of Cuba of Americans conducting exercises in the Caribbean," Malinovsky ordered Pliyev, "take immediate steps to raise combat readiness and to repulse the enemy together with the Cuban army and with all the power of the Soviet forces, *except STATSENKO's means and all of BELOBORODOV's cargoes*."[2] (Emphasis added.)

For Maj. Gen. Igor Statsenko, who commanded the missile division from headquarters near San Cristobal, the 22 October order from Moscow only reconfirmed the standing limits on his freedom of action. Any decision to fire the R-12 medium-range rockets—"Statsenko's means"—had always been reserved to the Kremlin leadership. After Kennedy's speech, as before, that control remained firm.

In contrast, the reference to Col. Nikolai Beloborodov's "cargoes" signalled a tightening in policy. The order reasserted full Kremlin authority over all nuclear arms, rescinding the limited grant of authority over battlefield weapons that Khrushchev had delegated to Pliyev during their talk in July. Beloborodov was responsible for the storage of all nuclear munitions on Cuba, including the main depot at Bejucal where the warheads for thirty-six R-12 missiles, for twelve "Luna" rockets and for forty short-range cruise missiles (FKRs) were being kept. The colonel was also safeguarding forty FKR warheads assigned, but not yet deployed, to rockets and launchers in eastern Cuba and the six atomic bombs designated for the specially fitted Ilyushin-28s, which were to be based at the central airfield near Santa Clara. Twenty-four warheads for the longer-range

---

* "Trostnik," meaning "reed," was the communications code name for Soviet headquarters on Cuba.

R-14 missiles that never reached Cuba were kept in the hold of the *Alexandrovsk* in the port of La Isabela.

None of the "cargoes" under Beloborodov's control had been released by 22 October to other commanders; nor were they released at any time during the crisis. Until that day's telegram arrived, however, the tactical weapons were Pliyev's to deploy and, if he were cut off from contact with Moscow, to use as a last resort. On Friday night, 26 October, expecting an attack the next day, Pliyev did order a number of mobile technical support bases carrying nuclear warheads to move, under cover of darkness, nearer the rockets that might have to carry them.

After Pliyev advised Moscow of that decision, Marshal Malinovsky, again signing himself "Director," wired back on 27 October, specifically forbidding the Group of Forces to employ any nuclear weapons without explicit approval from Moscow. Sent at 4:30 P.M. Moscow time and requiring confirmation of receipt, the message said: "It is categorically reconfirmed that it is forbidden to use nuclear armaments for the missiles, the FKRs, the 'Lunas' and the aircraft without authorization from Moscow."[3]

In fact, of the delivery systems that could have carried atomic warheads or bombs, only some of the battlefield weapons were ready for action in the last, tense days of October. Of the thirty-six medium-range R-12s, for example, only about half were ready to be fueled—an eighteen-hour process—and not one of them had been programmed for flight. Most of the Il-28 bombers were still in crates, a long way from operational. The "Luna" rockets and FKR missiles, however, were in place and targeted on likely beachheads and ocean approaches. The nuclear warheads for them, moreover, had been moved closer to those emplacements.

What If?

Malinovsky's 22 and 27 October orders to Pliyev make it clear that, once the danger of combat seemed real, Soviet leaders took firm steps to lower the risk that atomic warfare would erupt on Cuba. Earlier Moscow decisions had created that risk, but the moves to reduce it came as quickly as had the original decision to send tactical nuclear arms along with the Soviet troops.

Both the July initiative to deploy battlefield atomic arms and the October restraining order were Khrushchev's. When Semyon Ivanov told me of the first decision, he only indicated that it came from "the top"; we never discussed what lay behind it. My own judgment is that Khrushchev and his top military advisors believed that the tactical munitions were needed as back-up defenses for Soviet forces in the Caribbean which were too far away to reinforce quickly by conventional means. Willing to gamble that the full missile deployment could be concealed until it was complete, Khrushchev, I believe, also thought that using the low-yield, short-range nuclear weapons in combat limited to Cuba would not provoke massive nuclear retaliation against the Soviet Union.

Fortunately, we will never know whether that calculation was sound or reckless. And fortunately as well, the onset of the crisis caused the Soviet leadership to reexamine and rescind the emergency authority over the tactical nuclear arms Khrushchev had given to Pliyev. But by then the weapons were on Cuba. The question is whether they might have been fired. My answer is that the probability of even one such explosion occurring on purpose was very low, and the chance of an unauthorized firing was only a little higher.

Had the United States struck Cuba without warning, as its leaders briefly contemplated doing, or on 29 October, if negotiations had collapsed, I very strongly doubt that any of our tactical nuclear armaments would have been used in combat. The two instructions to Pliyev would have had a very powerful inhibiting effect. Soviet soldiers do not disobey orders lightly.

Just as importantly, actual battlefield conditions would have made it extremely difficult to mount any kind of tactical atomic strike against invading U.S. forces. At a January 1992 conference in Havana of U.S., Soviet and Cuban participants in the 1962 crisis, an American expert revealed that the U.S. "air strike plan called for 1,190 strike sorties on the first day."[4] Such massive bombardments, planned to last as long as a week before an actual invasion began, would have wrecked the medium- and intermediate-range missile sites—their primary targets—as well as the airfields that housed our MiG fighters and Ilyushin bombers, the surface-to-air missile (SAM) batteries and many, if not all, of the coastal-defense rocket installations.

By 27 October, U.S. reconnaissance, it has been learned, had also identified at least one of the three short-range "Luna" emplacements. Bombing runs would probably have neutralized that site, and further overflights might well have located the other two "Luna" detachments. The U.S. attackers would have had a harder time finding all of the eighty small cruise missiles—the FKRs—or any of the nuclear warhead storage bunkers. Still, it is very doubtful that Beloborodov's regular troops, who guarded those depots, would have released a single warhead without authorization.

The greatest uncertainty, then, lies in the possibility that Pliyev's internal military communications would have been so disrupted that separate Soviet units would have had to fight largely on their own. That prospect, in fact, was seriously discussed at a meeting of the Soviet senior staff in the Havana headquarters on the night of 26 October.

Apprehension ran high at this Military Council session. Through Maj. Gen.

Aleksei Dementyev, whose responsibilities for training Havana's armed forces put him in steady contact with Cuban leaders, Fidel Castro had suggested that the time had come for Soviet troops to put on their uniforms. He thought the change from civilian to military clothing would give morale a major boost, showing both Cubans and their U.S. foes that the island's defenders did not stand alone.

Pliyev did not take the hint. Many years later, when we reminisced in Leningrad about our time on Cuba, he explained that he thought the Soviet uniforms would only have made it easier for U.S. forces to concentrate their fire on our men and positions. In the Cuban climate, moreover, lightweight civilian clothing was more practical for handling weapons than the heavy, standard-issue uniforms that most of the soldiers had brought with them.

His judgment was probably sound, but in the field, Soviet soldiers were readying for combat. Under an old Russian military tradition, soldiers bathe themselves on the eve of battle, a sort of ritual purification as important as giving their weapons a final cleaning. On Cuba, where, of course, we had none of our familiar steam baths, I often saw our troops showering or swimming in the days after President Kennedy's speech. They were not bathing for hygiene or relaxation, but in preparation for a fight.

They, and the commanders who met with Pliyev in Havana on the night of 26 October, thought that the battle for Cuba would begin as early as the next day. Castro and his advisors had reached the same conclusion. At Soviet headquarters, we agreed that the expected air assault and subsequent invasion would eventually overwhelm our defenses. We also resolved, however, that initial defeat would not end our resistance. The survivors would retreat into the interior of the island to fight to the end as guerrillas alongside our Cuban comrades.

That decision was not just eve-of-battle bravado. As a practical matter, we had no way of leaving Cuba, no avenue for withdrawal. But our plan for last-ditch resistance also embodied the spirit of our troops and the deep commitment we had all come to feel to the Cuban Revolution. Fidel Castro had inspired more than his own countrymen. We Soviets, too, were imbued by his ideals and resolution. We saw his cause as our own and the defense of Cuba as a sacred duty.

As guerrillas (if it had come to that), our soldiers would have been most unlikely to carry any battlefield nuclear weapons that escaped the U.S. air strikes. Guerrilla tactics stress surprise and mobility, not firepower. On the move or in hiding, small groups of Soviet and Cuban troops would not have wanted to burden themselves with bulky missile launchers.

Nonetheless, it is just possible to imagine circumstances under which Soviet defenders would have been both able and willing to fire a tactical atomic weapon. As the U.S. fleet massed off the northwest coast of Cuba to land troops near Mariel and Havana, or as Marine units moved out of the Guantánamo base, well-hidden FKR units that had weathered the bombardments could have chosen either concentration as a target. Had any of the commanders of those short-range cruise-missile detachments been able to acquire a nuclear warhead—although that would have been even less probable, given the distance between the storage areas and the launchers and the controls on releasing and moving the warheads—he could have decided on his own to fire against the enemy.

A Case in Point

The idea is far-fetched, but not impossible. Under great pressure, soldiers may not wait for orders. Indeed, with tension at a peak on the morning of Saturday, 27 October, a Soviet antiaircraft commander on Cuba took matters into his own hands and authorized an attack on an American spy plane. The U-2 was destroyed and its pilot killed, but the incident, originating in a misunderstanding, left a measure of confusion in its wake and a heightened fear in Moscow that a U.S. attack was imminent.

The episode began when Cuban antiaircraft artillery, following Fidel Castro's orders, opened up against low-flying U.S. planes on the morning of 27 October. Not one was hit. The Cuban gunners had no SAMs of their own and very limited radar. But the heavy firing seemed to indicate that fighting had started.

Lt. Gen. Stepan Grechko, who had command of Soviet air defense on Cuba, took his cue from the Cuban example. Although he could not reach Pliyev when our radar spotted a U-2, Grechko knew that the Group of Forces commander had ordered our antiaircraft defenses to maximum alert and had asked Moscow on Friday night for authorization to use "all available antiaircraft means in the event of attacks by American aviators on our installations."[5]

No reply from Moscow to that request had reached Havana when Grechko was confronted with the news that we had a U-2 in our sights. He gave the order to fire. The rest of the story is best told by an eyewitness, Col. Yevgeni Mikhailovich Danilov, who was stationed with a SAM unit near Holguin. His regiment's commander, Col. Yuri S. Guseinov, was absent that Saturday morning, attending a meeting in Santiago de Cuba.

In a letter to me, Colonel Danilov, now retired, recalled the events that followed. "On the morning of 27 October, the duty officer at the command post declared an 'Alert No. 1,' " Danilov wrote. "I ran to the post when target no. 33 showed up clearly on the artillery board. Immediately a command came from the division command post: 'Destroy target no. 33.' I recall how Lieutenant Colonel Morozov, head of the political department, said to me: 'Yevgeni Mikhailovich, it looks like something serious is starting.'

"Everything was so unexpected that I decided to double-check the order to destroy the target with the division command post. They confirmed the order, and I immediately gave the command to the third and fourth detachments to destroy the target. Lt. Col. Ivan Minovich Gerchenko, commander of the fourth detachment, reported that he understood the order, that he had the target in his sight, was aiming at it and then immediately reported that it was destroyed, and that three missiles had been expended. The height of the target was 70,000 feet. I personally reported to the division command post that the airplane had been shot down."

From General Grechko down to the level of lieutenant colonels like Danilov, Morozov and Gerchenko, the common view was that combat had begun and that the previous restraints on Soviet forces had been superseded. These officers did not so much disobey orders as react, in a reasoned military manner, as they understood the situation required. Appropriately, they were not punished for the initiative they showed.

Along with Gen. Georgi Titov, who headed the Group of Forces' operational department, I filed a report to Malinovsky about the destruction of the U-2. The "Director's" reply of 28 October said: "We believe that you were too hasty in shooting down the U.S. U-2 reconnaissance plane at a time when an agreement to prevent an attack on Cuba by peaceful means was already imminent."[6] Malinovsky did not pursue the issue beyond that mild rebuke.

Nikita Khrushchev did pursue it. He was clearly alarmed by the event, misinformed about its instigators and nervous about Fidel Castro's militant views. In an admonitory letter of 28 October, he scolded Castro for what Khrushchev then believed was a Cuban action. Fearing that "Pentagon militarists" would seize on the downing of the U-2 as a pretext for scuttling a peaceful resolution of the crisis, he warned that the episode "will be used by the aggressors for their own purposes."[7] Two days later, a calmer Khrushchev reassessed the incident and without acknowledging the truth—that Castro's ill-equipped antiaircraft batteries had played no role in bringing down the high-flying aircraft—wrote the Cuban leader, "The fact that an American plane was shot down over Cuba turned out to be a useful measure, since the operation was successfully executed. This is a lesson to the imperialists."[8]

What happened on Cuba and in the skies above it that Saturday morning, however, is an important reminder of what might have happened if U.S. air strikes and an invasion had been launched. Under combat conditions, in the terrible disorder of the battlefield, there is an outside possibility that an enterprising Soviet commander could have put a low-yield atomic warhead on a short-range cruise missile. If such an officer had also found a target for that weapon, it is hard to believe he would have waited long for approval from higher authority before firing.

It is impossible to know what the U.S. response to such an act would have been. At the Havana conference, Robert McNamara, who was U.S. secretary of defense during the 1962 crisis, said that the planned invasion force "would *not* [his emphasis] have been equipped with tactical nuclear weapons," although its commander had requested authority to carry them.[9] McNamara declined, however, to rule out the likelihood that an atomic attack on the landing force would have canceled that restriction.

The presence of Soviet tactical nuclear weapons on Cuba and Pliyev's discretion over their use, which I disclosed to the Havana gathering, McNamara said, created "an added element of danger, which some of us . . . (a) had not anticipated, and (b) would have been horrified to think of the consequences of. . . . It horrifies me to think what would have happened in the event of an invasion of Cuba!"[10]

Comrades and Controversy

Strangely perhaps, I did not experience a similar feeling of horror on Cuba even when the danger of war was at its height. I expected a fight. I realized there was a good chance I would die far from home, but as a soldier I had no choice in the matter. As a soldier, I also understood that any nuclear war that started would lead to mutual annihilation. And I felt confident that those who did have the choice—the leaders of the Soviet Union, the United States and Cuba—would not let their confrontation escalate to the point of suicide. That judgment was soon proved correct.

High among the things that reinforced my courage was the attitude of the ordinary Soviet soldiers under Pliyev's command. They showed no fear, only well-deserved pride in what they had already accomplished under extremely arduous conditions and genuine enthusiasm for the mission they had been assigned. Despite the difficult climate, the tropical storms and the unbelievable heat, they voiced no petty complaints and seemed completely ready to defend Cuba as they would their own Motherland. Repeatedly on my inspection trips, I thought how patient, resourceful, undaunted and militant our Russian, Soviet soldier is, no matter where fate casts him.

An antiaircraft detachment in the Pinar del Rio district of southwestern Cuba was a good example. I went there midway through the crisis week with Gen. Mikhail Naumenko, who had flown to Cuba with me, and Lt. Gen. Stepan Grechko, who commanded Soviet air defense on the island. We were met by the detachment commander, Col. Vassili Fyodorovich Kolesnikov, and Che Guevara, whose presence had an almost electric effect on our troops. When they found out that the bearded, energetic man dressed in a jump suit and black beret was Guevara, Fidel Castro's comrade in arms, the gunners we were inspecting seemed to get an extra infusion of stamina and pride.

At one battery, the crew put on a brilliant demonstration of readying a surface-to-air missile for firing. At top speed, they loaded the missile on the launching pad, locked it on an imaginary target and brought it right to the point of firing. Che was visibly pleased by their performance, and I was relieved to see how well the batteries were protected. Supplementing the cover provided by large-caliber machine guns and submachine guns, which were manned and ready to open fire, the battery commanders chained their missiles to tractors and to the launch pads at night in case U.S. commandos attempted a raid. What impressed me just as favorably, however, was the instant rapport our soldiers felt with Guevara, a measure of the attachment they had formed to the Cuban cause.

I shared those feelings. The inspection had been prompted in part by a talk with Fidel Castro at Pliyev's headquarters two days after the Kennedy speech. That was my first encounter with the Cuban leader, and it filled me with a deep, instinctive respect for him. Castro had called the conference of senior Cuban and Soviet officers to discuss the readiness of his troops and ours and the state of communications between them. The talk lasted about an hour and a half, and despite the stress we all felt, Fidel was completely calm. Listening to the reports, occasionally posing a question through an interpreter, constantly making notes on a memo pad, he was purposeful and completely unruffled, as though war were not imminent and his life's work not at risk.

I also saw Castro in the role of electrifying orator, addressing a Havana crowd of 100,000 when the crisis was at its height. So were his passion and his ability to charge his audience with his power and his emotions. While he was speaking, a heavy rain began to fall. Not only did no one in the crowd run for shelter, many shouted at Fidel to put on a raincoat and to continue his speech. He refused the raincoat and kept on talking. The performance made me remember a very different occasion. Nikita Khrushchev came to Leningrad to deliver a public speech, but after he had been talking for just twenty minutes, half the crowd in the large square had filtered away. At the end of Khrushchev's oration, only a thin knot of people remained clustered around the podium.

On the afternoon of 24 October in Havana, Castro's main interest was the readiness of the Soviet ballistic missiles for firing. He was worried, as I was, that the missile division was behind schedule, and he also wanted better coordination between Cuban and Soviet antiaircraft defenses, especially swifter exchange of radar data about U.S. overflights. But the conversation was in general terms, even the discussion about improving communications between Pliyev's head-quarters and the Cuban Army's General Staff and between Soviet field commanders and their Cuban counterparts, Major Almeida in Santa Clara and Raul Castro in Santiago de Cuba.

At the top of the chain of military command, in fact, relations between Soviets and Cubans were more strained than at the working level. General Dementyev, not General Pliyev, was the main Soviet liaison with the Cuban Army, and Pliyev never developed easy ties with Castro. Never having told his host about the tactical nuclear weapons we had brought to Cuba, the Soviet commander did not inform Castro on the morning of 23 October about the instructions that reestablished Khrushchev's full control over the warheads' use. "If I had been consulted," Castro remarked at the 1992 conference in Havana after I spoke about the "Luna" rockets without mentioning the FKRs or the bombs for the Il-28s, "I would have said that there was a need for more tactical nuclear weapons. . .

"[I]f it was a matter of defending Cuba without creating an international problem," he added, "the presence of tactical weapons would not have created the same problem that the strategic weapons did. It couldn't have been said that tactical nuclear weapons in Cuba represented a threat to the United States."[11]

The secrecy that cloaked all of Operation ANADYR was the main reason that neither Pliyev nor any other Soviet official told Castro precisely what weapons had been deployed to his island. That lack of communication was symptomatic of the broader nature of high-level Moscow-Havana relations before, during and, for a tense time, after the Caribbean crisis. The pattern established in May 1962—Khrushchev and the Presidium deciding on a course of action and then persuading the Cuban government to follow their lead—held true in October and November as well.

Although Castro and his government had cooperated fully in bringing the Soviet missiles to Cuba, he was only informed, not consulted, about Khrushchev's decision to remove them. Understandably, Cuba then refused to allow foreign inspectors on its soil to observe that withdrawal, and Castro balked angrily at subsequent U.S. pressure to have the Il-28 bombers removed as well. The two sharp disagreements damaged Cuban-Soviet ties at all levels, especially between Khrushchev and Castro, but also between Castro and Soviet military leaders and diplomats in Havana. Camaraderie forged in the face of great danger became bitterness in its aftermath.

Inglorious Exit

Tension between Havana and Moscow became acute in the last days of the crisis, fed by misunderstandings on both sides. The first source was Khrushchev's interpretation of an urgent message that Castro sent him on the night of 26 October. As released by the Cuban government in November 1990, the letter warned that U.S. "aggression" was "imminent" and predicted that it would take the form of "an air attack against certain targets [the Soviet missiles] with the limited objective of destroying them."[12] Terming an invasion "less probable although possible," Castro made a proposal that Khrushchev took to be a request for a preemptive nuclear strike against the United States. The actual text reads:

> If . . . the imperialists invade Cuba with the goal of occupying it, the danger that that aggressive policy poses for humanity is so great that following that event, the Soviet Union must never allow the circumstances in which the imperialists could launch the first strike against it.
>
> I tell you this because I believe that the imperialists' aggressiveness is extremely dangerous and if they actually carry out the brutal act of invading Cuba in violation of international law and morality, that would be the moment to eliminate such danger forever through an act of clear and legitimate defense, however harsh and terrible the solution would be, for there is no other.[13]

Kremlin policymakers were alarmed by this appeal. While they were working to resolve the crisis directly with Washington, they feared that Castro was seeking to escalate the conflict toward global nuclear war. The erroneous first report that Cuban forces had shot down the U-2 raised their anxiety even higher and prompted the Khrushchev letter to Castro of 28 October, urging him "at this critical juncture not to be overcome by emotion, to show restraint."[14] Rather than give the "Pentagon militarists" any pretext to disrupt an impending U.S.-Soviet agreement that would "guarantee Cuba against attack," Khrushchev wrote, "I would like to advise you in a friendly way: show patience, restraint and even more restraint."[15]

That "friendly" advice might have been better received if Khrushchev had kept his Cuban ally better informed of the exchanges between Washington and Moscow during the preceding days. As it was, the letter reached Havana only after the press announced on Sunday morning that Khrushchev had accepted Kennedy's terms: withdrawal of the missiles in exchange for a U.S. pledge not to invade Cuba. Castro was indignant.* On a brief visit to Soviet military headquarters, he could barely conceal his anger.

Sitting silently in Pliyev's office, Castro stroked his beard as the Soviet general confirmed that Moscow had ordered the removal of the weapons that so many

---

* A Cuban editor who telephoned Castro with the news of the Moscow announcement recalled that the Cuban leader responded with a string of curses.[16]

men had worked so hard to deploy. For a time, Castro said nothing. Then, referring to the missiles, he asked, "All of them?"

"All," Pliyev replied.

"Very well," Castro said. He stood up. "Fine. I'm leaving now." He appeared totally calm, but he must have been seething inside. For a time, he refused to see Ambassador Alekseyev and, when they did talk, Castro did not hide his displeasure. Writing to Khrushchev on 31 October, he suggested that his urgent appeal for action in the event of invasion had been misinterpreted, either not read "carefully" or mistranslated. "The Soviet troops which have been at our side," he also said,

> know how admirable the stand of our people was through this crisis and the profound brotherhood that was created among the troops from both peoples during the decisive hours. Countless eyes of Cuban and Soviet men who were willing to die with supreme dignity shed tears upon learning about the surprising, sudden and practically unconditional decision to withdraw the weapons.[17]

Although the substance of the Soviet response to Kennedy's pressure angered Castro, it was the lack of consultation that offended him the most. I believe he was correct. The stationing of the missiles had been coordinated between the two governments. The withdrawal should have been handled in the same way. On the other hand, Cubans should have understood that with the United States and the Soviet Union half a step from a global nuclear disaster, no one could afford to waste a minute. On the weekend of 27–28 October, there was no time for consultation with Havana, and when other issues arose—verifying the withdrawal and removing the Il-28 bombers—Castro insisted on his rights. He refused to allow foreign inspectors on Cuban territory, and he drew out the negotiations over the airplanes through two tense weeks.

He was not the only discontented commander on Cuba. The day after the withdrawal order was received from Moscow, I went to see how it was being implemented in the San Cristobal area. At the rocket regiment base commanded by Col. Yuri Solovyov, I found the launch pads which the soldiers had labored so hard to build being broken down. I also found General Statsenko, the chief of the rocket division, watching the work and grieving in his heart over the end of his mission.

"First, you rushed me with the building of these installations," he complained, "and now you're reproving me because we're destroying them too slowly." I had no ready reply. There were no words I could say to this man who had done so much to discharge his military duty faithfully.

That duty soon extended to diplomacy. U Thant, acting secretary general of the United Nations, came to Havana at the end of October to try to arrange for UN inspection of the missile withdrawal, and Statsenko gave him a full briefing on the status of his division, the numbers of R-12 rockets—twenty-four—and launchers—thirty-six—plus six training missiles and the timetable for taking them all back to the USSR. Although U Thant's mission included gathering such military intelligence, his main goal was to arrange for inspection of the actual withdrawal. Castro, however, would not agree. Inspection, the Cuban leader said, was an unacceptable attempt to humiliate his country.

Instead, it was the Soviets who accepted a terrible humiliation. As we loaded our missiles, we had to inform the United States how many rockets each freighter carried. Once our vessels left Cuban territorial waters, U.S. ships and planes would come alongside, and our troops would take the tarpaulin covers off the rockets to let them be counted. Carrying such heavy and awkward cargoes on deck was dangerous. Putting them on display for inspection was shaming. It amounted to a public slap in the face of the Soviet soldiers who had done so much incredibly difficult work. Under the circumstances, however, there was no alternative.

There was also no real possibility of refusing the American demands that the Il-28 bombers be withdrawn as the missiles had been. It did not matter that the planes were obsolete and would have been easy targets for U.S. antiaircraft defenses. We had brought them to Cuba exclusively to strengthen coastal defenses. Even the six that were specially fitted to carry atomic bombs would have only been useful against an invasion fleet. In theory, however, their range extended deep into the United States, and that capability made them offensive weapons in Washington's eyes. Until the bombers left, the U.S. naval blockade would stay and, with it, the threat of attack.

Although Khrushchev initially opposed Kennedy's demands for the planes' removal, he soon conceded the point and sent his confidant, Anastas Mikoyan, to Havana both to rebuild Soviet-Cuban relations and to persuade Castro to let the bombers be shipped back to the Soviet Union. Mikoyan, who had been the first high-ranking Soviet official to visit Cuba after the 1959 revolution, arrived in Havana on 2 November. He had to spend two weeks to win Castro's approval. A transcript of one of their conversations is included in Appendix 1.

A Bumpy Road Home

While their talks dragged on, the 7 November anniversary of the 1917 Revolution arrived, and, on the eve of the holiday, General Pliyev organized a large celebration at the headquarters of the Group of Forces, followed by a smaller reception for senior Soviet and Cuban officers. As was customary, the first toast offered was to the heads of state of our two countries: Nikita Sergeyevich Khrushchev and Fidel Castro Ruz. Sitting next to me was a Cuban captain who held a high military post. Softly, but audibly, he proposed that the toast should be to Fidel and Josef Stalin, not to Khrushchev. His barb was obvious: had Stalin been alive, the captain thought, the Soviet Union would have defied the United States and kept the missiles in Cuba.

I and my fellow Soviet officers overrode him, raising our glasses and our voices to Khrushchev and Castro, but the captain insisted. "To Fidel," he said, "and Stalin." It was an awkward incident, and a brief one, but I described the episode in my usual end-of-the-day dispatch to the defense minister. My report had unexpected and unpleasant consequences.

Late the next evening, 7 November, I received a telephone call summoning me to Mikoyan's villa the following morning at ten o'clock. I was told that several other senior officers, including Pliyev, would also be on hand. Reviewing all my work in Cuba, all the questions that Mikoyan might ask, I did not fall asleep until well after midnight.

The first question he actually posed when we gathered at his residence cleared up the mystery. Who, he wanted to know, had sent a telegram to Moscow about the way the October Revolution had been celebrated? I immediately understood what he was driving at and promptly told him the contents of my last report to Marshal Malinovsky. No one else spoke. To my enormous surprise, my fellow officers who had also heard our Cuban colleagues criticize the missile withdrawal only looked at Mikoyan in subservience and confusion.

The silence seemed to me to last a long time, long enough for me to understand that my entire career—my fate, in the final analysis—hung on Mikoyan's judgment. His first words were a reprimand. "After all," he said, "I'm a member of the Presidium of the Central Committee. I'm not here as a tourist. I am supposed to know who reports what to Moscow." His anger, however, seemed to pass quickly. "Let's finish this unpleasant conversation on that point," he said. "And we won't come back to this issue again. Let's just keep it among ourselves."

I wanted to take him at his word, but as soon as I could use the secure radio link to Moscow that our signal corps had finally been able to open on 8 November, I spoke with General Ivanov and told him what had happened as a result of my reporting. He calmed me down, telling me not to worry, that my dispatches went to the very "top" in Moscow and were much appreciated there.

His reassurance did help my nerves, but the whole matter resurfaced when I returned to Moscow and learned that Mikoyan, preceding me, had mentioned his rebuke of me to Malinovsky. I had to explain to the minister how the whole brouhaha had started. He, too, told me the matter was of no consequence. Nonetheless, when I commanded the Seventh Guard Army in the Transcaucasus District and Mikoyan came on a visit in 1967, I screwed up the courage to ask him why he had raised the matter with Malinovsky, opening what was supposed to be a closed book.

Silent for a time, Mikoyan finally said, "You know, Comrade Gribkov, there was nothing special about that, so let's just forget about it." Over the years since, I have tried to forget, but the memory does not fade. The incident made me feel absolutely powerless. Deserted by my military comrades, I was left at the mercy of a man whose membership in the Politburo entitled him to discard my years of service at a stroke. In connection with Cuba, I was to experience the Kremlin's casual exercise of supreme authority one more time.

My colleagues and I returned to Moscow in late November, flying on a Czechoslovak airliner that took us on a storm-tossed route via Gander in Newfoundland to an icy landing in Prague. Wanting to get a snack during our stop in Gander, we found ourselves in the airport restaurant with, as the saying goes, "the wind whistling" through our empty pockets. As in the heat of Dakar so many weeks before, we could only curse the defense ministry's Central Finance Directorate and the financial helplessness to which it reduced Soviet generals, admirals and colonels who had just risked their lives on the front line of what was nearly a nuclear conflict.

We were rescued by a kind woman, the wife of the famous Soviet poet Yevgeni Yevtushenko, who had been with her husband on Cuba and was, like us, homeward bound to Moscow. In addition to her beauty and simple, dignified demeanor, she had diamonds on her ears and fingers and a thick pile of U.S. dollars in her wallet. Showing them to us, she asked us to order the best dishes and to let her pay the bill. We did not seriously abuse her generosity, but we were only able to repay it, once our flight was announced, by carrying her substantial purchases to the airplane.

In Moscow, I made a full report to Marshal Malinovsky, who was so interested in even the smallest details—including warm letters sent to him, along with photographs and verses, by rank-and-file soldiers—that he kept me talking for two hours. Once, General Ivanov gave me the high sign to finish up, but the minister glared at him disapprovingly and told me to continue. He was specially taken with a soldier's letter written in the style of a famous Chekhov story. "Dear Grandfather Rodion Yakovlevich," the writer asked, "when are you going to bring us back home to our dear and far-away Russia?"

I do not know what answer the writer received, but many of our troops stayed many more months on Cuba training Castro's army to use the defensive weapons—artillery, radar, tanks, surface-to-air missiles, planes and other equipment—that the Soviet Group of Forces transferred to our hosts. As students, the Cubans were excellent once the Soviet instructors learned that it was best not to applaud a trainee too highly or criticize him too sharply. Praise would make him slack off, thinking he had already mastered the subject, and criticism would leave him depressed and unresponsive. The best formula was the golden mean: "Pedro, you did such-and-such not so badly today, but if you practice today and tomorrow and do thus-and-so, you'll be much better."

I saw this training taking hold when Malinovsky sent me again to Cuba at the end of March 1963 to open a new, non-stop air route. The flight lasted fourteen and a half hours, taking us from Moscow north to Murmansk and then south between Greenland and Iceland, paralleling the Canadian and U.S. coasts to Havana. My return visit to Cuba, involving some organizational matters in Pliyev's command as well as oversight of the military instruction work, lasted only a few weeks, and the flight back to Moscow went smoothly, paving the way for Fidel Castro to fly the same route soon thereafter on his way to restoring good relations with Nikita Khrushchev.

In between my return and Castro's arrival, Malinovsky summoned me to his office again. With a smile that softened his words, he told me, "Your luck ran out." I was taken aback. What had happened? The minister explained that he had proposed that Pliyev and I be awarded the highest military order, Hero of the Soviet Union, and that the Politburo had approved the commendation in principle.

Khrushchev and Malinovsky, however, had discussed the matter again, and Khrushchev had asked how many times General Pliyev had already received the same decoration. The answer was two. That gave Khrushchev pause. He had also been twice named a Hero of the Soviet Union. Although Khrushchev did not say so outright, Malinovsky understood that the Party leader did not like the idea that Pliyev would outstrip him. Without referring the matter back to the Politburo, Khrushchev simply decided to bestow a different order on me and the commander of the Soviet Group of Forces on Cuba. We received the Order of Lenin, the highest state award of the Soviet Union. I wear mine with pride.

PART II

The View from Washington

by
General William Y. Smith

Prelude to Crisis

Wherever President John F. Kennedy and his advisors looked in spring and early summer 1962, a cocksure Nikita S. Khrushchev seemed to be grinning back at them, taunting, scheming, pushing for advantage. No longer just a "specter haunting Europe," Soviet communism was an awesome military presence from the Baltic to the Adriatic, a front-runner in space technology, a disruptive and expansive force in Third World conflicts. It had even won a foothold on Cuba, challenging the traditional American primacy in the Caribbean and the hemisphere.

I had an unusually close view of this phase of the Cold War competition. Starting in July 1961, I served as a member of the staff of President Kennedy's most trusted military advisor, Gen. Maxwell Taylor. In that role, I watched Soviet strategy unfold and worked with others to help shape the West's response during two years that went from acute confrontation in Europe through dramatic crisis in the Caribbean to the first successful superpower arms control negotiations to limit the nuclear threat. The Cuban missile crisis brought peril to a peak, but the head-to-head rivalry between the United States and the Soviet Union had been building toward a military collision well before Soviet ballistic missiles appeared on Cuba.

That jockeying set the stage for the Cuban crisis and fixed the attitudes of many senior U.S. decision-makers toward Moscow. To understand why they thought and acted as they did in October 1962, it is necessary to know something of the Cold War history of the preceding years. I have therefore begun my account of the crisis with a summary review of East-West relations in the early 1960s and of Kennedy administration debates and decisions on how to deal with Moscow and with the perceived threats it posed.

Misapprehensions within the U.S. government, especially between White House officials and top armed forces officers, also rose in this period and played a part in determining the influence of U.S. military professionals during it. The seeds of these mutual misgivings were planted early. Constrained by the U.S. tradition of civilian authority, the troubled military relations with the Kennedy White House were nonetheless factors of some note in the making of policy. The part they played, however, has been little noted in many accounts of the crisis. I have tried to add that dimension to my story and, especially, to the record of U.S. military thinking and action during 1962.

That year was one of mounting Soviet challenge. In the strategic arms race the USSR was proclaiming itself equal, if not superior, to the United States in the technologies essential for producing and deploying thermonuclear weapons. In struggles for political influence in Southeast Asia, Africa and Latin America, Moscow was positioning itself effectively as the ally of discontented peoples, many of them emerging from or still contesting Western colonial rule.

Viewed in retrospect, the period marked the apogee of Soviet power. To contemporaries, however, the Kremlin seemed well along toward its proclaimed goal: global dominance of a socialist world.

That impression was built on real achievements. Along with the stunning launch of the first Sputnik in October 1957 and the glory of Yuri Gagarin's first orbital flight in April 1961, the USSR claimed industrial growth rates exceeding those of the United States. Although the early Soviet satellites had little military value and the pace of development proceeded from the urgent needs of a war-devastated economy, in space and on earth the USSR looked like a formidable power. The destruction of Francis Gary Powers' U-2 aircraft in May 1960, moreover, demonstrated the Soviet Union's ability to defend its territory against other hostile flights, including the U.S. Strategic Air Command bombers that gave American nuclear retaliatory doctrine a large measure of credibility.

Khrushchev seized on these advances to sing the praises of communism. The West, he constantly proclaimed, could not block the triumphant progress of the socialist ideal. "Whether you like it or not, history is on our side," he gloated just a few days after the suppression of the November 1956 anti-Soviet uprising in Hungary. "We will bury you."

As John Kennedy was preparing for his inauguration, Khrushchev announced his intention to speed the ultimate victory of communism by supporting colonial peoples in "national liberation wars" against their "oppressors."[1] The overthrow of French rule in Vietnam and Algeria had shown Western power to be in retreat and, claimed Moscow propagandists, inevitable decline. The appearance of Fidel Castro in Cuba and his political pressure on American interests across Latin America promised further opportunities.

Against the Soviet Union's apparent momentum and its voluble, mercurial leader, the Kennedy team took office very much on the defensive. Its members, particularly the professionals involved in national security affairs, felt that they had inherited a far more complex and dangerous world and time than the Eisenhower administration had faced in the early 1950s. Challenges in Laos, in the Congo and, above all, in Berlin during 1961 heightened that feeling. But in spring 1962, neither top strategists nor mid-level military aides such as I imagined that the most demanding test of U.S. power would come in just a few months and from Cuba, just a few miles away.

Cuba: Secret Obsession

The island and its flamboyant young leader had come to occupy two quite different places in official U.S. thinking after the April 1961 Bay of Pigs disaster. Formally and openly, the Kennedy administration treated Fidel Castro as a secondary irritant to be carefully watched, economically isolated and patiently undermined. Obsessively and secretly, White House officials saw him as a reminder of deep humiliation and a target for violent revenge. Behind this official schizophrenia lay a history of mutual disappointment, wounds dating back perhaps as far as before the Spanish-American War of 1898, recently reopened and allowed to fester.

When Castro triumphantly entered Havana in early January 1959, many Americans, private citizens and government officials alike, supported him as a welcome change from the corruption of Fulgencio Batista's dictatorial regime. Shortly after he gained power, however, Castro's nationalization of properties owned by U.S. citizens, his ranting against U.S. imperialism and his contentious attitude during an April visit to New York, Boston and Washington marked him as a source of trouble for U.S. interests in the hemisphere.

During 1960, Castro further provoked his giant neighbor. He agreed to a commercial aid pact with the Soviet Union, under which the USSR would purchase Cuban sugar and lend Cuba $100 million. Arranging a companion military assistance agreement to upgrade his armed forces, he opened diplomatic relations with Moscow's Warsaw Pact allies, as well as China and North Korea. "Our war," said Ernesto "Che" Guevara, Fidel's most outspoken comrade in arms, in March 1960, "is against the great power of the North."[2]

In response, President Eisenhower pursued a two-track policy. Openly, the United States first cut its purchases of Cuban sugar and then barred all exports to Havana except food and medicine. Secretly, the President approved a Central

Intelligence Agency (CIA) plan for the development of a three-hundred-man paramilitary force outside Cuba to mount future guerrilla action against Castro. The agency began secretly training Cuban exiles for this mission in summer 1960.[3]

In the fall of that year, the CIA abandoned the idea of victory through guerrilla warfare. Castro's tightening control made it virtually impossible to land, organize and resupply paramilitary forces on the island.[4] Changing tack, the Agency called for an overt amphibious landing backed by tactical air support. A force of six hundred to seven hundred and fifty Cuban exiles would come ashore near the southeastern city of Trinidad, maintain a visible presence, draw dissidents to it and, it was hoped, "trigger a general uprising."[5]

With this plan unfolding and Castro's provocation mounting, Eisenhower ended the formality of diplomatic relations with Havana on 3 January 1961. Taking office a few weeks later, Kennedy chose to follow the course his predecessor had set. The policy echoed the Democrat's campaign pledges and the covert actions of the outgoing Administration, but the early decision led directly to the Bay of Pigs disaster in April 1961 and, ultimately, to the October 1962 missile crisis.

Clashes elsewhere in the world nourished suspicion and distrust between Washington and Moscow, but the seeds of the 1962 confrontation were sown at the Bay of Pigs. The failure there left the Kennedy team with a burning obsession to overthrow Castro, a fixation acted out in many overt and covert ways. Meanwhile, Castro's success in repelling the invasion and his sense of destiny and propelled him to look ever more avidly to the Soviet Union for material and moral support. Finally, the episode ensured Castro's willingness to act as Moscow's proxy in tormenting a chastened and embarrassed U.S. President. The climax of that effort came when Khrushchev's use of Cuba to shift the strategic nuclear balance of power in his favor led to the most perilous confrontation of the Cold War.

As a member of Gen. Maxwell D. Taylor's staff, I had a close-up view of that crisis and of some of the decisions that led to it. Taylor served President Kennedy, first, as an in-house military advisor, starting in July 1961, and, after 1 October 1962, as chairman of the Joint Chiefs of Staff. As one of his personal assistants first at the White House and then at the Pentagon, I was supposed, among other duties, to keep an eye on the Soviet Union. In a sense both of us owed our jobs to the failure of the Bay of Pigs invasion.

President Kennedy held his first White House meeting on the CIA plan for Cuba on 26 January 1961, less than a week after taking office. The CIA operation begun under his predecessor seemed too far advanced to stop. He also inherited a group of senior military advisors—the Joint Chiefs of Staff—who had been brought into the Cuban planning only weeks earlier. At the time, Gen.

Lyman L. Lemnitzer was the chairman, with Gen. George H. Decker representing the Army; Adm. Arleigh Burke, the Navy and Gen. Thomas D. White, the Air Force. Marine Corps Gen. David Shoup, although not a JCS member, attended most of the Joint Chiefs' meetings.

Their voices were barely heard in the frenetic first days of the new administration, partly because the advice they offered lacked precision and clarity. Although the Chiefs played only a secondary or tertiary role in the Bay of Pigs planning, they received much of the blame for its failure. Among other things, the Joint Chiefs disapproved of the CIA's conducting a military operation that should have been a U.S. Department of Defense responsibility. Indeed, one of the very few pluses they saw in General Taylor's Bay of Pigs after-action report was that President Kennedy agreed on military primacy in military matters and so directed.[6]

Given the state of affairs at the end of January 1961, however, the Chiefs had no choice but to enlist in the planning already under way. In early February, they unenthusiastically endorsed the CIA's Trinidad plan in a report later scorned for its hesitancy and seeming inconsistencies.

After reviewing the Trinidad plan, the President directed that it be scaled down to make it less "spectacular" and less easily traceable to U.S. motivation and support. Following this White House guidance, the U.S. Department of State insisted that all air strikes should appear to originate either from Cuban airfields or nearby airfields in Central America. This restriction dictated a landing somewhere other than Trinidad. After three possible alternatives were examined, a consensus favored the Bay of Pigs. While concurring that the locale on the south coast was the best of the three new alternatives, the Joint Chiefs stressed that they still preferred Trinidad. Planning, however, continued to focus on the Bay of Pigs.

The modified plan still called for a decisive air attack against Cuba's small air force at the time of the landing. CIA and military planners knew that the Cuban air force could easily destroy the invasion party unless it was taken out of action early. To make the operation less "spectacular," however, the President decided that one air strike would take place two days before the landing and one on the morning of the invasion.

The Joint Chiefs of Staff and the CIA both demurred. They warned that a small, early attack would not destroy Castro's air force, but would alert him and give him time to disperse his remaining planes. The President, however, held to his own reasoning.

The air strike two days before the landing, launched from Nicaragua with the cover story that the pilots were defectors from the Cuban air force, had modest success at best. Because of adverse public reaction, Kennedy canceled the follow-up air strikes that had been planned to coincide with the landing. As predicted, the Cuban air force effectively pinned down the invaders. On 19 April, three days after the assault began, the effort collapsed. Of the invading exiles, 114 were dead; 1,199 were prisoners.

As far as the Soviet Union was concerned, solidifying Castro's hold over Cuba was paying off handsomely. As the invasion force was collapsing, Khrushchev wrote Kennedy, "There should be no misunderstanding our position. We shall render the Cuban people and their government all necessary assistance in beating back armed attack on Cuba."[7]

Foreshadowing moves he did not make for another year, the Soviet leader raised another point a few days later. While the USSR had no military bases in Cuba, he charged that the United States was using countries bordering the Soviet Union to threaten its security. If the United States was offended by events in Cuba, the Soviet Union had "no lesser grounds" to feel the same way about actions along its frontiers.[8] The implicit reference was to the nuclear-armed, 1,500-mile-range Jupiter missiles being deployed to Turkey under an arrangement dating back to an Eisenhower administration decision in 1959.

Castro, too, was jubilant. Having manhandled the colossus to his north, he could now foment revolution throughout Central and Latin America with new energy and enhanced stature. At a 1961 May Day parade, he proudly announced that Cuba was entering an "era of socialist construction." Later that year he proclaimed that he "believed absolutely in Marxism . . . and had for some time."[9]

Defeat and Disarray

Embarrassment, resentment and recrimination prevailed in Washington. The administration had suffered disaster abroad and enfeeblement at home. To make things worse, growing support from Moscow made any attempt to overthrow Castro both substantially more difficult and politically more important.

Within the government, the Bay of Pigs ravaged the relationship between President Kennedy and the Joint Chiefs of Staff and, to a lesser extent, between the President and the CIA. Kennedy believed that neither had served him well and held the Joint Chiefs the more responsible. In his eyes, their review of the military aspects of CIA planning had been cursory at best.[10]

Admiral Burke, most probably representing the opinions of the other Joint Chiefs as well, judged that the last-minute changes in the plan made by the President were the major reasons for the debacle.[11] Had the JCS been brought into the planning earlier, had the Trinidad plan been approved and, especially, had air strikes been conducted as originally planned, Burke and his colleagues thought, the landing would have been far more likely to succeed.

Nor was Cuba the only issue on which the Joint Chiefs found themselves out of step with their new President. Inside the Pentagon, they were also on the defensive. There Robert S. McNamara, the new secretary of defense, had begun a drastic reform of decision-making and funding priorities. Senior military officers saw these changes as downgrading their military expertise and judgment in deference to the advice of young, bright, relatively inexperienced analysts known as the "Whiz Kids." These newcomers believed that systematic and detailed analyses of what they called the estimated "cost effectiveness" of proposed courses of action were far better guides to decision-making than military experience. The latter they often dismissed as little more than old prejudices.

Their disdain was mirrored by the men in uniform. Gen. Thomas D. White, then U.S. Air Force chief of staff, reflected the prevailing attitude. He wrote that he was "profoundly apprehensive of the pipe-smoking, tree-full-of-owls . . . professional defense intellectuals." He questioned whether "these often overconfident, sometimes arrogant young professors, mathematicians and other theorists have sufficient worldliness or motivation to stand up to the kind of enemy we face."[12]

Procedural reforms, however, were not the only changes the Kennedy administration brought to the Pentagon. No longer were strategic nuclear weapons to be virtually the single deterrent to war with the Soviet Union and the Warsaw Pact nations. Flexible response, championed by Gen. Maxwell Taylor, would replace massive retaliation as the basis for security planning. Far greater reliance was to be placed on conventional military muscle.

The new strategy went further yet. President Kennedy believed that nuclear war was a remote possibility and that other types of conflict, such as Khrushchev's wars of national liberation, were far more likely. The Bay of Pigs failure reinforced this belief, and the President ordered his military services to devote more thought and resources to organizing and training forces to help friendly governments abroad in combating armed opposition. Counterinsurgency operations soon became central to U.S. military doctrine and training.

The President's plan to shift away from massive retaliation had to overcome one obstacle of his own making. In the 1960 campaign Kennedy had railed against the "missile gap" that allegedly left the United States inferior to the Soviet Union in strategic nuclear power. He charged McNamara with reviewing this premise and suggesting corrective measures.

McNamara's response, publicized without attribution to him in early February 1961, was surprising: he could find no evidence of a missile gap. The White House promptly denied this conclusion. No studies had been completed, it said; no final judgments could be made. While Republican leaders challenged that denial for several weeks, McNamara backed it, and the issue receded from the limelight.

Nine months later, however, it resurfaced when U.S. intelligence determined that McNamara's earlier position had been justified: the United States held a clear lead in intercontinental missile strength. Against an estimated Soviet ICBM arsenal of fewer than fifty missiles capable of striking U.S. targets, U.S. forces included forty-eight land-based Atlas ICBMs and an equal number of similar missiles on three of the five Polaris submarines available for sea duty at any one time.[13] Moreover, it was claimed that the Kennedy defense budget of April 1961 would maintain U.S. superiority in strategic nuclear forces and programs without requiring crash efforts. Although the Army and Navy readily accepted this forecast, U.S. Air Force leaders were less convinced. Within the Defense Department, debate continued.

Bruising failure and disruptive change thus pitted the professional military against its civilian superiors after the Bay of Pigs defeat. Humiliation abroad and dissension at home made contention rather than cohesion the watchword. To get independent advice in the analysis of the Cuban misadventure, President Kennedy summoned Maxwell Taylor to the White House to "insert" him as an authoritative figure "between himself and the Joint Chiefs."[14] Kennedy even invented a job description for his high-level recruit: Military Representative of the President. For that task, Taylor assembled a small staff that I was privileged to join.

In Freedom's "Hour of Maximum Danger"

In the immediate aftermath of the Cuban failure, Taylor—an experienced combat veteran—found the White House like a "command post that had been overrun by the enemy," a place of "glazed eyes, subdued voices and slow speech. . . ."[15] Its beleaguered occupants had minimal regard for the uniformed personnel who were supposed to serve as their apolitical subordinates. Recalling the mood of his fellow New Frontiersmen at the time, Arthur M. Schlesinger, Jr. wrote that it seemed to them that the senior military professionals were "taking care to build a record which would permit them to say that, whatever the President did, he acted against their advice."[16]

In contrast, General Taylor developed an almost instant rapport with the President and, notably, with his brother and confidant, Attorney General Robert F. Kennedy. Taylor had commanded American paratroopers on D-Day in Normandy, led occupation forces in Berlin and the Eighth Army in Korea and had spent four years as Army Chief of Staff before retiring in 1959. His advocacy of a shift in U.S. military forces and strategy away from almost sole reliance on nuclear weapons to the approach Kennedy and McNamara favored—a much larger role for non-nuclear weapons and conventional forces—also commended him to the President. Taylor's 1959 book, *The Uncertain Trumpet*, promoting this change, had made a deep impression on then-Senator John Kennedy.

By July 1961, when Taylor put his uniform back on and took his new and newly created post as Military Representative of the President, the shock of the Bay of Pigs defeat had largely worn off. The siege mentality, however, had not. The United States was definitely on the defensive and needed to change its ways. "We are in a life and death struggle which we may be losing," Taylor told the President in June 1961 in a top secret analysis of the failed landing in Cuba, "and will lose unless we change our ways and marshall [sic] our resources with an intensity associated in the past only with times of war."[17]

As a major in the U.S. Air Force, which I had entered in 1948, I took President Kennedy's inaugural admonition that we had "been granted the role of defending freedom in its hour of maximum danger" very seriously. Having flown 97 missions as a combat pilot in Korea before Chinese antiaircraft fire wounded me and brought down my plane, I had spent the next decade as a West Point instructor and a Pentagon war planner. I came to General Taylor's staff in the Old Executive Office Building prepared for new clashes with Soviet power and expecting them imminently. I did not think a direct military challenge as likely as an indirect one, made through surrogate forces.

As I moved into a high-ceilinged, third-floor office two doors down from General Taylor's suite, I had little time to admire the shaded view across the green Ellipse to the Jefferson Memorial. Among the President's men and my Pentagon contacts, I picked up only faint whispers of the administration's continued obsession with Fidel Castro and his Cuba. We were all preoccupied with the status of Berlin, the future of the fragile nation of Laos and, increasingly, South Vietnam.

The early months of Kennedy's presidency saw a number of East-West skirmishes, each one seeming to force the United States and its allies into increasingly precarious positions. Khrushchev spoke and acted with a boldness that kept the West constantly on guard. The murder of the Congo's Patrice Lumumba in February 1961, for example, prompted a threat of intervention from the Kremlin and a Kennedy counterthreat. Soviet arms shipments, meanwhile, were fueling the Pathet Lao insurgency and its steady gains against the U.S.-supported regime in Vientiane.

Laos, in fact, commanded most of the President's attention during the early months; the installation of a neutral administration to defuse the crisis became his goal. It was not Khrushchev's. By late April, Kennedy was weighing the possibility of U.S. military intervention.

Very much on the defensive over their Bay of Pigs role, the Joint Chiefs of Staff entered the internal debate over Laos convinced that any commitment of U.S. military forces or resources there should not suffer from the fatal flaw of inadequate firepower that had doomed the Cuban invasion. They foresaw the danger of U.S. involvement in an extensive land war in Southeast Asia, including possible confrontation with China's huge army, and recommended that if combat forces were to be deployed, they should go in convincing strength—some 60,000 men.

The White House found those numbers excessive, and the President decided on a much less confrontational alternative. He ordered that a contingent of 10,000 U.S. Marines in Japan be readied for dispatch to Laos. Combined with continued diplomatic pressure, the gesture of military intent got Moscow's attention. Khrushchev accepted a neutral Laos, perhaps expecting the country eventually to fall into Communist hands by default. Whatever the reason, the Laotian crisis receded. It left behind, however, a new residue of vexation between the Joint Chiefs and Kennedy's civilian national security team.

Testing Time in Berlin

Exacerbated by quarrels in the Third World, the gap between Washington and Moscow continued to widen. When Kennedy and Khrushchev actually met in Vienna in early June 1961, the rift became a chasm. On his side of the divide, the Soviet leader left the summit convinced that his opponent was both inexperienced and weak.

At the summit Khrushchev reopened the issue of Berlin in dramatic terms. In the January 1961 speech that signalled his support for wars of national liberation, he had revived a variation of a threat first made in November 1958. Either the Western powers agreed to negotiate an end to their occupation of West Berlin, he warned, or he would act unilaterally. Specifically, he voiced an intention to sign a peace treaty with the German Democratic Republic, effectively undercutting the legal status of Allied forces in the divided city and the independence of West Berlin.

In Vienna, Khrushchev repeated this threat. Had he carried it out, the German Democratic Republic would have gained control over access to Berlin. It could then, in theory, forbid Berlin-bound Western military convoys from crossing GDR territory. Under such a challenge, Washington, London, Paris and Bonn would have to decide whether to use force to open the road. Khrushchev let it be known that armed action in such a case would be considered an attack on the Soviet Union. He confronted the West—and Kennedy as its principal representative—with a Hobson's choice, as *The Economist* described it, "between ignominious retreat and nuclear devastation."[18]

During the summer and fall after the Vienna meeting, Berlin became an almost daily preoccupation for Kennedy and his advisors. The city was the symbol of the U.S. commitment to defend Western Europe, the centerpiece of Allied co-hesion. It was widely accepted that if the United States backed down in Berlin, the action would signal a fatal weakness in American resolve. That the former German capital was isolated and virtually impossible to defend militarily served mainly to raise the stakes—possibly to the nuclear level.

That danger, in turn, underscored the urgent need to find a political solution to the problem rather than a military one. As he had done for Laos, the President devised a way to send a firm message without actually engaging military forces. By calling U.S. reserve units to active duty and positioning some of them in Europe, he indicated his intent to use force if necessary and to strengthen non-nuclear U.S. capabilities on the continent. He also brought the four NATO partners most concerned with Berlin into negotiations aimed at developing a common policy to maintain access to Berlin short of war.

While diplomatic talks continued, the Soviets indulged in periodic acts of harassment against Allied forces moving through the ground corridor to Berlin. They also took two dramatic actions that epitomized the tensions and risks in-herent in the crisis. The first to provoke Western outrage was the erection of the Berlin Wall in August 1961. The second was an incident in mid-October; when East German police tried to block the unimpeded entry of a U.S. diplomat into East Berlin, armed U.S. troops escorted him across the border. Three days later, another attempt to assert East German control over the "Checkpoint Charlie" crossing brought U.S. and Soviet tanks into a direct, nerve-testing con-frontation one hundred yards apart.

It was the first time in Cold War history that the armed forces of the two superpowers had been so close and so close to firing on each other. After a day of high tension and urgent messages from Kennedy to Khrushchev, the tanks gradually drew apart. The face-off ended as a critical test of nerves and resolve and, in a sense, a rehearsal for the test that would come one year later in the Caribbean.

Target: Castro

On the list of likely flashpoints for U.S.-Soviet confrontation, Cuba occupied a relatively low place. In purely military terms, the island was of secondary concern throughout 1961 and the early months of 1962. The memory of the Bay of Pigs gnawed at the Kennedy team's collective psyche, however, and Cuba secretly be-came the focus of an elaborate enterprise aimed at toppling the Castro regime.

McNamara revealed the depths to which the humiliation reached when he told a Senate inquiry into the CIA some years later, "We were hysterical about Castro" and under "pressure" from the President and his brother "to do something about Castro."[19] Ray Cline, the deputy director for intelligence at the CIA during the Kennedy years, once recalled that the Kennedy brothers believed "they had been booby-trapped at the Bay of Pigs, and it became a constant pre-occupation, almost an obsession, to right the record somehow." The brothers, he surmised, took a guiding precept from their father: "Don't get mad. Get even."[20]

Only a handful of officials were in on the secret planning and covert actions the Kennedy team was mounting against Castro. General Taylor was very much among them as Chairman of the Special Group (Augmented), responsible for the Cuban and other clandestine enterprises. The SGA also included Robert Kennedy, CIA Director John McCone, JCS Chairman Lemnitzer, National Security Advisor McGeorge Bundy, Undersecretary of State U. Alexis Johnson and Deputy Secretary of Defense Roswell Gilpatric. Collectively, in the words of historian James G. Hershberg, they "mingled the caution of the once-burned with frustration and fury toward the upstart [Cuban] revolutionaries. . . ."[21]

As head of the SGA, Taylor was completely familiar with the development of anti-Castro policy and operations. Most members of his small staff were not. To summarize the U.S. actions that fed Khrushchev's fears both for the survival of a valued ally and for Soviet credibility in the Third World, I have no personal recollections on which to rely. Instead, I have consulted the extensive published record of what has entered history as Operation MONGOOSE.

Preceded by the Joint Chiefs' contingency planning during summer and early autumn 1961 for either or both a blockade or a full-scale invasion of Cuba by some five or six Army and Marine divisions, MONGOOSE was actually conceived late that November. It was then that Attorney General Robert Kennedy told the SGA that "higher authority" wanted higher priority for Cuba.[22] This bureaucratic jargon did little to hide the President's own hand or the brothers' fierce intent.

To both Kennedys, the master of Havana represented a nearly intolerable reproach. More than a "bearded nuisance,"[23] as the dismissive judgment of Kennedy speechwriter and advisor Theodore C. Sorensen would have it, the Cuban revolutionary stood as a dynamic, ideological contrast to the trade-and-aid emphasis of the Alliance for Progress that Kennedy offered Latin America. Moreover, Castro was a domestic political irritant. Republicans could and did use the Cuban ruler's very existence to deflate Kennedy's inaugural promise to "pay any price, bear any burden . . . to assure the survival and the success of liberty."

Institutional disarray, however, handicapped the President in trying to make reality of his rhetoric in the Caribbean. At the CIA, both Director Allen Dulles and Richard Bissell, deputy director for operations, had to take primary responsibility for the Bay of Pigs. After a decent interval, both men resigned. On a number of issues, relations with the Joint Chiefs continued to be characterized by a muted but mutual chariness that was not eased by the appointment of Taylor to the White House staff. On the contrary, the Chiefs could view their colleague's recall from retirement only as further evidence of lost rapport with the President.

Such disharmony—as the White House, the armed forces and the intelligence community embarked on an effort that demanded seamless cooperation—got Operation MONGOOSE off to a rocky start. One thing was certain. No department or agency was going to allow a repetition of the misunderstandings that had produced the Bay of Pigs. All the participants in the return match wanted to make certain that their advice was carefully formulated, clearly expressed and fully understood.

MONGOOSE planning started from assumptions fundamentally different from those that guided the Bay of Pigs effort. Most striking was the understanding that overt U.S. military participation might be needed to overthrow Castro. The Joint Chiefs of Staff were directed to refine further their detailed contingency plans for such open intervention. For its part, the Defense Department wanted to be certain it had a plan that could be executed "as rapidly as possible, quickly confronting enemy forces with sufficient strength to be clearly beyond Cuban capability to resist. . . ."[24]

If Soviet agents picked up rumblings of these plans, perhaps they, and Nikita Khrushchev, would consider them evidence of intent. So much the better, military men at the time thought.

Pleased at the prospect of keeping the Kremlin's attention focused on Castro's survival rather than on exporting revolution, the Pentagon made no effort to hide the two-week, 40,000-man Marine and Navy maneuvers that engaged forces from North Carolina to the Caribbean in April 1962. The action culminated with an amphibious assault on the island of Vieques off the coast of Puerto Rico. Two smaller exercises that tested air and naval coordination took place in May. U.S. press accounts of these maneuvers alone would give Soviet intelligence enough information to feed Khrushchev's anxiety about American plans and Castro's future.[25]

Operation MONGOOSE

Another fundamental change called for a much more assertive covert program to undermine Castro and encourage insurrection. Brig. Gen. Edward Lansdale, an acknowledged expert in counterinsurgency and guerrilla operations, was designated chief of operations for the new effort. He was given authority from the SGA to task other government agencies as needed and instructions to develop a long-range program of action.

Lansdale delivered his recommendation on 20 February 1962, defining Operation MONGOOSE's aim as follows:

> **The Goal.** In keeping with the spirit of the Presidential memorandum of 30 November 1961, the United States will help the people of Cuba overthrow the Communist regime from within Cuba and institute a new government with which the United States can live in peace.[26]

Stressing that the intent was to foment and support a revolution from within, Lansdale laid out a six-phase plan. Although his schedule envisaged an uprising on Cuba in October 1962 and set target dates for the completion of each phase, he emphasized that he was not drawing a rigid timetable. His outline went as follows:

> Phase I. **Action.** March 1962. Start moving in.
>
> Phase II. **Build-up.** April-July 1962. Activating the necessary operations inside Cuba for revolution and concurrently applying the vital political, economic, and military-type support from outside Cuba.
>
> Phase III. **Readiness.** 1 August 1962, check for final policy decision.
>
> Phase IV. **Resistance.** August-September 1962, move into guerrilla operations.
>
> Phase V. **Revolt,** first two weeks of October 1962. Open revolt and overthrow of the Communist regime.
>
> Phase VI. **Final,** during month of October 1962. Establishment of a new government.[27]

Along with this broad framework, Lansdale presented a more detailed plan that would link sabotage, intelligence gathering and political, psychological and economic subversion by Cubans on the island with action by the United States. His conclusion showed, however, that he was still uncertain about the depth of the U.S. government's commitment to Operation MONGOOSE. Some hard realities remained unacknowledged.

The most vital was the willingness of the United States to use overt military force in support of Cubans attempting to overthrow Castro. Lansdale put it bluntly when he asked the SGA ". . . will the U.S. respond promptly with military force to aid the Cuban revolt? . . . An early decision is required, prior to deep involvement of the Cubans in this program."[28]

In mid-March, Lansdale received the "vital decision" he requested. Already some weeks behind schedule, the SGA approved the guidelines for Operation MONGOOSE, directing that the operations proceed on the basis of two fundamental assumptions. The first was that the United States would "make maximum use" of Cubans to overthrow Castro, while recognizing "that final success will require decisive U.S. intervention." Flowing from the first, the second assumption stipulated that the Cubans involved would take actions that would prepare for and justify U.S. intervention and then would assist in making the U.S. attack a success.[29]

In the sense that the SGA's 14 March memorandum acknowledged that U.S. military participation was crucial to success, Lansdale achieved what his predecessors had not: an early, top-level recognition and seemingly early resolution of the tough choices. Almost certainly, bitter memories of Kennedy's handling of the Bay of Pigs prompted Lansdale to insist on this key point and the overseers' group to agree.

The commitment, however, turned out to be less firm than it seemed. The Special Group hedged its bets from the outset by formulating go-slow operational mandates. It defined the acquisition of hard intelligence on Cuba as the first task. And although the SGA authorized political, economic and covert measures, it required that they be "short of those reasonably calculated to inspire a revolt within the target area, or other development which would require U.S. armed intervention."[30] In other words, Washington wanted to undermine Castro but, the directive notwithstanding, its leaders had not definitely made up their minds to use military force to do so.

This hesitancy did not keep the Joint Chiefs from applying themselves industriously. Taking earlier contingency planning further, they produced in April a study "on how to establish a 'total blockade' of Cuba," and the CIA analyzed that action's likely impact on Castro's regime.[31] A special Pentagon group drawn from the staff of the Commander-in-Chief of the Atlantic Command (CINCLANT) and the Defense Intelligence Agency (DIA) began coordinating the contingency planning.

As events unfolded, Lansdale's early timetable for Operation MONGOOSE proved optimistic. When he presented a review of the project on 25 July, he described it as a report at the end of phase I, the stage he had hoped would be over in March. Lansdale had originally planned for a period of some six months from start-up to actual revolt; slippage had made the October date for Castro's overthrow improbable, if not impossible.

The Reckoning

The July progress report put the prospects of an uprising further in doubt. In every aspect except military contingency planning, Lansdale detailed problems and shortcomings. The process of gathering recruits and gaining hard information as well as of developing guerrilla resistance in remote areas "was short of the hoped-for goal." Castro's security precautions and, "to some degree, policy limitations on the risks to be assumed" were cited as the causes.[32] The SGA's basic caution and hesitancy were interfering with its professed aims.

In the political field, the report reluctantly observed, State Department attempts to counter Castro's May Day propaganda and to arouse hemispheric reaction to Castro's suppression of a hunger demonstration in June had brought very limited results. As to psychological warfare, also overseen by the State Department, the MONGOOSE team lamented that the United States had no effective means to get information to the Cuban people. Few Cubans had good short-wave radio sets, and medium-wave broadcasts might prompt Castro to interfere with commercial broadcasts over a wide area in the United States. Clandestine radio within Cuba was just beginning; its transmissions had yet to gain much in the way of either audience or credibility.

Finally, MONGOOSE operatives still lacked authority to distribute propaganda leaflets from the air or on the ground. Sabotage activities were similarly frustrated. Only the Joint Chiefs of Staff could be complimented on substantial progress in their assigned tasks—developing plans and increasing readiness "for a decisive capability for intervention in Cuba."[33] Again recalling the Bay of Pigs, the military obviously wanted no misunderstanding about the comprehensiveness of these contingency plans.

In concluding his July report, Lansdale underscored his strong concern "that time is running out for the U.S. to make a free choice on Cuba, based largely on what is happening to the will of the Cuban people."[34] Expecting official guidance, America's Cuban supporters were beginning to wonder whether their future or U.S. security was Washington's chief concern. Lansdale warned that if they "become convinced that the U.S. is not going to do more than watch and talk, I believe they will make other plans for the future."[35] Those inside Cuba would lose hope; exiles already in the United States would decide to settle there.

Clearly, its chief saw Operation MONGOOSE languishing. Trying to generate a renewed and firm decision on how to proceed, he offered four possibilities:

a. Cancel operational plans; treat Cuba as a Bloc nation; protect Hemisphere from it, or
b. Exert all possible diplomatic, economic, psychological, and other pressures to overthrow the Castro-Communist regime without overt employment of U.S. military, or
c. Commit U.S. to help Cubans overthrow the Castro-Communist regime, with a step-by-step phasing to ensure success, including the use of U.S. military force if required, or
d. Use a provocation and overthrow the Castro-Communist regime by U.S. military force.[36]

Lansdale did not suggest that the SGA adopt any of his alternatives, nor did he express a preference among them. He recommended only that the overseers use his complete report as a basis for developing guidelines and objectives for phase II. In the original plan this was to be the build-up phase, the period when operations inside Cuba began and pressures mounted from without.

With phase I a half-hearted effort, and phase II's form and substance still undecided some six months after the top-priority program had been mandated, Lansdale's progress report could not hide the frustration of MONGOOSE personnel. They were becoming increasingly skeptical of their chances for success. Castro was getting stronger. U.S. actions seemed pusillanimous. The SGA manifested an apparent unwillingness to take the steps necessary to achieve the objectives that had been set.

That phase II, no matter which option was selected, would push further into the future any consideration of direct U.S. military intervention merely confirmed their doubts. It offered more evidence that although the Kennedy administration had set in motion an extensive operation for the overthrow of Castro, it meant to keep U.S. military involvement at the planning level. There were detailed plans for the invasion of Cuba, but evidently no willingness to execute them in any foreseeable future.

It was as if some SGA members and MONGOOSE operatives hoped that their presumed readiness to commit U.S. forces would somehow give the Cuban people enough encouragement to overthrow Castro by themselves. While National Security Advisor McGeorge Bundy, for one, may not have believed that the Cubans alone could overthrow Castro, he did not favor invasion.[37]

Even Robert Kennedy, his intense attention to Operation MONGOOSE notwithstanding, seemed not to have invasion in mind. At the height of the crisis later that fall, when the Soviets offered to remove the missiles in exchange for assurances that the United States would not invade Cuba, he commented, "We've *always* given those assurances. We will be glad to give them again."[38] A skeptic might claim that Kennedy was only playing word games; "assurances" meant nothing. Still, the intense pressure of the crisis and the imminence of events that neither the United States nor the Soviet Union controlled lend weight to the supposition that he meant what he said and that he never intended to invade Cuba.

According to Sorensen as well, the President for some time had had no urge to invade. He counted more on isolating Castro than on overthrowing him.[39] With some of the most influential U.S. leaders holding this attitude, Lansdale had reason to be concerned about the future of MONGOOSE.

Whatever suspicions they harbored, Lansdale and his associates continued their work in late July. The SGA began to grapple with the task of choosing among Lansdale's four options. As they did so, observers noted a massive influx of ships to Cuba from the Soviet Union.[40] The U.S. intelligence community responded with fresh efforts to determine what this new activity meant.

Storm Clouds in the Caribbean

As July turned into August, most of us on General Taylor's small White House staff focused on two issues: Berlin and Vietnam. We paid only passing attention to the developments on Cuba that aroused long-standing concerns among the Joint Chiefs and began to awaken the suspicions of CIA Director John A. McCone. Because we looked at Cuba and the noticeable increase in Soviet shipping to it in terms of the NATO-Warsaw Pact rivalry, my closest colleagues and I related Khrushchev's moves in the Caribbean to his designs on Europe. We gave far higher priority to the latter.

Ours was the conventional wisdom, and it was shared, even when the missile crisis broke months later, by many of the President's senior advisors. To us, the build-up on Cuba seemed largely a sideshow. Berlin was the main draw, and Southeast Asia a coming attraction.

More imaginative than we, some staff members for the Joint Chiefs had been worried that the Kremlin's support for Fidel Castro was part of a strategic design to turn the island into a military base and an eventual site for medium- and intermediate-range missiles. A prescient JCS representative had even tried to introduce this prospect into a 26 February 1962 draft of a joint Defense and State Department memorandum to the President on the possible use of U.S. military forces in support of Operation MONGOOSE. A State Department staff officer, however, objected. He was reluctant, he noted, "to agree to language which is speculative or alarmist."[1]

On 10 August John McCone brought the idea up again. He raised the possibility that the Soviets would move some medium-range missiles to Cuba in a meeting with Secretaries Rusk and McNamara, National Security Advisor Bundy, General Taylor, and others.[2] McCone voiced misgivings that had been aroused by intelligence gathered during a U-2 mission five days earlier over Cuba. It was the first such inspection since four flights that McCone had ordered in June had looked for evidence to confirm repeated rumors that the Soviets were building underground facilities for missiles or aircraft.

That comprehensive early-summer surveillance doubled the normal rate of two U-2 flights a month.[3] While using up the July quota for use of the delicate aircraft, the CIA found nothing to support the accumulating reports of suspicious activity. The 5 August U-2 mission told a different story. It brought home unsettling intelligence of the sudden increase in shipments of military material, and, revealing the presence of Soviet military personnel, prompted McCone's 10 August forebodings.[4]

No action followed the 10 August discussion. The same group, plus Attorney General Kennedy, met again eleven days later to hear McCone report that the Soviet supply effort was much larger than earlier estimated and extended to construction work of an unknown nature. Still, CIA analysts held that no offensive weapons were included. They concluded rather, that the construction was for "highly sophisticated electronic installations or COMINT [communications intelligence] and ELINT [electronic intelligence] and possible electro-counter measure efforts or missile sites, probably ground-to-air."[5]

In the ensuing conversation, the question of appropriate U.S. response to the placement of Soviet MRBMs in Cuba came up, apparently for the first time. The policymakers discussed imposing a partial or full blockade on shipping to Cuba, but Rusk and Bundy, at least, demurred. Believing that there was a "very definite inter-relationship between Cuba and other trouble spots, such as Berlin. . . ," they "felt that a blockade of Cuba would automatically bring about a blockade of Berlin; that drastic action on a missile site or other military installation of the Soviets in Cuba would bring" retaliation against "our bases and numerous missile sites, particularly [in] Turkey and southern Italy."[6]

The following evening, McCone and Taylor briefed the President, whom the CIA chief found "quite familiar with the [Cuban] situation"[7] and ready for a full-dress review of it with Rusk, McNamara, Bundy, Taylor, McCone and Undersecretary of Defense Roswell Gilpatric the next day. Requesting continuing analyses of Soviet personnel and equipment in Cuba, Kennedy asked particularly whether construction of surface-to-air missile (SAM) sites differed from that for ground-to-ground missiles. McCone said they were hard to tell apart.

What, the President then wanted to know, could the United States do against "missile sites" in Cuba? Could an air attack destroy them? Would a ground offensive be necessary? Could "a substantial guerrilla effort" do the job?[8]

Kennedy's questions were only that, an early exploration of alternatives. One consequence of the meeting, however, was an order directing the Department of Defense to study various available options for "executing a decision to eliminate any installations in Cuba capable of launching a nuclear attack on the U.S."[9] But there seemed little urgency. Many of the President's advisors at the 23 August policy review "related action in Cuba to Soviet actions in Turkey, Greece, Berlin, Far East and elsewhere," McCone noted.[10]

Only he regarded Cuba "as our most serious problem . . . the key to all of Latin America" and felt that "if Cuba succeeds, we can expect most of Latin America to fall."[11] And only McCone pressed for "aggressive political action" that would either bring the self-destruction of the Castro regime or, that being admittedly improbable, would set the stage for a MONGOOSE-inspired uprising and "the instantaneous commitment of sufficient armed forces to occupy the country, destroy the regime, free the people, and establish in Cuba a peaceful country . . . a member of the community of American states."[12]

These top-level discussions remained secret until many of the records were declassified in connection with the 1992 anniversary of the missile crisis. Except for those actually working on Cuban matters, such as our colleague, Tom Parrott, the discreet CIA representative, General Taylor's staff remained as much in the dark as was the public at large. In 1962 President Kennedy ordered a close, need-to-know hold on all information about the Soviet build-up in the Caribbean. He hoped to avoid providing ammunition to his political opponents while keeping maximum flexibility on Cuba for himself during the fall congressional elections.

It was a vain hope. The Republican campaign committees for the Senate and the House had already announced that Cuba policy would be "the dominant issue of the 1962 campaign."[13] Republican Senator Homer Capehart, campaigning for reelection from Indiana, told a rally there on 27 August that Soviet personnel on Cuba numbered three to five thousand—combat troops, not civilian specialists. Chiding the President for concealing the truth and masking the threat, Capehart demanded an American invasion.[14]

Political Heat, Dawning Light

Six days later, Democratic Senator George Smathers of Florida, a Kennedy intimate from their bachelor days and a politician with a vocal constituency of Cuban exiles, echoed Capehart's call. Smathers appealed for decisive but international military action to be engineered and led by the United States. That same day, his Republican colleague, Strom Thurmond of South Carolina, advocated a quick U.S. invasion. Texas Republican John Tower shortly thereafter lashed out at the Kennedy administration's "massive appeasement" of Cuba and the Soviet Union.[15]

The pressure from Capitol Hill may have been unwelcome, but so were the intelligence reports. On 29 August, a day on which President Kennedy characterized the Soviet presence on Cuba to inquiring journalists as "an expanded advisory and technical mission,"[16] a U-2 plane flew over the island for the second time that month. Its photos, presented and explained to Robert Kennedy two days later, showed eight sites for surface-to-air missiles being built in western Cuba.

McCone had no doubt that more would follow, and that their installation had a purpose. "They're not putting them in to protect the [sugar] cane cutters," he told the aide who brought him the news. "They're putting them in to blind our reconnaissance eye."[17]

My ears heard the rumble of partisan contention in Washington and also registered Moscow's angry denunciation of "trigger-happy Senators and Congressmen . . . whipping up anti-Cuban hysteria,"[18] but my eyes were on Europe and Vietnam. Early in 1962 and again in July, Soviet fighter aircraft harassed Western flights to and from Berlin, giving the West an airborne reminder of Khrushchev's threats to turn Soviet rights of control over to the East Germans. Not long afterwards, the Soviets rejected an Allied proposal to convene a conference on the divided city's status and called East German leaders to Moscow, it was assumed, to discuss Khrushchev's threatened separate peace treaty.

In Vietnam, summer 1962 brought heightened concern and deepened U.S. involvement. North Vietnam broadcast orders to the Viet Cong to destroy the strategic hamlets that the Americans and South Vietnamese were creating as rural refuges and political bulwarks. Although U.S. personnel in Vietnam were still nominally in advisory roles, their status did not protect them. Three Americans died in a U.S. helicopter shot down in the central highlands on 16 July.

Nine days later, Secretary McNamara returned from a visit to the region to declare that he was pleased with the progress being made. Early in August, the United States deployed a company of jet helicopters to South Vietnam. U.S. involvement was on the rise, and Vietnam, along with Berlin, dominated official Washington's attention.

I was not alone in paying little attention to Cuba. Most of those involved in national security matters shared the judgment of McGeorge Bundy, who later commented:

> When we thought of Cuba during 1962, at least until September, most of
> us thought first of our own frustrations, second about Castro's ambitions,
> and only after that about how Cuba might look to the Russians.[19]

Even in weighing that issue, officials tended to see Castro as a Caribbean pawn
in a European chess game. Secretary of State Rusk, for one, later said he had
reason to believe that the Soviet missiles in Cuba were "a part of Khrushchev's
policy on Berlin."[20] Paul H. Nitze, assistant secretary of defense, held the
same view.[21]

Most of us on Taylor's staff shared this perception even as the daily intelligence reports documented a sudden increase in Soviet military supplies bound
for Cuba. Twenty-one Soviet freighters carrying military cargoes arrived in July
1962, a volume of shipping more than three times as high as the preceding year.
By 3 September, the CIA believed that as many as sixty-five ships with military
equipment had reached Cuba since mid-July.[22] By 13 September another twenty-
six were en route.

We all badly wanted to know how the Cubans intended to use this new-
found strength. What did Khrushchev and Castro have in mind? But while our
curiosity rose, it was circumscribed by the assumption that Berlin and Cuba
were part of the same problem, with Berlin still the centerpiece.

Others in Washington might have had a different outlook, but they did not
share their thinking widely. Those involved in Operation MONGOOSE, including General Taylor, kept their counsel. So did the CIA personnel, who
had been involved since 1960—with or without the knowledge of Presidents
Eisenhower and Kennedy—in another scheme that demanded the utmost secrecy: a plan for the assassination of Fidel Castro.[23]

Even if analysts had been freely sharing data and assessments, the flow of
reliable information from and about Cuba was thin until late in summer 1962.
Only two U-2 flights were scheduled in August, and caution began to impact on
aerial intelligence gathering late in the month. Weather interfered with some
September missions. President Eisenhower had begun the flights—at the rate of
one a month—in 1960, and President Kennedy had doubled their frequency
in early 1962. The State Department, however, worried about the risks such
surveillance entailed.

Diplomats remembered all too well the downing of Gary Powers' U-2 over
Russia in 1960 and the subsequent U.S. embarrassment; they did not want a
repeat. State's reserve was reinforced by two incidents during the last week of
August and the first week of September. First, a U.S. U-2 strayed over Sakhalin
Island, and Soviet interceptors launched against it. The U-2 escaped unharmed,
but the scare left its mark. About a week later, a U-2 ostensibly belonging to
Nationalist China was lost over mainland China. With both events public

knowledge, the State Department feared that a third incident, this time over Cuba, would bring widespread condemnation of the United States.

The U-2 missions were thus mounted under careful scrutiny. The 5 August flight generated no unusual excitement, even though McCone saw early portents of trouble in the results. The photographs taken on 29 August did arouse concern. They showed eight SAM installations under construction in the western half of the island and also disclosed a site unfamiliar to photo interpreters at Banes in the east.

Its appearance sounded an alarm signal, but a muffled one. Hurricane season in the Caribbean put heavy cloud cover over Banes during a 5 September U-2 overflight. Although the weather was checked each day, no other mission could be flown until 26 September, and that one was similarly hampered. Both September surveys did bring back evidence of new SAM sites—three more on each date—raising the total to around seventeen. Between the two sorties, McNamara put off action on a CIA request for low-level reconnaissance by military aircraft, waiting for information that might more adequately balance the international and domestic political risks as well as those to the pilots.

Claims of Soviet missile deployments came primarily from refugees and CIA agents on the island but lacked credibility. As of January 1962, the Agency had already logged two hundred and eleven missile sightings. Not one of them was borne out by U-2 photography.

Often coming from untrained observers and in insufficient detail even in August, raw intelligence from agents made it hard to ascertain whether offensive or defensive missiles—or, indeed, any missiles at all—had actually been observed. The CIA, therefore, did not disseminate allegations about missile sites unless photographic evidence backed them up. Even as observations on the ground multiplied—one hundred thirty-eight human intelligence reports from May to August; nearly nine hundred in September—almost all seemed connected to SAM or cruise-missile installations and related equipment. The three reports that could not be so explained were "negated" by photographic intelligence.[24]

The requirement that refugee, defector and agent reports be crosschecked against photography meant delay in circulating their claims in top-level Washington circles. The number of such reports also generated a growing number of intelligence community requests for photography, but weather conditions, caution—and probably an unconscious desire not to challenge long-held perceptions of Soviet priorities and practices—kept U-2 overflights of Cuba on a business-as-usual schedule until mid-October.

The Pull of Conventional Wisdom

Only later would observers and analysts such as I realize that the administration had fallen prey to a common fault. It saw in Cuba what it wanted and expected to see, not what was actually taking place. It interpreted Soviet military assistance to Castro as a little-modified rerun of past Kremlin endeavors in the Third World.

Surface-to-air missiles, for example, had shown up in earlier Soviet deliveries of defensive hardware to Egypt, Indonesia and Tanzania. The SAMs on Cuba therefore seemed only a continuation of Soviet practices and a confirmation of past U.S. policy judgments. The massive increase in deliveries of military equipment through August and September did not shake the wide agreement within the U.S. government that the mission of the expanding Cuban military forces had not changed. Thus, the conventional wisdom, challenged in the higher reaches of the U.S. government only and inconclusively in those months by John McCone, had it that the Soviets would readily help Castro prepare to defend against a possible attack from the United States but would not provide offensive military capabilities.

As a corollary, we also believed for a number of other reasons that Khrushchev would not deploy medium- or intermediate-range missiles so far from the Soviet Union. Moscow had never attempted such a move before, and the risks involved—of discovery, of loss of control, of violent confrontation with Washington—seemed far too high for a rational Soviet leadership to ignore. Whatever the particular goals of the expanding military support for Cuba, they did not point to a dramatic departure from established Soviet patterns. Or so we thought in August and September and, in the case of most senior Kennedy advisors, right up to the mid-October discovery of the Soviet MRBMs.

Even when the medium-range missiles were discovered, their military significance remained a subject of debate. In political terms, they were extremely provocative. The first ballistic missiles spotted—the fourteen-hundred-mile range SS-4s—posed an undoubted threat to U.S. cities on an arc from El Paso in Texas through Cincinnati to Washington, D.C. From sites in central Cuba that were photographed later, the twenty-eight-hundred-mile range SS-5s could have hit civilian targets throughout the forty-eight contiguous states. But the power to rain terror on American civilians did not automatically translate into a decisive Soviet advantage or tilt the strategic nuclear balance against the United States.

That stability rested basically on the relation between U.S. and Soviet long-range atomic forces. U.S. strength in both intercontinental ballistic missiles (ICBMs) and strategic bombers so vastly overshadowed that of the USSR that neither the missiles on Cuba nor those on their way were capable of decisively altering the strategic balance in favor of the USSR. It seemed that Khrushchev was risking a great deal to achieve only a small gain. It was hard to see why he would gamble so unless he expected to use the missiles as bargaining counters to swap for Western concessions on Berlin or for the withdrawal of U.S. missiles from bases near the Soviet Union.

Moscow already was stationing large numbers of MRBMs and IRBMs in western Russia. These weapons could wreak havoc in Europe without having much impact on the U.S.-Soviet strategic equation. The United States had about one hundred and seventy-five intercontinental ballistic missile launchers and just over one hundred submarine-launched Polaris missiles, as well as more than fourteen hundred long-range B-52 and medium-range B-47 bombers that could be refueled in the air. Estimates at the time gave the Soviet Union around one hundred and fifty long-range bombers and between fifty and one hundred intercontinental ballistic missiles that could reach the United States in about half an hour. Later information put the number of Soviet ICBMS at only twenty.[25]

Despite the U.S. advantage in ballistic missiles, American strategy in 1962 still relied heavily on the aircraft in the USAF Strategic Air Command (SAC). A number of these were on ground alert near the end of runways at all times; a few were airborne with nuclear weapons aboard, able—if the President directed—to proceed directly to the Soviet Union, refueling in the air. The bombers on ground alert could be airborne before incoming Soviet missiles arrived. Additionally, SAC counted heavily on its ability to rapidly raise the level of readiness of forces not on alert, dispersing them to selected bases and positioning them to launch immediately toward the Soviet Union.

Time was key to that retaliatory capability—time to disperse planes and to get them airborne. As the Soviets fielded more ICBMs, more and more U.S. aircraft not on airborne or ground alert would become vulnerable to missiles launched from the USSR; but that added danger was an issue for the future, not for the Kennedy administration in its first years. If missiles were deployed in Cuba, their flight time to U.S. targets would be ten to twenty minutes less than that of ICBMs fired from Soviet territory.

By themselves, those few minutes would make no real difference, since U.S. bombers not on alert could probably not even survive an attack launched from Soviet territory—once the USSR had sufficient missiles in its arsenal. In 1962, however, the Soviets had only a handful of such ICBMs and higher priority targets for them than bombers in the United States.

The major significance of Soviet missiles on Cuba therefore would come from their added numbers, not from their ability to reduce America's warning time. With missiles on Cuba to use in a preemptive nuclear strike, Khrushchev would almost triple the weight of atomic firepower he could quickly place on U.S. targets, particularly on air bases. Conceivably, the extra force could severely, perhaps fatally, limit U.S. ability to retaliate and thus make the idea of a devastating attack much more tempting to the Soviets.

In summer 1962, however, few of us had reason to believe we would face such a threat from the south. On 1 August, the U.S. intelligence community—CIA, Pentagon and State Department analysts combined—published an estimate on Cuba that concluded that Moscow and its allies were "unlikely" either to provide Castro with forces sufficient to conduct independent military operations or to station combat units in Cuba, at least for the next year or so.[26]

Such help was not needed for internal security, the assessment held, because Castro was not threatened from within nor likely to be. His armed forces could suppress any likely insurrection, contain and control guerrilla action and repel any invasion "short of direct U.S. military intervention in strength."[27] Although Cuba's economy was "in deep trouble," the analysts doubted the success of any uprising against the regime in the absence of "substantial outside support for the insurgents."[28]

Their 1 August estimate had clearly been in the works for some time; obviously, it did not fully take into account the upsurge in Soviet activity on the island in late July. Once data from the 5 August U-2 mission and other sources were in hand, CIA's Office of Current Intelligence acknowledged on 22 August that Cuba's military forces were being strengthened measurably.

Still, the agency held that there was no indication of Soviet military units in Cuba. The Soviets who had been observed were thought to be construction personnel, not troops. As to what they were building, the limited evidence suggested that the Soviets might be simply beefing up Cuban air defenses with SAMs, as they had done for other Third World clients.[29] Nowhere in the three-and-one-quarter-page memorandum were offensive military capabilities mentioned. It did, however, note that the economic and military assistance seen "amount to the most extensive campaign to bolster a non-bloc country ever undertaken by the USSR."[30]

Mounting deliveries of Soviet military equipment to Cuba over the next weeks reinforced the Agency's concern. The volume far exceeded the CIA's first estimate, and reports about it bred an understandable demand throughout the U.S. government to get a handle on what was going on.

MONGOOSE in Limbo

While the Soviet build-up moved forward, covert U.S. efforts to overthrow Castro went into a stall. CIA's repeated findings that no internal uprising was likely or would succeed without determined and forceful outside support confronted the supervisors of Operation MONGOOSE with the same fish-or-cut-bait challenge that General Lansdale had been putting before them one way or another since the spring. The issue was whether the administration would commit to intervene militarily in the event of the insurrection it wanted to inspire.

The answer, given by the President on 23 August, was—again—continue planning on the basis that it might be necessary to use U.S. military force to overthrow Castro.

To help reach that decision and get a go-ahead from the SGA for at least one of the options he had laid out at the end of July, Lansdale had the Defense Department prepare a paper on the consequences of U.S. military intervention in Cuba. Although the resulting memorandum predicted that Cuban defensive responses would range from "strong initial resistance" to guerrilla warfare, its tone suggested that such resistance would present no real problems. The paper warned that Cuban capabilities would improve with the flow of modern Soviet equipment, implicitly arguing for action as soon as feasible.[31]

With no Cuban government-in-exile to assume power after Castro's ouster, the Pentagon planners also contemplated a possible need for a U.S. occupation force. The U.S. Army would play the principal part in such a force, whose role and length of stay on the island would depend on the guerrilla resistance Castro and his followers were able to mount and the time required to "reconstitute an effective friendly Cuban government."[32]

In itself, the Pentagon's sanguine approach to a U.S. military role on Cuba did not move MONGOOSE far ahead. On 21 August, probably in preparation for his meeting that day with his Special Group colleagues and with the President the next evening, McCone put on paper his dissatisfaction with MONGOOSE planning. He began by commenting that, in the view of the CIA's Board of National Estimates, a "stepped up" version of Lansdale's second (b) option—diplomatic, political and economic pressure short of open U.S. military intervention—would not achieve the stated objectives. After so much visible effort, such a failure would cost Washington dearly in terms of prestige. A more aggressive program to improve U.S. intelligence gathering and impede Castro's economic progress would also fall short. "[S]ubstantial Soviet technical assistance," McCone judged, meant "that with the passage of time, it is possible there will evolve in Cuba a stronger rather than a weaker Castro dominated communist state, fully oriented to Moscow. . . ."[33]

McCone preferred a three-part strategy: an aggressive worldwide political program to alert Latin America and the world to the dangers of Castro; a second, still secret group of actions, presumably involving a focused and sizable sabotage effort within Cuba; and, when appropriate, the "instantaneous commitment" of U.S. military forces to destroy the regime and occupy and free the country. He closed by urging that his proposals should "go forward with all possible activities" envisaged in Lansdale's "plan (b)."[34]

McCone's ideas flowed logically from the 1 August national estimate in which all intelligence community members, including the military, had concurred. Nonetheless, his push for action ran up against the worries of Rusk and Bundy, in particular, that U.S. military involvement in Cuba would trigger Soviet countermoves against Berlin and, perhaps, attacks on U.S. overseas missile sites in Turkey and Italy. During the 21 August session in Rusk's office, McCone noted Bundy's view that all U.S. operations in Cuba must be covert, because "overt actions would involve serious consequences throughout the world. . . ."[35]

Even so, McCone must have pressed his case at the White House the next day, winning a presidential directive on the future course of MONGOOSE. At the end of the 23 August session, Kennedy ordered up a range of options he could choose from to get rid of Castro and called for "plan b-plus" of Operation MONGOOSE to "be developed with all possible speed."[36] Specifically, the President also asked for planning moves "to deliberately seek to provoke a full-scale revolt against Castro that might require U.S. intervention to succeed."[37]

Those decisions, however, did not put the matter to rest. On 3 September, Walt W. Rostow, who had moved from his post as Bundy's deputy on the National Security Council staff to head policy planning at the State Department, responded to a Kennedy request for advice by offering recommendations for a different way to broaden the effort to get rid of Castro. Sharing McCone's goal, Rostow argued for political, diplomatic and economic means to achieve it. If the President had chosen military options a few days earlier, his number two advisor on national security affairs had not heard the decision as a final order.

Rostow, on the contrary, believed the United States could and should work more diligently with Latin American governments to identify and interfere with Castro's subversive activities. At the same time, he recommended increasing economic pressure on Cuba. Its trade with the free world, already low, should be further cut, primarily to signal Moscow that the United States was committing itself to the "drawing of a line." Next, Rostow wanted to tell the Soviets directly that if they raised tensions in places such as Berlin and Vietnam, the United States might take action against Cuba. Finally, he suggested convening a hemispheric or Caribbean meeting on Cuba.[38]

Believing that the United States should and could achieve its Cuban objectives without direct use of military force, Rostow proposed a "two track" redefinition for MONGOOSE. Track one—"a heightened effort to move along the present lines"—would have harassment of Castro as its minimum objective. The maximum goal would be to trigger Castro's overthrow from within. Track two would consist of getting more Cubans involved in anti-Castro activities, both on the island and off it. Mindful of the previous attempt to enlist Cubans in such efforts and of the Bay of Pigs debacle, Rostow believed that a patient build-up of resistance from within could preclude a repeat of past errors. Lansdale, he urged, should be directed to look at track two very carefully, no matter what had apparently been decided less than two weeks earlier.

Political Pressures, Political Response

Even before the Rostow memorandum reached him, the President appeared to be backing away—at least in public—from the orders he had given to foment an uprising in which U.S. forces might have to intercede to assure success. Under mounting pressure to explain press reports of the Soviet build-up, administration spokesmen in August stuck to the line that the activity was defensive and probably involved no Soviet troops. Cuban exile leaders in Miami claimed otherwise, alleging specifically that 4,000 Soviet soldiers had landed since 29 July, but that report was promptly denied by "U.S. officials."[39]

After Senator Capehart took up the cause with his public call for an invasion to remove Soviet combat troops from Cuba, the President entered the fray. At a 29 August press conference, Kennedy said there was no evidence that such forces were on the island. In response to a question, he said that he was not for invading Cuba "at this time," adding that his phrasing had no special meaning. He believed it would be a mistake to invade Cuba.[40]

Those of us not in MONGOOSE saw nothing unusual in the President's declaration. But to Lansdale's operatives, who had just been ordered to develop plans that might call for U.S. use of force, the press conference statement could have come as a blow. Embittered, they might then have decided to use a classic Washington instrument—the leak—to force the President back to the policy approach he appeared to be disowning.

Whether he got his initial information from MONGOOSE leaks, other knowledgeable government sources or only from the Cuban refugees he cited, Senator Kenneth Keating, a respected New York Republican, began a series of detailed attacks on U.S. policy toward Cuba, starting 31 August on the Senate floor. Referring to U.S. policy as a "look-the-other-way" one, Keating cited refugee reports on the flow of Soviet military equipment and personnel into Cuba. He specifically mentioned missile bases, but spoke only of defensive sites to discourage attacks on Cuba by other countries in this hemisphere.[41]

Warning the President that Americans wanted to know what was going on in Cuba, Keating declared that "the answers received are unsatisfactory."[42] The effect of Keating's oratory and his efforts to make the administration have the Organization of American States take "prompt and vigorous action"[43] was to make Cuba just what the President did not want it to be: a campaign issue. All of us in the White House could feel the pressure rising, the nervousness over Cuba mounting.

Although Keating identified only refugee reports as his source for this first speech, he later stressed that his information either came from or was confirmed by government sources. This claim disturbed the Kennedy people; it had the ring of truth. His information corresponded very closely to the reports the administration was receiving through regular intelligence channels. The Senator never revealed his sources, and efforts to identify them have been unsuccessful,[44] but there can be little doubt that he had solid, inside information, far more complete than what government channels were providing to officials such as myself.

Both Republican outcry and new intelligence findings kept pushing Cuba into the limelight. A week after the 29 August U-2 flight photographed SAM sites, White House press secretary Pierre Salinger acknowledged the presence of the antiaircraft missiles and supporting electronic gear in Cuba. His statement, however, stressed that the government knew of no Soviet combat forces in Cuba, nor of "other significant offensive capability." Should such potential be detected, Salinger added, "the gravest issues would arise." Unappeased, Keating renewed his attack on 6 September, urging that the United States institute a complete economic boycott of Cuba and consider imposing a limited blockade on all military shipments to the island.[45]

Apparently alarmed by the noise level in Washington, the Kremlin moved to reassure the Kennedy administration. On 4 September, Anatoli Dobrynin, then beginning his 23 years of service as Soviet ambassador to the United States, paid a call on Robert Kennedy to deliver a message from Khrushchev for the President: no surface-to-surface missiles or other offensive weapons would be emplaced in Cuba. The military build-up in Cuba was not of any significance, Dobrynin vowed, adding Khrushchev's pledge to do nothing to disrupt relations during the congressional elections.[46] Two days later the Soviet diplomat, asking urgently to follow up a previous get-acquainted visit, met with Kennedy speech writer and confidant Theodore Sorensen to repeat the message he had already communicated through the Attorney General.[47]

In between the diplomat's two meetings came the Salinger statement, itself motivated by the Attorney General's feeling that the President needed to make an unequivocal public statement about the unacceptability of offensive weapons in Cuba. To add some emphasis to the White House words, on 7 September the President asked Congress to renew the authority it had given him during the 1961 Berlin crisis to call military reservists to a year of duty.

As if in response, on 11 September Nikita Khrushchev gave a predictably verbose statement to *The New York Times* warning the United States that an attack on Cuba might bring nuclear war, but promising to do nothing—specifically, nothing in Berlin—that would interfere with the upcoming congressional elections. He reminded the world, however, that soon after the election the Berlin issue had to be resolved.[48]

Meanwhile, in the upper echelons of the administration, rumblings heard only by a select few continued. While on his honeymoon in Paris, McCone learned about the missile installation at Banes that had puzzled analysts, and on

7 September he cabled his opinion that the site might be for short-range, portable surface-to-surface missiles that could attack the southeastern United States or areas in the Caribbean.[49]

Four days later the agency's Board of National Estimates replied to the director. The message from his senior analysts was that they were "still persuaded that costly crash operation to install SA-2's is reasonably explained by other than desire to hide later build-up and the Soviets likely to regard advantage of major offensive build-up not equal to dangers of U.S. intervention."[50]

The efforts by the Soviets to calm the waters and the reassurances from inside his administration did not relieve the political pressure on President Kennedy. He had to show that he was not, as Republicans were charging, "soft" on Cuba. He used a 13 September press conference, therefore, to issue a more definitive warning, one that some historians argue would have had decisive effect in the spring, but came too late to head Khrushchev off.[51]

Noting that shipments to Cuba to date posed no threat to the United States, Kennedy spelled out the developments that would. The last one was ". . . if Cuba should . . . become an offensive military base of significant capacity for the Soviet Union, then this country will do whatever must be done to protect its own security and that of its allies."[52] The President would return to this warning more than once, reminding the Soviets that they had been put on notice—if not before the missile deployments began, certainly before they were completed. They could have been stopped.

In truth, Kennedy's warning was vague, promising no specific action. It did nonetheless draw a clear distinction—as Rostow had suggested earlier in the month—between defensive and offensive equipment for Cuba, and it foretold some type of U.S. action if the Soviets overstepped the line. The United States might abide improvement in Cuba's defenses, but it would not condone the presence of a significant offensive capability. It was a position the Taylor staff could understand and accept, although, except for Taylor himself, we had not been in on its formulation.

On 16 September, McCone returned to the possibility of Soviet MRBMs in Cuba. From Paris he asked the Agency to study the possibility of secret MRBM placement under a basing plan that would make the missiles operational after only a few hours' overt preparation. Stating that he did not wish to be alarmist, he nonetheless believed it necessary for the CIA to keep the administration thinking about the dangers of a surprise. He also wanted others to understand that once Cuba had an air defense system installed, the United States might not be able to acquire the necessary information on MRBM missile site construction.[53]

As McCone had noted in August, he, for one, was very worried about the proven vulnerability of the U-2 to SAMs. The President, however, continued to doubt that the Soviets would take drastic steps in Cuba. And, except for

McCone, Kennedy's senior intelligence advisors saw no heightened danger. On 19 September, to demonstrate its continued attention to the increasingly explosive issue, the intelligence community issued a new special national intelligence estimate to update its 1 August report.

Assessing the significance of the buildup and "the possible future development of additional military capabilities"[54] on Cuba, the analysts held that the main aim of the Soviets was to strengthen Castro's defenses against any attempt by the United States to overthrow him. That conclusion indicated that the U.S. military exercises conducted in April, May and early August as well as others being planned for the fall were having the desired effect of keeping Castro and his Soviet protectors worried about potential U.S. action against the Cuban regime. The Pentagon policymakers who wanted to keep their adversary distracted in the Caribbean could feel that their tactic was working.

Gauging the possibility of a Soviet deployment of offensive weapons to Cuba, the 19 September estimate said any such action would be "represented to be defensive in nature" even if the arms were "of a more 'offensive' character: e.g., light bombers, submarines, and additional types of short-range surface-to-surface missiles (SSMs)."[55] Any such move by Moscow, the experts held, would turn on whether the Soviets thought they could introduce such weapons without provoking a U.S. military reaction. The estimate also considered the military advantages the Soviets could derive from medium- and intermediate-range missile bases on Cuba, and those to be derived from a submarine base, concluding that establishment of a submarine base was the more likely.[56]

For several reasons the analysts saw placement of long-range missiles as unlikely: the Soviets had not installed such weapons even in Soviet satellite territories; to do so would raise serious problems of command and control; if offensive weapons were in Cuba, many more Soviets would have to be on the island than there were; finally, the Soviets almost certainly would expect a strong reaction by the United States to the appearance of offensive weapons at its back door.[57]

The estimate concluded by underscoring the argument that placing MRBMs in Cuba would run counter to policies the Soviets were pursuing in Latin America. Moscow did not propose to take over the region with military force; it planned instead to build up Communist or "Communist-allied" leaders with mass followings to replace existing governments.[58]

All these arguments had been made before; together, they continued to seem convincing. Given the public and private assurances that Khrushchev had been sending, administration officials had every reason to feel as September drew to a close that, whatever was going on in Cuba, no explosive revelations would disrupt U.S-Soviet relations or the 1962 elections. Theirs and mine was a false confidence. We had been lulled into it by the conventional wisdom and the trickery of Nikita Khrushchev. Our wake-up call was soon to ring.

Cuba: Front and Center

The first day of October, Maxwell Taylor's first day as chairman of the Joint Chiefs of Staff, brought the start of a new, top-level military attention to Cuba and a new concern about Soviet intentions there. An intelligence briefing delivered to McNamara, Taylor and the service chiefs that day made the prospect of Soviet ballistic missiles in the Caribbean—so recently and regularly dismissed as unlikely—suddenly appear all too probable. The case was not air-tight, but it was persuasive. It launched Taylor's term at the JCS on a dramatic note.

Until then, most senior officials at the White House, the State Department, the CIA and the Pentagon, and those in the intelligence community that advised all four institutions, had seen only what they wanted to see: a continuation in the Caribbean of familiar Kremlin maneuvering in the Third World. Even Fidel Castro's 25 September announcement of a Soviet-Cuban agreement to build a large fishing port on the island as a base for the USSR's Atlantic trawler fleet generated little alarm among insiders. Although the public statement made some suspect that a secret Soviet submarine base was what was actually being planned, that prospect, too, fit with parallel developments in Egypt and Indonesia.

So close to America's coastline, the activity was hardly innocent. Yet to most senior policymakers the build-up did not seem to signal any new degree of menace. Among the foresighted exceptions were John McCone and some mid-level CIA and Defense Department analysts. Also alarmed, or wishing to appear so in the weeks before the Congressional elections, were the senators and representatives who adopted a nearly unanimous resolution in September to use force, if needed, against Cuban-based Communist subversion or aggression.

Within the administration, the conventional wisdom was only dispelled after the 14 October U-2 overflight of western Cuba. Two weeks earlier, however, its hold began to loosen dramatically. The change, coinciding with his new duties, quickly thrust General Taylor and his small personal staff on which I served from advisory roles into the center of the action.

As he moved to the Pentagon from the White House, where the position of Military Representative of the President was abolished, Taylor retained a sound and friendly professional relationship with McGeorge Bundy and the National Security Council staff. More important, he had the evident respect of the President. With Robert Kennedy his ties were even closer. The work they had done together—first on the Bay of Pigs investigation, then on Operation MONGOOSE, on other covert actions, on counterinsurgency and on a host of political and military issues—had transformed their solid official dealings into a warm, personal bond.

Their two personalities could not have been more dissimilar. Taylor was a handsome, cultured, scholarly, highly decorated and highly successful military professional who kept himself in excellent physical condition through his favorite sport, tennis. In 1962 Bobby Kennedy was still the young, confident, often impatient, often rumpled, brash younger brother, a strong influence on the President, dedicated above all to ensuring his brother's success.

Yet a special chemistry linked the Attorney General and Taylor. As a measure of friendship, respect, and affection, the younger man named one of his sons after the general. Even away from the White House, Taylor could count on easy access to the President, directly or through Bobby, an informal arrangement that benefitted him, the Attorney General and, most importantly in the coming crisis, the President.

Across the Potomac River, Taylor already had sound working ties, though not close personal ones, with Secretary of Defense McNamara. With the uniformed service chiefs, on the other hand, Taylor's position was delicate, his reception edgy. His after-action report on the Bay of Pigs, cautiously critical of the Joint Chiefs but nonetheless damning, had left a sour taste. Additionally, Taylor had retired from active service. Senior military professionals naturally wanted their own turn at the top position. The Army, Navy and Air Force heads, including Gen. Earle G. Wheeler who took the post of Army Chief of Staff at the beginning of October, also wondered whether Taylor would be their advocate with the President or a White House enforcer in their councils.

The actual crisis brought that ill will close to the surface. On more than one occasion during the tensest days, General Taylor made sure that the Chiefs had the opportunity to deliver their advice to President Kennedy directly. As JCS chairman, he kept the channels of communication open, but his more bellicose colleagues nevertheless doubted that he shared their attitudes and feared that he did not always represent the military's point of view effectively.

The intelligence briefing Taylor heard on his first day in office sharply shifted the Pentagon's view of Cuba. New evidence pointed most probably to the introduction of medium-range Soviet ballistic missiles on the island. The briefing, reflecting similar conclusions reached by CIA experts, was the work of Col. John R. Wright, Jr., the Defense Intelligence Agency's (DIA) analyst assigned to watch the build-up on Cuba. In his careful review of the films from the August and September U-2 flights, Wright found patterns of Soviet equipment and construction pointing to preparations for a missile site. He shared his suspicions with the DIA director, Lt. Gen. Joseph F. Carroll. Carroll took Wright's concerns and a recommendation for urgent U-2 inspection of the San Cristobal area to Taylor's first official meeting with McNamara and the Joint Chiefs.

Reinforcing Colonel Wright's findings, the CIA had also received two reports, originating on 12 and 17 September, that extra-long, tarpaulin-covered, cylindrical objects had been spotted on roads leading from the port of Mariel to the interior of Cuba. Unlike the hundreds of earlier accounts of Soviet missiles on the island—starting even before Soviet military aid began—these two sightings were too detailed to be dismissed as exaggerations. The agents, whose messages were frequently hand-carried, invisible-ink notes that reached the CIA station and debriefing center in Opa Locka, Florida, weeks after they were written, had clearly seen something larger than cruise or surface-to-air missiles.

This kind of information from Cuba could not be discounted. Supplementing Colonel Wright's analysis, the reports pointed to a possible missile site in the Sierra del Rosario mountains near the large town of San Cristobal, fifty miles west-southwest of Havana. Like General Carroll, the CIA wanted the area subjected to U-2 reconnaissance. The 14 October mission brought back the evidence that triggered the Cuban missile crisis.

Half Speed Ahead

The U.S. military, however, did not wait for that confirmation to step up the pace of planning. At the 1 October Pentagon meeting, Robert McNamara and the Joint Chiefs agreed that what they already knew and what they now suspected meant that U.S. military force might soon be needed against Cuba. It was time to accelerate preparations for such an intervention. On 2 October, the Secretary of Defense sent the JCS a memorandum listing the circumstances that could require U.S. military action against Cuba and requesting appropriate contingency plans and heightened readiness to execute them.

McNamara listed six eventualities that were likely to trigger a U.S. military response: Soviet actions in Berlin; Soviet offensive weapons in Cuba; an attack against the Guantánamo naval base; an uprising in Cuba that called for U.S. assistance; Cuban armed subversion in the western hemisphere; and a presidential decision that "the situation in Cuba is inconsistent with continuing U.S. national security."[1] For each possibility, McNamara asked the Chiefs what forces would be needed to carry out which missions and what preparations the different services should be making to mobilize for such assignments.

With an eye on Berlin and on the first reports of U.S. casualties in Vietnam, he also instructed the Chiefs to factor in the consequences of acting against Cuba on U.S. ability to deal with threats elsewhere in the world. Stressing that for all six contingencies "we can assume" that the political objective would be the removal of Soviet systems from Cuba or the removal of Castro from power or both,[2] McNamara acknowledged that the second goal was the more difficult. The Joint Chiefs, he directed, should focus on that objective and on the military capabilities to achieve it.

As the Pentagon leapt into action, others remained unconvinced that there was a problem. As late as 5 October, McGeorge Bundy believed the Soviets would not place offensive weapons on Cuba. In a discussion with McCone that day, he stated that he did not "feel" the Soviets would go that far. According to McCone's account, Bundy "was satisfied that no offensive capability would be installed in Cuba because of its world-wide effects. . . ."[3]

McCone disagreed. He believed that the Soviet construction would end up with MRBMs in Cuba. He now thought this ". . . a probability rather than a mere possibility." He had the civility to note, however, that many in the intelligence community agreed with Bundy.[4]

Indeed, on 8 October, the Board of National Estimates again stated its belief that the Soviets would not move offensive missiles to Cuba. Assessing the implications of a proposed presidential announcement of U.S. overflights to gauge the build-up on Cuba, the CIA's top analysts forecast that although such a declaration would earn disapproval from "free world" public opinion and at the United Nations and "create new strains in Soviet-American relations," it would also impress Soviets and Cubans alike with Washington's "evident willingness to raise still further the level of tension over Cuba and to commit itself to further risks." Neither the announcement nor the actual overflights, the board held, "would cause the USSR to alter its Cuban policy in a direction which increased the provocation offered to the US, e.g., the provision of medium-range missile bases."[5]

Behind the idea of openly claiming a legally suspect right to patrol the skies over Cuba was heavy pressure from the CIA and the Joint Chiefs to get a clear picture of the situation on the ground and of the extent and meaning of the

Soviet build-up. It was early October, and the Chiefs had little more hard data on the strength and disposition of Castro's forces than they had had at the end of August. All they could be certain of was that Soviet and other ships continued to arrive in Cuba in unprecedented numbers.

Formally charged with planning an invasion, the Joint Chiefs needed to see the face of the enemy. The Army and Marines had to have up-to-date information on how well fortified and defended were the projected landing sites U.S. troops would storm, what back-up forces were in place, what other defenses were being constructed. The Air Force and Navy required the latest photography of surface-to-air missile (SAM) sites and of airfields and their defenses so that pilots could map out their attack runs.

The first credible agent reports of medium-range missiles in Cuba only made the military commanders even more anxious. MRBMs in Cuba would add a dangerous new dimension to the situation and raise the stakes exponentially. The stakes were already very high—and the U-2s were still on the ground.

Bad weather—the worst hurricane season in years—was partly responsible. It led to the last-minute cancellation of four scheduled U-2 flights in September and impeded photography on a 17 September mission. Not until eighteen days later did a U-2 bring back usable intelligence—the discovery of four more Soviet anti-aircraft missile (SA-2) bases—and confirm conclusively what had become apparent over the preceding month: "an island wide SA-2 defense was being constructed."[6]

From the Joint Chiefs' viewpoint, however, weather was a secondary problem. In their view, one shared by many CIA officials, the primary difficulty was the obsession in the White House and State Department about the political costs America would supposedly have to pay if a U.S. reconnaissance plane were shot down over Cuba, as Powers' craft had been over the USSR in 1960 and as another plane presumably had been on 8 September in China.

In top-level discussions of the need to gather intelligence during August and September, Dean Rusk kept returning to this possibility. How, he asked, would the Kennedy administration explain its actions to its Latin American allies and before the United Nations? The outcry, he anticipated, would be long and loud. Once the SAM defenses were discovered, Rusk saw the risks of losing a U-2 heightened; even more caution was required. He won agreement to conduct only peripheral reconnaissance flights of Cuba, no closer than twenty-five miles—SAM range—to its coasts.[7] Similar caution led to the transfer of the U-2s from the CIA to the Air Force's Strategic Air Command (SAC) on 12 October. There would be less embarrassment if a downed U-2 were found to have a military pilot.[8]

Those peripheral flights produced little or no useful intelligence. Increasingly anxious, the CIA and Joint Chiefs sought alternatives. One was to use high-speed drone aircraft. Bundy, Rusk and McNamara, however, were opposed. Low-level military reconnaissance was too risky, but flights twenty-five miles offshore by RB-47s, B-52s, Navy F8Us and F3Ds were unproductive. A still camera with a 100-inch focal length was mounted in a large Constellation aircraft, but vibration blurred the photographs beyond utility. Next, a 240-inch focal length camera was tried, but the results, although better, were of little value.[9] As reports of missile sightings continued to arrive, the cameras that could confirm or deny such observations remained shuttered.

If the intelligence community was of two minds about the presence or prospect of missiles on Cuba, Kenneth Keating was not. On the Senate floor on 9 October he made an impassioned plea for President Kennedy to inform the American public fully about developments in Cuba and to take action against the growing military threat there. He proposed that the United States be prepared to act with or without the support of the Organization of American States and raised the prospect of blockading Cuba if all else failed.[10]

The next day Keating spoke to the Senate again. He declared that overnight he had confirmed that six intermediate-range missile bases were under construction in Cuba and would be operational in six months. Ratcheting up his criticism of the Kennedy team, he fumed that the "American people are being kept in the dark . . . . Let us have all the facts," the New York Republican demanded, "and have them now."[11]

The Administration again denied the Senator's charges, but the public dispute had its effects. At the White House it made the President even more sensitive to leaks. The day after Keating made his second speech, McCone brought Kennedy photographs of crates unloaded in Cuba in early October and thought to hold Ilyushin-28 medium bombers. The President's first reaction was to ask that the information "be withheld at least until after the election . . . [if it] got into the press," in McCone's words, "a new and more violent Cuban issue would be injected into the campaign" that "would seriously affect his independence of action."[12]

In fact, the CIA director pointed out, the photos had already been disseminated to the intelligence community and several military commands. Resisting Kennedy's request that all such information be "restricted,"[13] McCone did agree to restrict the future circulation of reports about Il-28s in Cuba to top presidential advisors. The limitation mirrored the one Kennedy had imposed earlier on dissemination of U-2 intelligence about the island.

MONGOOSE Loses Steam

For those of us at lower levels, it was the Keating bombshell, rather than any intelligence we saw, that had already made us sniff a crisis in the making. Because we were not intimately involved in the planning that McNamara had set in motion, those of us who belonged to General Taylor's personal staff did not know what we did not know. We did know that there was a puzzle and that we were missing some pieces of it.

Having asked Cmdr. Worth Bagley (later Vice Chief of Naval Operations) and me to move with him from the White House, Taylor put us and Army Col. Bernard W. Rogers (later Army Chief of Staff and Supreme Allied Commander Europe) to work with the chairman's in-place staff group—two colonels and a Navy captain—who had served his predecessor, Gen. Lyman Lemnitzer. Col. Julian J. Ewell (later Lieutenant General, U.S. Army) remained Taylor's executive officer.

Representing all three services, the enlarged chairman's staff group divided up a range of geographical responsibilities—Europe, Asia, Latin America and other trouble spots—and was assigned as necessary to handle operational matters such as budget issues, force dispositions and the like. Col. Laurence J. Legere, Taylor's principal European advisor with whom I worked closely at the White House, joined Bundy's National Security Council staff and became an on-going liaison with General Taylor.

During the first days in his new post, Taylor himself was still feeling his way. As he oversaw the movement of U.S. forces toward a war footing, he worked mostly within the existing JCS command structure, leaving his personal staff more on the sidelines. Meanwhile, our former White House colleagues and our new officemates on the second-floor, E-Ring hallway that was the domain of the Chairman of the Joint Chiefs kept their knowledge of Cuban affairs to themselves.

From my desk just inside the Pentagon entrance nearest the Potomac River, I could sense from the tempo of activity in the sealed-off Joint Staff area that something very unusual and possibly dangerous was stirring. With more advanced Soviet military equipment arriving in Cuba daily and with the media and Congress giving it more attention, I could see Castro becoming an even larger headache than before. But as I got more curious by the day, I learned nothing that pointed definitively to the crisis ahead.

Operation MONGOOSE planners were almost equally at sea. Entering the month that General Lansdale had initially—optimistically—scheduled for the final stages of Castro's overthrow, the field operatives and the senior policymakers were all still struggling, sometimes with one another. At a 4 October meeting of the top-level oversight group, General Taylor heard McCone and Robert Kennedy quarrel over the reasons for Operation MONGOOSE's "lack of forward motion."[14]

The heated exchange began after the Attorney General, according to McCone's account, noted his brother's dissatisfaction "with lack of action in the sabotage field [and] went on to stress that nothing was moving forward."

General Lansdale and McCone answered that no sabotage had yet been attempted because none was authorized in phase I. McCone added his view that the "lack of forward motion [was] due principally to 'hesitancy' in government circles to engage in any activities" too easily traced to the United States.[15]

The imputation of indecisiveness—similar to the charges that Republican campaigners were making in public—obviously stung the younger Kennedy. The Special Group, he countered, had not "withheld approval on any specified actions . . . but, to the contrary, had urged and insisted" that Lansdale's operatives move. Without actually resolving the issue of who was to blame or for what in the past, the two men moved on and, with their colleagues, agreed that "more dynamic action was indicated" for the future. But they also agreed that the guidance for action approved as recently as 6 September was "outmoded." Lansdale was instructed to set existing sabotage plans in motion and conceive new ones, including possible operations to mine Cuba's harbors and capture and interrogate some of Castro's troops.[16]

What the meeting really showed was how little progress had been made in satisfying the President's directive of 23 August to come up with a "plan b-plus." McCone acknowledged as much in a talk the next day with Bundy. Both the Defense Department and the CIA, its director reported, felt that the "activist policy" that had launched MONGOOSE was gone, a casualty in part of the State Department's "extreme caution." McCone worried particularly that "decisions to restrict U-2 flights" over Cuba were keeping Washington from seeing what McCone suspected was under way: the build-up of "an established offensive capability, including MRBMs," a development—as noted earlier—that he thought "a probability more than a mere possibility."[17]

Unconvinced of that likelihood, Bundy did agree that U.S. policy "was not clear" and, consequently, U.S. efforts "were not productive." After reviewing Walt W. Rostow's "Track Two" proposal and Lansdale's more activist approach—without coming down firmly for or against either one—Bundy spelled out the alternatives as he saw them. Either "we would have to go in militarily (which seemed to him intolerable)," McCone recorded, or "we would have to learn to live with Castro, and his Cuba and adjust our policies accordingly."[18]

Early in October, therefore, Operation MONGOOSE planning stood essentially where it had at the end of July. There had been much conversation, some directives for additional plans and, apparently, some irritation in the White House that more had not been accomplished. The major U.S. effort launched in February to get rid of Castro by October had led, as Bundy remarked, to little more than frustration.

When the full crisis burst on official Washington just eleven days after McCone's talk with Bundy, the Attorney General turned to MONGOOSE once more, still displeased with its progress but still hoping to make it an effective policy instrument. Summoning General Lansdale and State, CIA, JCS and other aides to his office at 2:30 on the afternoon of 16 October, Robert Kennedy— fresh from the first meeting of the executive committee of the National Security Council (ExComm) missile-crisis managers—voiced the President's "general dissatisfaction" with a year's worth of "discouraging" results in fomenting unrest and executing sabotage on Cuba. His remedy, he said, would be to give MONGOOSE more of his "personal attention" and meet with its supervisors daily at 9:30 A.M. from then on.[19]

Even given such stimulus, MONGOOSE remained an operation without a mandate. As the CIA representative at the meeting, Deputy Director for Plans Richard Helms observed that his agency was "prepared to get on with the new action program" and "would execute it aggressively." But its objective, he said, "would have to be determined at some point since the Cubans . . . were seeking a reason for risking their lives in these operations . . . ." Basically, unless they were convinced "the United States, perhaps in conjunction with other Latin countries, would bail them out militarily," they would not consider any plan of action "sensible."[20] The Attorney General then asked for new ideas, noting "in passing" and without amplification "the change in atmosphere in the United States Government during the last 24 hours." Perhaps thinking of possible U.S. military action, he also asked what percentage of Cubans "would fight for the regime" if the island were invaded.[21]

Ten days later, when the prospect of invasion seemed very real, Operation MONGOOSE was all but a dead letter. General Lansdale was complaining that the CIA and the Defense Department had snatched his authority away, leaving him "not in channel of either operations or information." His immediate concern was a plan for a submarine to put fifty Cubans—none of them his recruits— on the island to gather pre-invasion military intelligence. Although that reconnaissance was put on hold and eventually scrubbed, the MONGOOSE overseers decided on 26 October to give the State Department responsibility secretly to create a political office to plan for a post-Castro Cuban government.[22]

Late October was the effective end of the road for the Administration's long-running covert effort to overthrow Fidel Castro. The firm commitment to assist dissident Cubans with U.S. troops had never materialized. Without such support, a MONGOOSE-sponsored uprising most probably would have been a replay of the Bay of Pigs. And with the discovery of Soviet ballistic missiles on Cuba, the U.S. military was gearing up to do the job on its own—without manufacturing an insurrection on Cuba as the excuse for action.

Enter OPLANs 312 and 314

The U.S. military plans for Cuba for which Secretary McNamara on 1 October asked increased readiness to execute were already well advanced. The Joint

Chiefs had given them top priority since Operation MONGOOSE had begun in February and had carefully reviewed the outlines for action developed by field commanders. But those plans, seemingly so finely honed, had to be substantially revised after the influx of Soviet arms in August and September.

That work fell first to the U.S. Atlantic Command (CINCLANT) and its chief, Admiral Robert L. Dennison, headquartered in Norfolk, Virginia. Charged with conducting any military operations against Cuba, Dennison had forces from all the military services at his disposal and flexible plans envisioning different levels of combat and size of forces, depending on the degree of resistance encountered on Cuba.

Until early October, CINCLANT's Contingency Operation Plan 314, or OPLAN 314, called for simultaneous airborne and amphibious assaults in the Havana area by Army, Marine, Navy and Air Force units. As it had since February, CINCLANT intended to field two Army airborne divisions and two Marine division/wing teams while keeping a third Army division in ready reserve. Tailored armor and artillery detachments, Navy ships and aircraft and Air Force tactical air units would support an invasion force of several hundred thousand.

The general concept had been tested, at least in part, during the spring of 1962, in two amphibious Marine landings on the island of Vieques, east of Puerto Rico, and related Navy operations at sea, as well as in exercises along the southeastern coast of the United States. Early in October, a naval task force carried out a command-post, joint Navy and Marine exercise that simulated troop movements of the size scheduled to involve some 20,000 naval personnel and 4,000 Marines during the two weeks beginning on 15 October.

Like the spring maneuvers, the October rehearsal was to mount a shore assault and associated naval operations in the area of Vieques. The opponent was openly identified as "Ortsac"—Castro spelled backward—a loud signal to Soviets and Cubans alike that U.S. forces were practicing for a landing in Cuba.[23]

Throughout the summer, the U.S. Army also improved its posture. In early August it conducted a major two-week exercise with the Air Force. This Operation Quick Strike involved 65,000 troops and 10,000 vehicles, including 8,000 troops and 6,000 tons of cargo airlifted from Fort Carson, Colorado, to the Carolinas. The most significant change affected the Air Force. Given the small size and limited effectiveness of Cuba's air force and air defense, early contingency planning had assigned the U.S. Air Force only a limited role, supporting the invasion force with tactical air units "as required." The initial OPLAN provided only for separate air strikes at the time of a landing, as had been approved (and then curtailed) in connection with the 1961 Bay of Pigs assault. Admiral Dennison and the Joint Chiefs evidently thought that Cuban defenses could be overwhelmed without massive, early use of air power.

In late July and throughout August, however, as new intelligence uncovered the defensive build-up on the island, and especially after SAMs were discovered by the 29 August U-2 flight, the Air Force took a fresh look at the part it would play. On 7 September, the commander of the Air Force's Tactical Air Command (TAC), Gen. Walter C. Sweeney, directed a working group to prepare a "well-planned, thoroughly coordinated tactical air offensive to be launched against Cuba *well in advance* of an airborne assault and amphibious landing."[24] (Emphasis added.)

By 27 September, the TAC's air strike plan had been approved by Gen. Curtis LeMay, U.S. Air Force Chief of Staff, and by the commander of the U.S. Strike Command, the "unified" or joint service U.S. military commander who had day-to-day operational control of TAC forces. LeMay directed Sweeney to present the plan to Dennison. Doing so on 28 September, Sweeney also offered to become a subordinate air commander to CINCLANT for Cuban operations. Dennison accepted, and within forty-eight hours the Air Force proposal was designated as CINCLANT Contingency Operation Plan 312 (OPLAN 312).

The OPLAN contained many options, from one air strike against a single target such as a SAM installation to large-scale attacks against any number of targets. By 10 October TAC fighter units were training at bases in Florida. At those locations, moreover, they began stockpiling the bombs, ammunition and other supplies needed to conduct combat operations. Even before the MRBMs were detected, TAC was moving to a war footing.

As the tempo quickened but before the conclusive evidence from the 14 October U-2 mission could be analyzed and disseminated, the Joint Chiefs met to assess their preparations for invasion and to consider possible additional steps. On the afternoon of 15 October, they decided on a number of actions. Concerned about the Il-28 bombers and MiG fighters in Cuba, they asked the air defense commander, the commander-in-chief of continental air defense (CINCONAD), to estimate the U.S. casualties from a Cuban air strike and to recommend further steps to improve the air defense posture in the southeastern portion of the nation.

The Joint Chiefs also recommended calling up the 150,000 reserves that Congress had authorized the President to mobilize a few weeks earlier. Additionally, they requested Admiral Dennison to make certain revisions to his operations plans in line with the improved state of readiness of U.S. forces that McNamara's early October orders had generated. And they determined to impose absolute secrecy between the time of any decision to move against Cuba and the implementation of the air strike and invasion plans.[25]

With these decisions made, the Chiefs were ready for the military action that seemed increasingly likely on 15 October and all but certain when they met the next afternoon. In the interim, the photo interpreters at the National

Photographic Intelligence Center (NPIC) in Washington had analyzed the U-2 films and realized that they had a major discovery on their hands.

The document that officially announced the NPIC findings opened with a straightforward sentence of the utmost importance: "Photography of 14 October 1962 has disclosed two areas in the Sierra del Rosario mountains . . . which appear to contain Soviet MRBMs in the early stages of deployment."[26] With that declaration, the 1962 Cuban missile crisis moved into full swing.

Preparing to Strike

The discovery that Soviet missiles were in Cuba ended all hesitation about putting the U-2s to work, and seventeen overflights were conducted in the next five days. The bad weather lifted, and more than 98 percent of the island was photographed cloud free, giving U.S. military commanders sorely needed, valid information on which to do their detailed planning for air attacks and invasion. But the increased coverage must also have alerted Soviet and Cuban personnel to the heightened U.S. interest in their activities and caused them to accelerate efforts to ready their missiles for action.

That probability was among the factors that drove the first debates in the National Security Council's ExComm about how to respond to the provocation. The initial consensus—reached after the President's advisors recovered from what Robert Kennedy called "the dominant feeling . . . of shocked incredulity"—was that "an air strike against the missile sites" without prior notice to the Soviets or Cubans "could be the only course."[27] Listening to the discussion of a surprise attack that began in the Cabinet Room of the White House at 11:30 on the morning of 16 October, and feeling, "We had been deceived by Khrushchev, but we had also fooled ourselves," the Attorney General slipped his brother a note. "I now know," he wrote, "how Tojo felt when he was planning Pearl Harbor."[28]

Few of the other ExComm members initially shared his concern. For them, the United States would not be the aggressor; it was the victim of a surprise maneuver, one which the Soviets had publicly and privately forsworn and against which they had been explicitly warned in September. Even Dean Rusk agreed that "we have to set in motion a chain of events that will eliminate this base. I don't think we can sit still."[29]

Rusk did lean against "a sudden, unannounced strike."[30] So did Bundy, but McNamara, Taylor, Treasury Secretary C. Douglas Dillon and the President himself all tended initially to accept the inevitability of an air attack against the MRBMs. "We're certainly going to do number one—we're going to take out the, uh, missiles," John Kennedy said, "[S]o it seems to me that we don't have to wait very long. We ought to be making *those* preparations."[31] (Emphasis in original.)

In this first ExComm session, the open question seemed less whether to strike Cuba than when and with how much force. Taylor agreed with Rusk that any air strike should cover the missile sites, airfields, and nuclear sites. As for timing, such an attack would require careful study, which the Joint Chiefs had not yet had time to make, of the latest U-2 photography and also the laying out of a coordinated attack plan. U.S. military forces were not yet ready to attack, he said, but they soon would be. He and the Chiefs planned to meet later that day to discuss the matter and give McNamara and the President their best judgment.[32]

McNamara added that although the Joint Chiefs preferred several days for preparation, the United States could launch an air attack "literally within a matter of hours." The air strike "could continue for a matter of days following the initial day, if necessary. . . . In any event we would be prepared . . . for an invasion both by air and by sea."[33] Taylor thought the decision to invade would be "the hardest question militarily in the whole business,"[34] but as he and the Secretary of Defense returned to the Pentagon, they expected that some form of military action would be required and were anxious to ready the Chiefs for such eventual orders.

When the Joint Chiefs met later that afternoon, they spent most of the time answering twelve questions McNamara posed. The basic issue was the same one that had been the center of discussion at the White House earlier that day: What kind and level of U.S. military response was most appropriate? Should it be a limited strike against MRBMs only, as many of the President's closest advisors favored? How about hitting the MiG aircraft as well as the MRBMs? Or striking MRBMs, all combat aircraft, nuclear storage sites and PT boats? What did the Chiefs think of a naval blockade to accompany a large-scale attack?

Other questions dealt with the time required to execute CINCLANT's air attack and invasion plans, and whether it was preferable to attack the missiles piecemeal, as soon as they were identified, or wait until most or all of them were exposed. What about possible Soviet reaction, and what general war preparatory actions would the Chiefs recommend? Should reserves be mobilized?

In their answers, the Chiefs strongly and repeatedly recommended against an initial piecemeal attack against MRBMs only, or against only a portion of the military threat. They considered that approach militarily unsound and instead advocated an initial powerful air strike against all militarily significant targets that could affect the United States or its military forces.

Included in their target list were not only MRBMs, all combat aircraft and nuclear storage sites but also tanks and PT boats. Such an attack could be conducted shortly after the pilots received their target folders. The Air Force and

Navy needed that intelligence in their hands to build those folders as soon as possible.

Concluding that the security of the United States was in unquestionable jeopardy, the Joint Chiefs held that the MRBMs should be attacked even after they became fully operational, and that after the initial large-scale air attack, any other MRBM sites should be hit as soon as they were identified. They also endorsed a naval blockade accompanying the air strikes to seal Castro off from outside support. As for invasion, it would be sixteen to eighteen days before U.S. Army and Marine forces would be in position and ready, but they were already moving forward. To a man, with no second thoughts, the Joint Chiefs rejected the prospect of living with the threat of a missile attack from the Caribbean.

Not ready to estimate what the Soviet reaction would be to any U.S. attack on Cuba, they recommended certain precautionary, preparatory actions for general war. Among them were the dispersal of strategic nuclear offensive and defensive weapons systems and action to raise the level of U.S. military readiness worldwide once the President announced that the United States had discovered the missiles. Finally, along with a recommendation to consider declaring a national emergency, they urged that the 150,000 reservists assigned for mobilization be called up.[35]

On all the questions McNamara raised, the Joint Chiefs' firm stance signalled their conviction: the time and the opportunity to get rid of Castro had arrived. The moment needed only to be seized. They were ready to do so.

Divided Councils

The Joint Chiefs of Staff were consistent and united in recommending the use of overwhelming military power against the Soviet and Cuban military on the island. From the onset of the crisis to its climax, the Chiefs were firm advocates of using force. Diligently they prepared for the air strike and possible invasion that they correctly understood to be the President's initial preference as well. Indeed, as late as Sunday morning 21 October, nine of the sixteen ExComm members who met with John Kennedy favored such a course.[1] When the strike and invasion plan was rejected in favor of the less-provocative naval blockade, itself soft-pedaled as a quarantine, the Chiefs accepted the decision dutifully, but disappointedly.

They continued in the following days to mobilize a vast attack force; by the weekend of 27–28 October, the Joint Chiefs were ready to launch a massive air and sea assault. By that Sunday, U.S. intelligence indicated that all medium-range SS-4 missiles were operational, ready to launch within six to eight hours. Adding to the sense of urgency, a Soviet missile brought down a U-2 plane over eastern Cuba that Saturday, killing the pilot, Maj. Rudolf Anderson, Jr., one of the two flyers who had first photographed the MRBM sites on 14 October.

The Joint Chiefs thought that the moment had come. They asked that the decision be made to begin air attacks early in the next week. Again they were overruled. Before opening fire, the President wanted to learn Khrushchev's reply to the U.S. message accepting the Soviet leader's apparent offer to withdraw the missiles in exchange for a U.S. pledge not to invade Cuba.

Kennedy's decision reflected, among other things, a difference between his objectives and those of the Joint Chiefs. They had pursued three clear purposes from the start: remove the missiles, oust Castro and win back the President's respect, so much diminished since the Bay of Pigs. In the end, two of their goals eluded them. In their view, the United States lost an opportunity to reassert its power in the Caribbean. Primed to deliver a knockout blow, the leaders of the U.S. armed forces were obliged to pull their punch. They were good soldiers and they followed orders. But the rejection stung, and resentment lingered.

Some of it was directed at Maxwell Taylor. At least a few of his new Pentagon colleagues saw him more as a White House loyalist than as their champion. That suspicion missed the reality: Taylor was an independent thinker who took his responsibilities to both the President and the armed forces with equal seriousness. His first duty, however, was to his own conscience. When Taylor put the Joint Chiefs' case to the ExComm, he would make clear where his views and theirs parted company. Although such differences emerged formally only once or twice, some senior military professionals feared that Taylor was giving their arguments less than full support across the board.

Still learning my duties in that third week of October and of my new assignment, I sensed the friction between the chairman and the Chiefs dimly if at all. I knew that adding members of Taylor's White House staff to his Pentagon retinue, doubling its size, had caused some resentment. As an added irritant, my two colleagues and I had taken over an office on the outside corridor, the E-ring, close to the chairman's. Until our arrival, the room had belonged to an elite group of Marines, supporting their commandant when he attended JCS meetings. The Marines' office had been pushed deeper into the building, farther from the center of things, and they were not happy.

Even in my prime location, however, I did not detect as much as a hint of change in the status of U.S.–Soviet relations until the morning of 19 October. As I reviewed military and diplomatic cable traffic, I came across a Department of State message to our Moscow embassy. Although it made no mention of missiles in Cuba, the report of the 18 October meeting between President Kennedy and Soviet Foreign Minister Andrei Gromyko nonetheless had an unusual and ominous ring to it. Knowing about the Soviet build-up of equipment in Cuba only in general terms and knowing nothing of Operation MONGOOSE, I still sensed from the cable the existence of some new developments, perhaps significant ones, that I did not understand.

As I normally did when I saw something out of the ordinary, I called the message to General Taylor's attention, both to inform him and to see if I should take any follow-up action. He told me there was nothing I need do, and our discussion ended. The next morning, I took him a follow-on message from either State or the Moscow embassy—I do not recall which—and, again, he asked for no further exploration of the matter.

Only on Monday, 22 October, did I learn of the crisis brewing over Cuba. The chairman called me into his office, briefed me on the situation in outline and told me that he needed my help. I was taken aback by his news. Like many others, I interpreted Khrushchev's actions primarily as an attempt to improve Soviet strategic nuclear capabilities, and I knew that any confrontation on that front carried the highest risks of miscalculation and ensuing, unbelievable disaster. My first reaction was to wonder about Khrushchev's state of mind. If he were losing self-control, the potential for miscalculation was greatly magnified. I anticipated a period of the highest tension and danger.

My assignment was to keep General Taylor informed of the latest intelligence on Soviet and Cuban activities, of the status of U.S. readiness for military action and of developments elsewhere in the Pentagon and in national security policy-making circles. The third of those tasks put me in very close contact with Paul H. Nitze's personal assistant, Elmo Zumwalt, then a Navy captain, later an admiral and Chief of Naval Operations. Nitze was then Assistant Secretary of Defense for International Security Affairs and, like Taylor, a member of the ExComm.

I was by no means Taylor's only source of information. The primary responsibility for keeping him and the Joint Chiefs abreast of developments fell on the Joint Staff and its supporting elements of some two thousand uniformed personnel, the Defense Intelligence Agency and other elements of the government. Serving basically as an outside observer for Taylor, I was not admitted to the Chiefs' closed-door deliberations around a large table in the "tank," the security-tight conference room down the hall from the chairman's office.

There, the service Chiefs sat in assigned positions, each one usually accompanied by a three-star deputy. Working through a previously set agenda, they discussed issues in turn, and their decisions were recorded by an officer from the JCS Secretariat. Normally during the crisis, I was not briefed on their decisions and recommendations. Instead, my duties were to give the chairman information that could assist him in making independent judgments and to help him prepare for the frequent and lengthy ExComm meetings.

Information about field unit readiness came through a myriad of separate and often uncoordinated channels. Intelligence on Soviet and Cuban moves also arrived from many sources. And the thinking within the government was constantly changing. Keeping ahead of so many variables was literally impossible. Just keeping track often meant rushing the latest report or proposal across the Potomac to be passed to Taylor in an ExComm meeting.

From 22 October to the end of the month, I spent most of my time in the Pentagon. Days ran into nights, ran into days, interrupted only by snatches of sleep on a cot in my office. Occasionally, I had time to drive the few miles through Northern Virginia to my Falls Church home to change clothes, shower and check in on my wife and two very young sons. Usually, with too much to do and too little time in which to do it, I felt that I was falling behind the power curve, missing some element of insight, information or analysis that might help point a way out of the heightening crisis.

Differing Priorities

One key judgment involved gauging the likely Soviet reaction to a U.S. attack on Cuba. Of the twelve questions Secretary McNamara put to the JCS on 16 October, the issue of Moscow's probable rejoinder was the only one to which the Chiefs did not formulate a reply the same day. After meeting for most of 17 October, they reached two conclusions that guided their deliberations over the next weeks: first, the Soviets would not go to general war over Cuba; second, fresh Soviet pressure was most likely in Berlin, but moves against the island of Quemoy off China's coast, or against Iran, Turkey or Korea were also possible.

   The Joint Chiefs put those estimates in a paper drafted for them by their group of senior strategic thinkers, the Joint Strategic Survey Committee (JSSC), for submission to the ExComm later that day. The JSSC forecast of "sharp and strong encroaching [Soviet] actions at Berlin, short of direct seizure"[2] if the United States attacked Cuba reflected a view that was widely held in civilian circles as well. The related estimate that Moscow was not likely to move to general war to avenge losses in the Caribbean—and the willingness to formulate decisions and actions based on that judgment—was more controversial. It touched off the first direct clash between the Chiefs and President Kennedy.

   Called to the White House on 18 October to attend part of an ExComm meeting, the Chiefs, Robert Kennedy recalled, were "unanimous in calling for immediate military action" and "forcefully" opposed to a naval blockade they doubted would be "effective." Gen. Curtis LeMay was the most vigorous in making the case for attack. When he assured the President that "there would be no reaction" from Moscow to a U.S. air strike and invasion, the President was skeptical. He thought the Russians *would* react, somewhere, somehow.

> They can't, after all their statements, permit us to take out their missiles, kill a lot of Russians, and then do nothing. If they don't take action in Cuba, they certainly will in Berlin.[3]

After the Joint Chiefs left the meeting, according to Deputy Secretary of Defense Roswell Gilpatric, the President was "just choleric" about LeMay's comments. Kennedy told his aide, Kenneth O'Donnell, "These brass hats have one great advantage in their favor. If we . . . do what they want us to do, none of us will be alive later to tell them that they were wrong."[4]

Behind the President's scorn lay more than recollections of the Bay of Pigs. In October 1962, the Chiefs, as noted, were actually pursuing two central goals, while the President was committed to only one. The President and the military men wanted, first of all, to remove the missiles. But the Chiefs also wanted to remove Castro.

Reflecting on the crisis twenty-five years later, McGeorge Bundy identified this crucial divergence of priorities. He pointed out that some Pentagon and CIA officials were convinced that the overthrow of Castro was both a very important objective in its own right and one that could be readily justified and achieved now that Soviet missiles were in Cuba. The President, according to Bundy, agreed that ousting Castro was desirable, but he and his closest advisors did not think the time for it had arrived. At this stage of the game, with the missiles their primary concern, they thought of Castro as

> a hostile pawn, to be captured, threatened, or spared as the central purpose might dictate. It was not Castro's existence that had created the crisis; it was Khrushchev's missiles.[5]

The Joint Chiefs can be forgiven for pursuing the broader objective. Operation MONGOOSE, though seen to be stalled by high-level indecision, seemed to reflect a Kennedy Administration resolve to rid itself and Cuba of Fidel Castro. As part of this commitment, U.S. military services had begun conducting extensive exercises in spring 1962, and had developed detailed contingency planning for the removal of Castro. While it was true that the exercises were designed primarily to distract Castro from exporting revolution by making him worry for his own safety, the activity also improved U.S. ability to act against Castro should the opportunity arise. To the Joint Chiefs, the Soviet missiles in Cuba provided that opportunity.

Pondering how the Kennedy Administration might have misread Kremlin concerns about Castro, Bundy wrote, "We knew that we were not about to invade Cuba." But, he added, "Khrushchev certainly knew of our program of covert action against Cuba, and he could hardly be expected to understand that to us this program was not a prelude to stronger action but a substitute for it."[6]

In taking the view that the time really had come to oust Castro, the Joint Chiefs may have fallen into wishful thinking, a desire to see their priorities and those of the White House in harmony. But given the hard evidence available to them, the fault was excusable. Unfortunately, the civilian-military misunderstandings that predated the missile crisis persisted through its escalation and resolution. Not only located on the opposite side of the Potomac River, the President's military advisors were also on a different course.

The record of the Joint Chiefs' daily deliberations during the missile crisis, now largely declassified, is full of evidence of this widening breach. High among the Chiefs' concerns was an effort to preclude any repeat of the criticism that, as in spring 1961, they had been less than clear in the advice they gave. Those Bay of Pigs scars still ached. The Chiefs did not want a second Cuban episode to leave a second set of similar wounds.

They began their campaign on 17 October by sending McNamara written confirmation of the views they had given him the day before. The statement opposed an air strike against the missiles alone. Rather, it advocated an air attack against all missile sites, all combat aircraft, combat ships, tanks and other appropriate military targets in Cuba, including the nuclear storage sites that the Joint Chiefs believed would soon be built. The comprehensive air strike, the JCS said, should be mounted in tandem with a complete blockade. Eliminating Castro, the Chiefs also advised, would require an invasion, preferably under their OPLAN 314.[7]

Over the next weeks, their determination to give sound, understandable advice led them to focus on four aspects of the crisis: acquisition and analysis of intelligence on both the Cuban build-up and other Soviet activities worldwide; the readiness of U.S. forces; nuclear weapons aspects of the crisis; and the strength and clarity of their recommendations to the President. The last of these concerns may have been the most persistent. It reflected the Chiefs' natural desire to give the necessary strategic direction to the field commanders in the most professional military way. The Joint Chiefs thought of those military operations as essential. Now was the time to get rid of Castro. The military could do that job. All that was needed was presidential approval.

Holding Fire

That go-ahead never came. What had seemed a near-consensus in the ExComm on 16 October in favor of military action began to erode the next day. Early that morning, while the other Joint Chiefs were still meeting, General Taylor joined McCone, McNamara, Bundy, Robert Kennedy, Undersecretary of State George W. Ball and Assistant Secretary of State Edwin Martin in Ball's conference room.

There, the JCS chairman at first seemed to support McNamara's position that the missiles in Cuba "had no great military significance" in light of the ability of each superpower to inflict nuclear devastation on the other, even without added weapons on Cuba. Later, however, Taylor expressed greater concern about the altered threat. McCone agreed with him, but the discussion moved to other issues, leaving the question of how to assess any change in the strategic nuclear balance unresolved.[8] More significantly, during the three ExComm sessions on 17 October, sentiment began to grow in favor of blockading Cuba to prohibit the introduction of any further offensive weapons. McNamara emerged as the "strongest advocate" of such a course.[9]

At the start of the day, McCone had found the President "inclined to act promptly if at all, without warning, targetting on MRBMs and possibly air-fields."[10] Meeting without him, the President's advisors debated a range of alternatives. With varying degrees of conviction, former Secretary of State Dean Acheson, McCone, General Taylor and Secretary Rusk argued for military action, commencing with air strikes against the medium-range missiles and Soviet bombers.

Charles E. Bohlen and Llewellyn E. Thompson, both former ambassadors to the Soviet Union, took an opposing view. They suggested making a diplomatic approach to Khrushchev and Castro before any military moves. As the conversation continued, Thompson reconsidered and joined Edwin Martin, McNamara, Robert Kennedy and, for a time, General Taylor in favor of a blockade as a first step in a campaign of pressure.[11] Summarizing the fragile consensus, McCone advised other intelligence community officials that "a limited blockade . . . of additional arms" was "probable." But, he noted, the decision "is by no means unanimous. The opinions range from doing nothing on the one hand, to immediate military action on the other."[12]

With different participants and shifting positions, the contentious high-level discussion continued into the weekend, sometimes with the President's participation, sometimes in his absence. Historians and memoirists have tended to scant the views and activities of the one set of participants who took a firm position at the outset and held it to the end: the Joint Chiefs. They wanted to stage massive air strikes and follow them with an invasion. When the President opted to start with a naval blockade instead, they continued to urge—and to prepare for—decisive military action.

But they were also realists. Briefed by their chairman on the trend of civilian thinking during the 17 October discussions, the Chiefs requested Taylor the next day to inform the ExComm that if an all-out air strike had been vetoed, the minimum raid ought to target the Il-28 medium bombers as well as the missiles. All offensive weapons that could reach the United States should be attacked.

Later that morning, with intelligence in hand that revealed a continuing build-up of missiles in Cuba, the military leaders had their first opportunity to present their recommendations to the President himself during an ExComm meeting. Among the variants under consideration, they preferred action without diplomatic preliminaries, a comprehensive air strike, evacuation of dependents from Guantánamo and its defense, readiness for invasion and a blockade of Cuba.[13]

The sharp LeMay-Kennedy exchange at that session indicated that the President's and the Joint Chiefs' thinking was far apart. But after returning to their Pentagon offices, the Chiefs continued working to determine when they would have sufficient, up-to-date intelligence and detailed operational plans in hand to launch military action against Cuba. By day's end, the JCS had decided that the earliest feasible date for a large-scale air attack was 21 October; the preferred date was 23 October. The earliest feasible date for an invasion was 28 October, but 30 October would be better.[14]

During the evening of 18 October, the Joint Chiefs received new intelligence that reinforced their conviction that the crisis required a military solution. CIA experts confirmed that sixteen Soviet-manned, medium-range, ballistic missiles were deployed in western Cuba and—heightening anxiety in Washington— were near enough to operational status that half of them could be fired within eighteen hours of a command from Moscow and the rest five hours later. The same report noted that two other sites were being prepared for intermediate-range missiles that the analysts did not expect to be operational until December.[15] Although no nuclear warheads had been seen, the evaluation continued, the United States had to assume their availability, with "yields in the low megaton range."[16] In the CIA view, the Soviet Union intended to make Cuba "a prime strategic base," not a token symbol of strength.[17]

The next day, the intelligence community issued a special estimate of Soviet reactions to various U.S. moves against Cuba. It offered more backing for the Joint Chiefs' case for early military action. The analysts concluded that the Soviets wanted "to demonstrate that the world balance of forces has shifted so far in their favor that the US can no longer prevent the advance of Soviet offensive power even into its own hemisphere."[18]

Forecasting a continued flow "of strategic weapons" to Cuba if the United States acquiesced in the first part of the build-up, the CIA paper also predicted that notifying Khrushchev of U.S. knowledge about the MRBMs would not "halt the deployment" but would produce threats to Berlin and demands for negotiations on all foreign bases.[19] U.S. military action, on the other hand, would "most likely" provoke "broad retaliation" by Moscow against Berlin, but not— except through Kremlin miscalculation—either general war or "military measures, which in [Soviet] calculation, would run the gravest risks of general war."[20]

With that CIA judgment as reinforcement, the Joint Chiefs met with President Kennedy again on 19 October to press their case for what they had agreed was the "only satisfactory solution" to the Cuban problem: an air attack accompanied by a complete blockade and followed by invasion. To preserve surprise but retain the support of U.S. allies in the North Atlantic Treaty Organization, the Chiefs also recommended notifying British Prime Minister Harold MacMillan and possibly his West German counterpart, Konrad Adenauer, some two hours before any direct military action.[21]

On the use of ground forces, the Chiefs and their chairman held slightly different views. Taylor favored an air strike, but did not yet want to make a final decision to invade. He preferred to be ready for such action if the air attacks failed to bring the overthrow of Castro from within.[22]

This internal disagreement seemed a minor one, but it was not. Once again, the Joint Chiefs were becoming concerned that their chairman was not advocating their positions strongly enough before the ExComm; here was proof that his approach and theirs were not identical. No wonder their views found little support with the President. Their doubts and suspicions would build up over the next few days.

Decision and Dissatisfaction

The day after their second meeting with the President, the Chiefs weighed in again, sending Taylor to a 20 October ExComm session with a paper advocating a large-scale air attack on 23 October instead of either a strike limited to offensive weapons two days earlier or a blockade. Taylor returned to the Pentagon to inform the Joint Chiefs that their wishes had not prevailed. The ExComm planned to recommend a blockade of offensive weapons to be instituted twenty-four hours after a presidential speech on 21 or 22 October. President Kennedy actually decided on Sunday the 21st to impose a blockade, but to style it a quarantine, and to announce his action on Monday evening.

At three o'clock that Monday afternoon, Kennedy explained his decision to a full National Security Council (NSC) meeting. He said he had not given up the idea of an air strike until Sunday morning and had done so then only because there could be no certainty that U.S. planes would destroy all the MRBMs before any could be launched. The quarantine, although "a very tricky course," was "far less likely to provoke a nuclear response," the President said.[23]

Although they were not statutory members of the NSC, the Joint Chiefs sat in the Cabinet Room for the climactic meeting. They had been invited at Taylor's suggestion as a way of allaying any fears that he was not vigorous enough in presenting their recommendations. When Kennedy asked for their comments on his plan of action, the military men answered with a few statements, but no strong objections. Taylor later remarked that, face-to-face with the President, "the JCS tigers turned out to be pussycats." General LeMay saw it differently. He commented that he knew a set-up when he saw one and that Taylor had waited until all the President's plans were formulated and agreed on before giving the other service Chiefs a chance to talk to the President.[24] He was not mollified.

As Chief of Naval Operations, Adm. George W. Anderson, Jr., had already been tasked with implementing the blockade. In the Cabinet Room, the President addressed him directly. "This is up to the Navy," Kennedy said.

"Mr. President," Anderson responded, "the Navy won't let you down."[25] He then explained the procedures U.S. ships would follow in intercepting Cuba-bound vessels. The approaching ship would be hailed and signalled to stop for boarding. A failure to respond would first bring a shot across the bow and, if that warning were ignored, a shot into the transgressor's rudder. That technique, the admiral assured the President and the NSC, would cripple but not sink the vessel.

With all present seemingly satisfied, Secretary McNamara formally approved the Navy's plan.[26] Three days later, however, the procedure no longer seemed to him quite so simple or reassuring. On 24 October, the day the quarantine was to take effect, McNamara went to the Navy's Flag Plot Room for a briefing during which he asked Admiral Anderson to review the procedures outlined in the White House on Sunday.

With a backdrop of wall charts displaying the location of the Cuba-bound ships under U.S. surveillance, Anderson said the opening step would be to hail vessels trying to cross the quarantine line. Among Soviet ships, the *Bucharest* was due to be the first. The two men's conversation, as McNamara recalled it twenty-four years later, quickly became tense.

> "In what language—English or Russian?" I asked.
> "How the hell do I know? . . . I suppose we'll use flags."
> "Well, what if they don't stop?" I asked.
> "We'll send a shot across the bow," he said.
> "Then what, if that doesn't work?"
> "Then we'll fire into the rudder," he replied, by now clearly annoyed.
> "What kind of a ship is it?"
> "A tanker, Mr. Secretary."
> "You're not going to fire a single shot at a tanker without my express permission is that clear?" I said. That's when he made his famous remark about how the Navy had been running blockades from the days of John Paul Jones. . . . I rose from my chair and walked out of the room, saying that this was not a blockade but a means of communication between Kennedy and Khrushchev; no force could be applied without my permission; and that would not be given without discussion with the President.
> "Was that understood?" I asked. The tight-lipped response was "Yes."[27]

Events were soon to prove McNamara correct; the quarantine was more a means of communication than a blockade. Gen. David Burchinal, an Air Force officer who worked for General LeMay, later reported that when the first ship, a Swedish vessel, reached the quarantine line, it ignored the signal from an American destroyer to heave to and identify its cargo and continued toward Cuba. When the destroyer captain reported that he was ready to shoot, the Pentagon ordered him to hold his fire and let the freighter pass.

In fact, only one ship was boarded during the quarantine, in an act that Burchinal said was "mainly theater." The freighter *Marucla* had earlier been selected by the President as the first ship to be stopped and inspected. Registered as Lebanese, not Soviet, it could be boarded without challenging Khrushchev's pride or possession.[28] According to Burchinal, the *Marucla* was found to be carrying military equipment but was nonetheless allowed to proceed.[29] If so, the *Marucla* was exceptional. Soviet policy was to use Soviet ships for such cargo.

The McNamara-Anderson exchange was an unusually open display of the tension that gripped all the U.S. participants during the missile crisis. Open or suppressed, strain marked many of the dealings between the President's civilian and military advisors and left those relations more frayed than before. A policy analyst relying on the published record and on interviews with a number of the decision-makers seven years after the crisis, found that the "Joint Chiefs advocated . . . a massive air strike, leading to an invasion and the overthrow of Castro . . . with an abandon that amazed other members of the ExCom."[30]

It also upset the President. "Impressed with the effort and dedicated manner in which the military responded," John Kennedy was disturbed, his brother recalled, by the failure of the Joint Chiefs, Taylor excepted, to consider fully the implications of the steps they were recommending. "When we talked about this later," Robert Kennedy remembered,

> he said we had to remember that they were trained to fight and to wage war—that was their life. Perhaps we would feel even more concerned if they were always opposed to using arms or military means—for if they would not be willing, who would be? But this experience pointed out for all of us the importance of civilian direction and control and the importance of raising probing questions to military recommendations.[31]

On Alert

The President's decision to quarantine Cuba as an opening move did not rule out other follow-up options. Indeed, Kennedy was himself uncertain that the quarantine would succeed.[32] For this reason, the military was directed to prepare for a variety of actions. Following the President's 20 October instructions, JCS plans included limited air strikes (against the missiles only) to be executed either without warning or after twenty-four hours' notice as early as 22 or 23 October. To hedge further against a failure of the blockade, the Chiefs were also readying the massive air attack and invasion plans developed by CINCLANT and were under orders to be primed to move to a general war footing.[33]

Confirmation of the quarantine plan only heightened military concerns about readiness and led to a request, which McNamara approved, to disperse U.S. aircraft from their home bases throughout the United States and to strengthen the number of air defense units in the southeast and position them for action. By nightfall on Sunday, 21 October, some 60 additional Air Force interceptor aircraft had been moved south, bringing the total number in Florida to over 120. To bolster ground defenses, eight more HAWK surface-to-air missile battalions were also ordered to move south.

At the time of the President's 22 October speech, twenty-two planes equipped with "Genie," low-yield, nuclear air defense weapons were airborne off the Florida coast. An atomic burst from one of those rockets would make up in destructive power what the air-to-air missiles of the time lacked in accuracy. If MiG aircraft or Il-28s from Cuba attempted to attack the United States, they would confront an armed-to-the-teeth air defense force.[34] McNamara had also agreed to a Strategic Air Command airborne alert, and by early afternoon of 22 October, sixty-six SAC B-52s were aloft, carrying nuclear bombs and flight plans that could take them to targets in the Soviet Union.

With the approval of the President, the Joint Chiefs also ordered U.S. military forces worldwide to move from their normal posture—Defense Condition (DEFCON) 5—to a state of higher readiness, DEFCON 3, that would permit effective response to any Soviet use of force, whether in the Caribbean, Europe or the Pacific. On 24 October, SAC went to DEFCON 2. The Joint Chiefs also ordered that all communications between military units be held to essential messages only, unless otherwise directed.[35]

For SAC, heightened readiness meant that battle staffs were manned twenty-four hours a day; personnel were recalled from leave and no new leaves were approved; nonessential maintenance and training were discontinued; and combat elements and their supporting units began actual preparations for combat. The other commands, at DEFCON 3, were somewhat less ready, but they were prepared, if ordered, to move to DEFCON 2.

With all these actions under way and, at least from 21 October onward, hard to conceal from Soviet intelligence, President Kennedy moved to guard against accidentally triggering conflict with Moscow. Since the very first ExComm session on 16 October, the President had been concerned about the Jupiter missiles in Turkey that later became a stumbling block to the resolution of the crisis. Kennedy worried both that Khrushchev might try to strike the Jupiters if U.S.

planes attacked Soviet weapons in Cuba and that the missiles that Turkish officers were just then getting set to operate and maintain might be fired against
Soviet targets without his authorization. The Jupiters' atomic warheads were
physically separate from the rockets and kept under the control of U.S. personnel, but any missile—nuclear-armed or not—fired from Turkey would greatly
escalate tension.

Standard procedure, dictated by U.S. law, prohibited any such missile launch
without explicit presidential approval. At that time, however, no electronic safeguards physically prevented such a firing. Instead, at every level of command,
two military personnel were to get instructions separately and to confirm them
with one another before acting on firing orders received through normal military
channels. Electronic measures, called permissive action links, were then being
installed in the U.S. nuclear arsenal, but not on the Jupiter missiles.

Anxious that war should not begin with an unauthorized firing from Turkey,
President Kennedy was not satisfied that standard procedure was insurance
enough against accident. He told the Joint Chiefs to reinforce the existing safeguards. The Chiefs, in turn, directed the U.S. commander in Turkey to make
the Jupiters "inoperable"—to destroy the missiles immediately—if any attempt
was made to fire them without specific presidential authorization.[37]

Searching for Nuclear Warheads

The other nuclear warheads that preoccupied the President and his advisors
were ones they could neither control nor even locate. U-2 photography had
found three suspected nuclear storage sites in various stages of construction on
Cuba, but analysts judged none of them completed as of 21 October. Still, voic-
ing a widely shared view, the CIA held that "one must assume that nuclear weapons could now be in Cuba to support the operational nuclear capability [of
MRBMs and IRBMs] as it becomes available."[37]

Beginning 23 October, the U.S. Navy and Air Force began to fly low-level
reconnaissance missions over Cuba, partly to intensify the search for nuclear
weapons and weapons depots but primarily to provide targeting data more accurate than the high-level U-2s could supply. The Pentagon wanted intelligence
collected on the ground as well, and officials accordingly asked the CIA to
transport fifty Cubans by submarine to the island and put them ashore to gather
information on the status of Soviet forces, especially the ballistic missiles.[38] This
was the request that so upset General Lansdale that the proposed mission was
cancelled.

I also personally got in the hunt for Soviet nuclear weapons, an excursion that
did neither lasting good nor great damage. The question of whether there were

nuclear warheads on Cuba was one of the most pressing concerns. An answer would greatly influence the preferred U.S. course of action. Throughout the crisis, therefore, I looked for evidence that would confirm the arrival of warheads on the island.

I found none, but my search led me down a number of interesting avenues. For example, during the early stages of the quarantine, as I was reviewing message traffic from U.S. intelligence sources on Soviet military activity, I noticed a report that a U.S. Navy ship had picked up suspicious levels of radioactivity emitted by a Soviet freighter, the *Poltava*. I suggested to General Taylor that he ask Admiral Anderson if the emanations meant the ship was carrying nuclear warheads; at the 8:00 A.M. Joint Chiefs' meeting, Taylor posed the question. Anderson, somewhat embarrassed, replied that he had not seen the message.

He was displeased; being asked a question about his service that he could not answer placed him in a position he did not relish. Later that morning, Anderson's office informed me that the report had little significance, that I had misread it. I passed this new information immediately to Taylor, who was displeased in turn. Seemingly, he had raised a red herring. Firmly but politely, he told me that he did not want to be put in such a position again, an unnecessary admonition since I had earlier reached that conclusion on my own.

Still later, the Navy reversed its earlier call to me. My report, it was now agreed, was meaningful; the *Poltava* was assumed to be carrying nuclear warheads, but it was no longer headed toward Cuba. It had turned back. I immediately reported these new facts to Taylor, a service that did not seem to overcome his earlier discomfort. Understandably, the subject did not come up again.

Nuclear weapons did. Low-level photography of 25 October, available in Washington on the 27th, confirmed the presence in Cuba of FROG ["Luna"] tactical missiles, a twenty-to-twenty-five-nautical-mile-range unguided rocket that Soviet ground forces were known to arm with both conventional and atomic charges.[39] The same reconnaissance found that the nuclear bunkers at the MRBM sites were "not yet ready for storage, assembly or checkout" of warheads, but construction at all Soviet installations was moving at a "rapid pace."[40]

The Joint Chiefs asked Admiral Dennison whether, in light of this new intelligence, he believed U.S. invasion forces should be equipped with tactical nuclear weapons. Dennison replied that he would want the ability to retaliate with such munitions if his forces were attacked by nuclear weapons and said that he was modifying the CINCLANT plans accordingly.[41] The Joint Chiefs responded by authorizing him to equip invasion forces with *nuclear-capable* delivery systems, specifically, eight-inch howitzers and "Honest John" rockets, roughly comparable to the FROGs.

The order, however, prohibited the introduction of nuclear weapons into Cuba without further JCS approval,[42] and the Joint Chiefs did not plan for U.S.

forces to employ atomic armaments in either the air attacks or invasion of Cuba. The authority given to Dennison went only so far as to position him to respond in kind if Soviet forces fired nuclear weapons in the defense of Cuba and if, under U.S. law, the President authorized nuclear force in retaliation. The guidance Dennison received reflected an official U.S. judgment that it was most unlikely that Soviets on Cuba would use tactical nuclear weapons. Their medium-range missiles were another matter, the danger on which Washington's eyes and fears focused.

I recall no conversation with General Taylor during the crisis in which the issue of tactical nuclear weapons—U.S. or Soviet—was raised. The U.S. invasion force did not need such arms to succeed, and given U.S. estimates of the small number of Soviet forces on Cuba, planners saw no sense in the island's defenders employing battlefield atomic weapons and thereby risking escalation. In analyzing prospects for McNamara and the President, the Joint Chiefs judged that such action by the Soviets, while a "possibility" to be accepted, was not "likely." If the Soviets did go nuclear, the Chiefs held, the United States "could respond with overwhelming force against military targets."[43]

Ready on the Firing Line

That combination of preparedness and precaution set the tone that prevailed in official Washington during the early and most dangerous days of the 1962 U.S.-Soviet confrontation. After the President's speech, the first diplomatic notes from Khrushchev were defiant and offered no prospect of early agreement. It was Soviet ships, as they halted their progress toward the quarantine line or turned back toward home on the 24th and 25th, that tentatively indicated a mid-week move to retard and perhaps defuse the crisis. After their move was reported, Secretary Rusk noted, "We're eyeball to eyeball, and I think the other fellow just blinked."[44]

The mid-ocean signal, however, was not echoed on Cuba. There, the CIA on 24 October found "rapid progress" in construction work at the missile and weapons-storage sites.[45] On the positive side, the Agency did not detect "crash . . . measures to achieve a higher degree of [combat] readiness for Soviet and bloc forces" in other parts of the world.

In contrast, U.S. preparations reached a point on the decisive Saturday, 27 October, at which the Joint Chiefs could confidently report to the President that their forces were ready to execute the Cuban contingency plans and poised for attacks on the island. The Navy's blockade forces—two aircraft carriers accompanied by nine escorts, plus a separate task force of some twelve destroyers and cruisers—were on station. Three Marine battalions had reinforced Guantánamo; three more were on ships off the coast of Cuba. Additionally, a Marine expeditionary brigade was en route to the Caribbean from the West Coast.

At this point, the U.S. unified Air Defense Command had 183 interceptors in the southeastern United States. Twenty-two were on five-minute alert; another 72 were on fifteen-minute alert, and 48 on a one-to-three-hour alert. Four interceptors were airborne at all times, augmented from one hour before first light until one hour after it by five additional aircraft.

Among them, to carry out air attacks against Cuba, the Navy, the Marine Corps and the Air Force's Tactical Air Command had some 850 aircraft in Florida. Those assigned to OPLAN 312 were on a one-hour alert, but could go to a higher readiness level if directed. Along the east coast, the Army had assigned CINCLANT four of its divisions plus supporting artillery. Additionally, a task force of infantry, armored and artillery units was on its way east from Texas.[46]

For its part, SAC had 52 B-52s airborne with 196 nuclear weapons "effectively covering targets" in the Soviet Union should general nuclear war erupt. On 15-minute ground alert were 271 B-52s and 340 B-47s, with 1,630 nuclear weapons, as well as 136 single-warhead Atlas and Titan intercontinental ballistic missiles. Within another 24 hours, SAC expected to have a total of 172 missiles and 1,200 aircraft with 2,858 weapons in the highest state of readiness.[47]

In the air, on land and at sea, a massive U.S. force of close to one million personnel stood ready for combat. They had been readied and deployed with extraordinary speed and now waited only for direction to execute their plans. They did not underestimate the dangers. Since the Soviets were presumed to have nuclear warheads on Cuba, even perhaps for the FROGs, it was also conceivable that a U.S. invasion force would meet a nuclear response. In this context, McCone had reminded McNamara and other ExComm members as early as 17 October that, according to espionage reports from Col. Oleg Penkovsky, Soviet field commanders had "much more" autonomy over the use of nuclear weapons than did their U.S. counterparts.[48]

On that Saturday morning, 27 October, McNamara reported disturbing news to the ExComm: some Soviet ships continued to move toward the quarantine line and might have to be intercepted in the very near future.[49] In the afternoon came word that a U-2 was missing over Cuba, presumably hit by a SAM. Earlier in the week, the President had asked to be informed immediately if a U-2 were shot down, and, as Bundy wrote in the minutes of the 23 October ExComm meeting, "it is expected . . . the recommendation will be for immediate retaliation upon the most likely surface-to-air site involved in this action."[50]

In the White House that Saturday afternoon, however, decision was deferred. Advised that the SAMs on Cuba were Soviet manned and controlled, the President saw the firing on the U-2 as "an escalation by them," but chose to put off immediate retaliation.[51] "It isn't the first step that concerns me," his brother recalled Kennedy saying, "but both sides escalating to the fourth and fifth step—and we don't go to the sixth because there is no one around to do so. We must remind ourselves we are embarking on a very hazardous course."[52]

The decision to defer a sortie against the Soviet surface-to-air missile batteries on Cuba surprisingly met with the approval of the Joint Chiefs. Led by LeMay and Wheeler, they judged that since the SAMs were in clusters, it would be "impracticable" to attack just one. Even the small danger of Soviet nuclear retaliation made a single strike seem a poor risk.[53] The Chiefs did not favor piecemeal attacks; they wanted to proceed with an all-out assault on the 29th.

At the Eleventh Hour

The immediate and more important question before the President was how to answer the two different messages from Khrushchev. The first, a rambling, almost plaintive letter—McNamara called it "twelve pages of fluff"[54]—had arrived in Washington in four parts between 6:00 and 9:00 P.M. on Friday evening. It outlined a possible deal: if Kennedy, on behalf of the United States, would promise not to attack Cuba, "would restrain other [nations] from actions of this sort [and] would recall your fleet," Khrushchev wrote, ". . . the question of armaments would disappear [and] the question of the destruction of the armaments . . . would look different."[55] The second message, broadcast as a communique over Radio Moscow at 10:00 A.M. Saturday Washington time, was both tougher and more formal. It hedged the earlier offer with a demand for the removal of U.S. missiles (the Jupiters) from Turkey under United Nations inspection procedures that would parallel those applied in Cuba. It seemed to pull back the Friday olive branch and even to raise the prospect that Khrushchev had been overruled, if not overthrown.

While the ExComm was debating the proper response to the Soviet leadership, the Joint Chiefs submitted a formal request for authority to launch an air strike two days later, with invasion to follow. Ready to attack, they were convinced that attack was imperative. Evidence that the Soviets were continuing to build nuclear storage facilities on Cuba reinforced the Chiefs' decision to accept the conclusion of the Defense Intelligence Agency that the missile deployment foreshadowed other Soviet challenges at America's back gate.

Behind the Kremlin's moves, judged the DIA, was a plan to improve Moscow's capability to stage a nuclear attack and a calculation that the United States could not prevent the advance of Soviet offensive power into the western hemisphere.[56] In the eyes of the Joint Chiefs, either of those propositions put U.S. security profoundly at risk. Together, they were intolerable.

General Taylor again disagreed in part with the Joint Chiefs. He would delay deciding that Saturday, as his colleagues wanted, to authorize the start of the air strike on Monday and he preferred, as well, to withhold a decision to invade.[57] He nonetheless made a straightforward presentation of the Chiefs' views to the ExComm. The transcript of the meeting records his words and the reception they received from Attorney General Kennedy and others:

> TAYLOR: Mr. President, the chiefs have been in session during the afternoon on—really the same basis as we have over here. This is the recommendation they give as follows: that the big strike, Op Plan 312—be executed no later than Monday morning the 29th unless there is irrefutable evidence in the meantime that offensive weapons are being dismantled and rendered inoperable; that the execution of the Strike Plan be part of the execution of 3–16, the Invasion Plan, [excised] days later.
>
> RFK: That was a surprise. (Laughter, mixed voices)[58]

Brushing the Joint Chiefs' views aside almost as comic relief, the ExComm turned back to the task of finding a politic way to answer Khrushchev and a diplomatic way out of the crisis. Not many minutes earlier, a different kind of military alarm had also provided a brief distraction. An Alaska-based U-2, it was reported, had mistakenly flown into Soviet air space in the Far East. Soviet fighters gave chase, but the American pilot got his plane back to safety. The accident could have raised the day's tension unbearably, but it was soon agreed that the Kremlin was unlikely to interpret the incursion as the prelude to attack.

The President, at least, quickly dismissed the problem. Speaking of the unfortunate U-2 pilot, he used words he might privately have applied to the Pentagon professionals who seemed that day so out of touch with him and his anxieties. Said John Kennedy: "There is always some son of a bitch who doesn't get the word."[63]

Climax and Aftermath

While the President and his top advisors debated their options late into Saturday evening, 27 October, I tried to reason my own way through the problem they faced. I wanted to see if I could make sense of the U.S.-Soviet impasse, even perhaps come up with some ideas that would help find our way around it. The more I analyzed the situation, however, the more bleak my thoughts became. As I read and re-read the two strikingly different messages from Khrushchev, I became convinced that the United States and the Soviet Union were on the brink of global nuclear war.

I read the Soviet texts at a desk in General Taylor's outer office as I waited through the night for word of developments. In those dark hours, I did not know that the President had sent Khrushchev a reply to the conciliatory first message, ignoring the second and the issue it raised of the Jupiter missiles in Turkey. Nor did I know that Robert Kennedy, on his brother's instructions, had met with Anatoli Dobrynin, the Soviet ambassador to the United States, to urge a quick and positive response from Khrushchev to the President's message and to offer a secret understanding on removing the Jupiters. I only knew that the ExComm had gone back into session after supper and that the President had signed an order putting twenty-four Air Force Reserve squadrons on active duty to carry troops.

All the signs that night pointed toward war—and not just war, but catastrophe. It was the only time in my life that I believed the world was headed for nuclear devastation, and the threat made me worry, once again, about my family. My wife Maria and our two sons were living just a few miles from the Pentagon, a prime target for any Soviet attack. My rank of major meant that no official provision had been or would be made for their evacuation, and I did not know whether Maria understood how grave the situation was.

I had not kept her advised of crisis developments. The information I held was very sensitive, and, besides, I rarely got home. Some days earlier, my brother Ray had called from Arkansas to ask Maria how concerned he and his family should be. She replied that she knew no more than they did and expected to be among the last to learn. If war did come, she told Ray, his family's chances of survival would be much greater than ours. Washington would certainly be destroyed immediately.

My view was the same. I doubted that any evacuation plans, even for the most senior of advisors, would be of much value. In the kind of nuclear exchange that seemed all too possible, there would be no safe place to hide, and only ruin would greet those who did survive.

I had faced the prospect of my own death once before, but then, as I lay wounded on the frozen ground of North Korea next to the wreckage of my fighter aircraft in February 1952, I knew that I had done all I could to ensure survival. Not long before, I had insisted that higher headquarters provide helicopters to rescue pilots downed behind enemy lines and had worked out emergency rescue procedures that the pilots in the 49th Fighter Bomber Wing would follow to fly cover until help arrived. No more than several weeks passed before I was shot down by ground fire. And soon after crash-landing on the mud flats of North Korea's west coast, I could see and hear F-84 Thunderjet fighters piloted by my friends circling overhead, strafing nearby enemy positions, shielding me until a rescue helicopter came.

In the relative quiet of my Pentagon office almost ten years later, I felt no such assurance. Instead, I asked myself then—and more than once later—if I had done everything possible in my work on the military aspects of national security to minimize the chances of a nuclear war. I did not question the need for the United States to have a strong nuclear deterrent posture. But it should be just that: a nuclear posture to prevent war, not to fight wars.

Maintaining that delicate deterrent balance was a challenging proposition; the problem had occupied much of my thinking for several years. On that Saturday night in October, the deterrent theory seemed on the edge of failure. Had I missed some key element in the equation, some words or actions that, in the hands of the proper U.S. officials, could have persuaded the Soviets ahead of time not to risk peace by provoking the United States in Cuba? Or had I and others misunderstood Soviet thinking all along? Had there never been a way to avoid this showdown?

Khrushchev's two last messages raised other questions. How rational was Soviet decision-making? Had Khrushchev lost control of himself and the situation? Was he flailing about, and thus more likely to try to exploit any element of the situation—the missiles in Turkey, the status of Berlin—that he thought he could use to his advantage? Was he trying to pressure the President, as he had in Vienna some sixteen months earlier, hoping that Kennedy would back down?

Until the combative Saturday morning communique from Moscow, U.S. analysts had assumed that we faced a mercurial but basically rational Khrushchev who, seeing the determined U.S. reaction to his ploy in Cuba, would understand that Soviet missiles there were intolerable to the United States. Within limits, such an enemy's responses could be fairly well predicted. Some, at least, felt that they could calculate the Soviet reply to U.S. military action on Cuba and that, if the Soviets did not back down, the United States could use force there with reasonable confidence that the conflict would not spread and escalate. Now that very fundamental assumption was in doubt. Would Khrushchev in his desperate hours launch a nuclear attack against the United States? How could we deal rationally with an irrational opponent? If it came to that, who was our opponent?

One way to read the conflicting Khrushchev messages was as evidence of a power struggle in Moscow. Who was in charge in the Kremlin? Had Khrushchev been replaced overnight by a hard-line group that was willing to go to war over Cuba? Across the Potomac, the ExComm thought as much. "While you were out of the room, Mr. President," McGeorge Bundy told John Kennedy that afternoon,

> We reached an informal consensus . . . last night's message was Khrushchev, and this [Saturday] one is his own hard-nosed people overruling him . . . they didn't like what he said to you last night. Nor would I, if I were a Soviet hard-nose.[1]

Whether Khrushchev had lost his composure or his hold on power, the net result was an apparently irresistible slide toward violent confrontation. I did not believe either side wanted this outcome, but I had grave doubts that it could be avoided. The pace of construction at the Soviet missile sites on Cuba was accelerating. The momentum of U.S. military preparations in response seemed inexorable. Diplomacy was going nowhere. The Cold War seemed about to end in a terrible explosion, and I felt that all of us who had worked so hard to prevent nuclear war were on the brink of failing our families, our country, ourselves.

Reprieve and Dissent

Despair turned to relief shortly after nine o'clock Sunday morning Washington time as Moscow Radio broadcast in English a new message from Khrushchev to

Kennedy. "The Soviet government," its leader declared, "has given a new order to dismantle the arms which you described as offensive, and to crate and return them to the Soviet Union." Making it clear that he linked the missiles' withdrawal to the pledge in Kennedy's letter the night before not to invade Cuba, Khrushchev also said he would cooperate in arranging United Nations verification of the disarming of the Soviet missiles. "Thus, in view of the assurances you have given and our instructions on dismantling," the Kremlin leader said, "there is every condition for eliminating the present conflict."[2]

Elation spread through Washington—but not to the E-ring of the Pentagon. In the offices of the Joint Chiefs of Staff, Khrushchev's message was suspect, perhaps a new piece of Soviet trickery, on a par with the repeated pre-crisis denials that Moscow was sending offensive weapons to Cuba. The Joint Chiefs felt that the Soviet leader's offer "might be an insincere proposal intended to gain time" to make his ballistic missiles fully operational.[3]

Brought to the White House that afternoon to be thanked by the President for "your advice and your counsel and your behavior during this very, very difficult period," the senior military men did not respond as the President expected. "We have been had," declared Admiral Anderson.[4] General LeMay was even more critical. His thundered advice was a question: "Why don't we go in and make a strike on Monday anyway?"[5]

That furious reaction flabbergasted the President, but intelligence reports from Cuba during the next four days appeared to back up the Joint Chiefs' suspicions. On 29 October, U.S. reconnaissance flights found no dismantling. On 30 and 31 October, with the quarantine and overflights suspended while acting United Nations Secretary General U Thant visited Cuba to try to negotiate verfication of a Soviet withdrawal, the CIA told the ExComm that available intelligence pointed to continuing "construction and concealment" work that could raise the missiles' readiness.[6]

The Joint Chiefs saw in these reports only another example of Khrushchevian deception. Again they recommended to the President that the United States destroy all Soviet offensive weapons on Cuba. Their 29 October advice was to remove "all nuclear capable delivery systems, including surface-to-surface missiles (including ship based), bomber aircraft, bombs, air-to-surface rockets and missiles, warheads for any of these weapons, supporting and operating equipment, and missile fuel."[7] On 31 October, the Chiefs urged that the quarantine be reimposed,[8] and on 1 November, after U Thant returned to New York without Cuban agreement to on-site inspection of the Soviet withdrawal, the President ordered the quarantine reinstated on a selective basis.

The next day finally brought overhead photographic documentation that the medium-range ballistic missiles (MRBMs) were actually being disassembled.[9] That work was the first step in fulfilling Khrushchev's Sunday-morning promise,

Major Gribkov in 1943.

Gen. Anatoli I. Gribkov in Moscow as Chief of Staff of the Warsaw Pact Forces.

Soviet troops from Operation ANADYR in Cuba, 1962.

Ruins of Maj. Rudolf Anderson, Jr.'s U-2, shot down over Cuba, 27 October 1962.

U.S. Air Force plane overflying homeward-bound Soviet ship off the coast of Cuba, November 1962.

Russian freighter with missiles uncovered inspected at departure from Cuba, 9 November 1963. *(Courtesy of Bettmann Archive.)*

Left to right: Fidel Castro, Lt. Gen. Pavel Dankevich and Gen.
Issa Pliyev, Havana, 1962

Raul Castro (in cap) with Col. Dimitri Yazov, commander of the 106th motorized regiment, Cuba,
1962. Marshal Yazov was dismissed as Soviet minister of defense in August 1991 and imprisoned until
1993 on charges of conspiring in the attempted
putsch against Mikhail Gorbachev.

General Gribkov with Fidel Castro in Havana, January 1992.

Raul Castro (center) meeting Soviet military officials in Moscow, July 1992. Foreground, left to right: Adm. Sergei Groshkov, Marshal Matvei Zakharov, Castro, Marshal Rodion Malinovsky, unidentified Cuban, and Marshal Sergei Biryuzov.

Left to right: General Gribkov, Raul Castro, and Robert McNamara, former U.S. secretary of defense, Havana, January 1992. Autographing the original photograph for General Gribkov, Raul Castro wrote, "The most important thing is that Cuba is and will always continue to be a socialist country, thanks to the efforts of the Cubans and to the great help we received from the Soviet Union."

Gen. William Y. Smith as Chief of Staff, Supreme
Headquarters Allied Powers Europe (SHAPE), 1979.

First Lieutenant Smith in the
cockpit of an F-84 Thunderjet,
Korea, 1951.

Maj. Smith being promoted to Lieutenant Colonel by Gen. Maxwell
Taylor (right), Washington, 1963.

but not the last. Still skeptical of Soviet intentions, the Joint Chiefs turned their attention to the issue of verifying the removal of the MRBMs from Cuba and, with them, what President Kennedy in his 27 October letter to Khrushchev had referred to as "all weapons systems in Cuba capable of offensive use."[10]

That definition was to prove particularly troublesome, but the first obstacle to be overcome was the U.S. demand to observe the departure of the Soviet missiles from Cuba. Fidel Castro was adamant; he would permit no inspection, even by the United Nations, on Cuba or in its territorial waters. The alternative, agreed on only after much contentious negotiation at the United Nations, was to have Soviet ships at sea submit to "close alongside observation by U.S. naval vessels."[11] With that procedure set, the Joint Chiefs marked the end of the most threatening phase of the crisis.[12]

The agreement and its implementation did not, however, end the confrontation. One other prickly issue remained, and it was not close to resolution: the removal from Cuba of the Il-28 light bombers. Capable of reaching the U.S. mainland, they were considered by the Kennedy administration to be among the offensive weapons that Khrushchev had pledged to withdraw. The Soviet leader objected. The bombers, he insisted as late as 11 November, were "12-year-old planes . . . incapable of offensive actions."

"We brought them to Cuba," he maintained in a letter to Kennedy, "only because they can be used as a mobile means of coastal defense under cover of antiaircraft fire from their own territory. They cannot however fly beyond the limits of that cover since they will immediately be destroyed."[13]

That argument had merit only if U.S. air defense forces around the Caribbean were to be kept on permanent alert, a burden no senior Washington official wanted to assume. Although agreeing that the bombers were less menacing than the missiles, the Joint Chiefs saw the planes' "continued presence" as "a long-term threat to the continental United States [that] would consequently require a higher level of air defense of our southeastern states and would give deep concern to many parts of Latin America."[14]

Through the first seventeen days of November, the fate of the Il-28s hung fire, the subject of intense U.S.–Soviet argument and, it was learned much later, of heated Soviet-Cuban exchanges. The stalemate caused the Joint Chiefs to renew their pressure for decisive military action and kept the crisis at a high pitch until Thanksgiving eve.

The Crisis Ends

The 2 November overhead photographs that confirmed the movement from the missile sites carried quite a different message on the Il-28s. The bombers were being uncrated and their parts pieced together; one was seen taxiing, another fully assembled, at the San Julian airfield in southwestern Cuba. Reconnaissance data available on 3 November revealed additional Il-28 shipping crates being transported toward San Julian. The next day, similar crates were seen at Holguin, an airfield in the eastern part of the island. At least thirty-seven and possibly forty-one Il-28s were definitely on Cuba, and the Soviets were continuing to assemble them and prepare them for action.

As long as the bomber issue remained unsettled, the Joint Chiefs pressed for frequent photographic flights over Cuba at both high levels and low. The death of Maj. Rudolf Anderson, Jr. and the destruction of his U-2 on 27 October had not diminished the military's insistence on reconnaissance. Only when U-2 photography of 7 November showed that surface-to-air-missile (SAM) batteries were apparently preparing to fire on overhead targets did the Joint Chiefs recommend conducting further flights in such a way as to expose no more than one aircraft at a time.[15]

This tactic would also allow the United States to pinpoint the source of, and to respond to, any single SAM launch. If attacks indicated broad resistance to U.S. overflights, the Chiefs recommended retaliatory strikes against all airfields and air defense systems in Cuba. For an isolated incident, they advised a more limited response. Both options were to remain open until the Soviets agreed to withdraw the Il-28s.[16]

Seeing no discernible progress toward that goal, the Joint Chiefs used their 8 November comments on a paper prepared by Paul H. Nitze, assistant secretary of defense, to recommend that after a "limited period" had passed without the removal of the bombers, the United States should attack and destroy them.[17] The next day, however, they proposed quite a different course. Let the Il-28s stay on Cuba; their presence would nullify the U.S. promise not to invade the island.

Obviously, the Chiefs thought that an opportunity might still arise to justify using overt military force to resolve the Cuban matter. On 12 November, they stated their case in a memorandum to the ExComm. Although they again called for the withdrawal of the aircraft, they added the view that their plans for an air attack and invasion of Cuba represented the only "long term solution."[18]

For a meeting with the President four days later, the Chiefs reviewed and renewed their recommendation: the Il-28s must go—"preferably by negotiation, otherwise by blockade and, if need be, by military action."[19] On 18 November, Khrushchev finally conceded both this point and the U.S. right to inspect the bombers' withdrawal at sea as it had done with the MRBMs.

In response, President Kennedy lifted the quarantine, and U.S. military forces began to stand down from alert and to return to normal activities. A week elapsed, however, before the Joint Chiefs felt they could relax fully. Overhead photography on 27 November confirmed that seven of the thirteen Il-28s at San

Julian were being disassembled; another twenty crates remained unopened. That evidence brought the second and final phase of the crisis conclusively to an end.

One loose end remained to be wrapped up: Operation MONGOOSE. Evidently discussed at a late November ExComm meeting,[20] the venture was phased out two months later. A "Standing Group" replaced both the ExComm and the Special Group (Augmented).[21] Covert actions continued against Cuba, but not under the auspices of General Lansdale and his group.[22]

In late May 1963, at a meeting of the Standing Group considering Cuba and steps to place pressure on Castro, Bundy summarized the situation. The task before the United States, he maintained, was "to decide now what actions we would take against Castro, acknowledging that the measures practical for us to take will not result in his overthrow."[23] He had said much the same thing nearly six months before. In his 5 October discussion with John McCone, the national security advisor had seemed "inclined . . . to play down" MONGOOSE-style tactics against Cuba, to view open military intervention as "intolerable" and to see only one other alternative: "we would have to learn to live with Castro and his Cuba and adjust our policies accordingly."[24]

A frightening crisis had proved that forecast correct. Watchful, armed coexistence with a hostile neighbor, whether a small nation, such as Cuba or a superpower, such as the Soviet Union, was the only safe course for the United States to pursue, year in, year out. The Cuban Missile Crisis of 1962 nearly forced another choice: violent confrontation. Assessing the danger of nuclear war inherent in the crisis, U.S. and Soviet leaders both drew back from what Nikita Khrushchev told John Kennedy was "the abyss we came to."[25] But it was a very close call.

Minority Views

In the final analysis, it was the President's call. Initially disposed to use force, he moved with most of his civilian advisors to a different course, leaving the senior military men a minority in administration councils. During the crisis, the Joint Chiefs had good access to the White House, but nothing like the casting vote. On four occasions from 18 October through 16 November, they met as a group directly with the President. In addition, Admiral Anderson attended a National Security Council meeting to discuss the quarantine and met twice separately with the President, once accompanied by Gen. David Shoup, Commandant of the Marine Corps. LeMay and three other senior Air Force officers also met once with the President.

From 17 October to 29 November, the Joint Chiefs sent Secretary McNamara twenty-four memoranda for use at the ExComm. Four of the documents went to the President as well. Unlike their Bay of Pigs experience, the Joint Chiefs could not feel that they had not been consulted soon enough or frequently enough. In the daily ExComm sessions, General Taylor had relayed their thoughts and recommendations. Although the service Chiefs believed that Taylor did not always present their views as strongly as they wanted, the real reason that their advice fell mostly on deaf ears was Kennedy's instinct, not Taylor's lack of ardor.

The top military professionals were heard, but their messages, although loud and clear, did not match the President's developing understanding of his options and of the grave dangers inherent in the use of force. In the earliest hours after the discovery of the Soviet weapons, most ExComm participants, including the President, seemed to favor an air strike to destroy the missiles.[26] As that consensus quickly disappeared, the Joint Chiefs were virtually alone in strongly advocating that the initial U.S. response be an air strike and subsequent invasion of Cuba.

They were not alone, however, in believing that at some point use of force might be necessary. The President himself considered that a distinct possibility.[27] Additionally, some other ExComm members who approved quarantine as the first step held views similar to those of the Joint Chiefs. Paul Nitze, for example, later said he did not rule out use of force. Rather, he was uncertain whether quarantine, air strike or invasion was the proper response. He favored the quarantine as the initial action, fully aware that if that did not work, an air strike would be conducted. If that did not do the job, Nitze believed, the United States would have to "contemplate" invasion. He saw no real conflict between the three options. For him, the correct policy was to achieve the objective with the minimum use of force possible.[28]

By 27 October, when the Joint Chiefs were still pressing for authorization to begin the planned assault, the ExComm faced a very different situation than the problem it had first confronted eleven days before. The quarantine had stopped, slowed or led Soviet ships to turn back. Khrushchev's two latest messages, however conflicting, seemed calculated at a minimum to keep negotiations going. In this setting, the Joint Chiefs became fully isolated. Their recommendations for an immediate air strike and invasion showed, in McGeorge Bundy's later and charitable judgment, "that they were out of touch with their commander in chief, but the fault was not primarily theirs."[29]

President Kennedy was less forbearing. Commenting afterwards on the role of the Joint Chiefs during the crisis and on their desire to invade Cuba, he remarked to Arthur Schlesinger,

> One thing this experience shows is the value of sea power and air power;
> an invasion would have been a mistake—a wrong use of our power. But the

military are mad. They wanted to do this. It's lucky for us that we have McNamara over there.[30]

Kennedy displayed the depth of his feelings even more graphically over dinner at the White House on 15 November with his friend and *Newsweek* correspondent Ben Bradlee. As Bradlee recalled the conversation, the talk, turning to Cuba, brought an explosion by the President about his forceful lack of admiration for the Joint Chiefs of Staff, except for Maxwell Taylor, whom he called "absolutely first class." As for the others, said Kennedy,

> The first advice I'm going to give my successor, is to watch the generals and to avoid feeling that just because they were military men their opinions on military matters were worth a damn.[31]

The President's praise for Taylor reflected both the friendship between the two men that had grown during Taylor's service at the White House and the JCS chairman's attitude toward using force in Cuba—a stance markedly less belligerent than that of the Joint Chiefs. At the start of the crisis, Taylor later recalled, he personally preferred an air strike to a blockade because he believed that over time Khrushchev would hide the missiles in Cuba and make it more difficult either to target them for attack or to ensure that all of them had been removed. As he participated in the ExComm debates, he, like many others, changed his mind. Moving away from the position of the Joint Chiefs, Taylor recommended delaying any binding decision to conduct an air strike or invade unless the Soviets unequivocally challenged the quarantine or flatly refused to withdraw the missiles.

His restraint was apparently bred of a conviction that Khrushchev would eventually have to retreat. "I was so sure we had 'em over a barrel," he said, "I never worried much about the final outcome, but what things might happen in between."[32] After the crisis subsided, he remarked that he was glad that the President had overruled him and the service Chiefs. The blockade, it turned out, was enough to achieve U.S. objectives.[33]

As noted earlier, unspoken disagreement over those objectives was the real source of the clash between military and civilian points of view in October 1962. The President and his principal advisors were willing to live with Castro, but not with the Soviet missiles. The Joint Chiefs, taking what they had good reason to think was also the view of both Kennedys and the Central Intelligence Agency, felt strongly that Castro, too, represented an intolerable danger to U.S. security.

The net result of the Joint Chiefs' advice during the crisis therefore was just the reverse of what they had intended. They had done their part; they had supplied clear and direct advice that was, in their military judgment, sound as well, but in the President's decision-making, their advice was overruled. At the end of November 1962, they found themselves held in lower regard than they had been after the Bay of Pigs.

The President, they ruefully learned, intended to listen to his civilian advisors and, on selected issues, to General Taylor, but not to the Joint Chiefs. In John Kennedy's view, the Cuban Missile Crisis had ended successfully. He had attained the U.S. objective—the removal of the missiles—while avoiding hostilities with the Soviet Union and the threat of escalation to global nuclear war. The President could have hoped for no more. The Joint Chiefs were out of step with him.

Going into their last meeting of the crisis period with the President, the Chiefs approved a set of points for General Taylor to make at the session. The immediate issue on 16 November was the removal of the Il-28 bombers, but the talking paper looked beyond that question to broader and more enduring dangers. Other Soviet "weapons systems" on Cuba, the document argued, are "of significant military importance. . . . [A]ir defense weapon systems . . . [pose] a constant threat to our surveillance," and the Soviet Army's weapons constitute a potential problem for the defense of Guantánamo or the conduct of "any invasion attempt."[34]

Even more troubling than the "equipment," to the memorandum's authors, were the Soviet military personnel on Cuba. They posed an especially sensitive problem, and the Chiefs urged that the United States "generate now all the pressure possible to get the Soviet personnel out."[35] Otherwise, they worried,

> When the extent of this presence is known and the weapons systems remaining in Soviet hands are thoroughly appreciated, it will be clear to the Western Hemisphere that it has indeed been invaded and remains invaded by the Soviet Union.[36]

Given that long-term political and military danger, the Joint Chiefs also argued against letting Castro off the hook too easily. They held that "it would be damaging to our national interest and the sense of security of our Latin American allies to create the impression of underwriting Castro for an indefinite period without careful qualification."[37] Any assurances to Castro should be based on Khrushchev's withdrawal of all his forces and his pledge to foreswear future military assistance to Cuba. Even with those conditions met, promises to Castro should be "linked to his good behavior" and his acceptance of continuing U.S. air surveillance.

This final warning from the Joint Chiefs to the President on the dangers posed by a continuing Soviet presence on Cuba and an unrepentant Castro was remarkably prescient. At least as a domestic political issue, the Soviet presence on Cuba cropped up regularly in later years and regularly embarrassed Kennedy's successors in the White House. The 1970 discovery of what appeared to be a Soviet submarine base under construction at Cienfuegos gave Richard Nixon anxious moments. Publicity about the combat brigade of Soviet troops on the island diluted the commitment of Frank Church, then chairman of the Senate Foreign Relations Committee, to ratification of the second Strategic Arms Limitation Treaty (SALT II) in 1979. Soviet shipments of modern aircraft— MiG-29s—to Cuba and of other military and nonmilitary aid also interfered with George Bush's and Mikhail Gorbachev's efforts a decade later to improve relations.

Foresighted though they were at the close of the 1962 confrontation with Moscow, the Joint Chiefs had not earned President Kennedy's trust. Within a year, Admiral Anderson would be gone from Washington, to serve as U.S. ambassador to Portugal instead of a second two-year term as Chief of Naval Operations. General LeMay fared a little better. When his first term as Air Force Chief of Staff expired in July 1963, the President extended his appointment for a third year. After Kennedy's assassination, Lyndon Johnson had LeMay stay at the Pentagon until February 1965.

Kennedy's initial decision to keep LeMay on may well have reflected the number of powerful friends the Air Force head had in Congress. To a Washington journalist, the President remarked in summer 1963, "it's good to have men like Curt LeMay and [Admiral] Arleigh Burke commanding troops once you decide to go in. . . . I like having LeMay head the Air Force. Everybody knows how he feels. That's a good thing."[38]

The President's public praise should be read in the political context of the time. He needed LeMay's support, and that of the other service Chiefs, for the Limited Test Ban Treaty that had just been negotiated in Moscow. Kennedy called the agreement among the United States, the United Kingdom and the Soviet Union to end atmospheric and undersea nuclear weapons testing a "step toward reason, a step away from war."[39] Many U.S. Senators, whose votes were needed for ratification of the accord, were skeptical, and the testimony of the Joint Chiefs would weigh heavily in their minds.

Maxwell Taylor was a driving force in winning their unenthusiastic, but unanimous, endorsement of the treaty. He arranged to have the President make his case personally to each service chief and, with Robert McNamara, negotiated the price for the Chiefs' consent. It was Kennedy's "unqualified and unequivocal assurances" that underground nuclear testing would continue and that the United States would maintain its nuclear laboratories, strengthen its ability to detect violations of the ban and stand ready to resume explosions in the atmosphere on short notice.[40]

The Underlying Debate

One result of this effort was that LeMay broke with his predecessor as Air Force chief of staff. Gen. Thomas D. White opposed the treaty and any limitation on nuclear testing. LeMay, in contrast, joined Taylor and the other Joint Chiefs in endorsing the limited ban. They were not enthusiastic. They had opposed the idea of a comprehensive prohibition on such testing, but they were willing to back President Kennedy on the modified agreement. Republican Senator Barry Goldwater, an Air Force reserve officer, was not. His reason echoed the warning the Joint Chiefs had given President Kennedy in November 1963: until the Soviet Union withdrew all its forces from Cuba, no treaty with Moscow deserved approval.[41]

Goldwater's suspicions were one enduring legacy of the Cuban Missile Crisis. The ExComm debates that led to the oversimplified classification of U.S. policymakers as hawks or doves formed a muffled prelude to the arguments over U.S.–Soviet relations that were to recur in different settings again and again in subsequent years. In 1962, the divisions of opinion were primarily attributable to different views of the Cold War, based on experience in living with and dealing with the Soviets.

Dean Acheson, Paul Nitze, Maxwell Taylor and Secretary of the Treasury C. Douglas Dillon, among the more resolute early advocates of a forceful response to Khrushchev, based their views on a central proposition. The United States had an unmistakable military advantage in conventional forces in the Caribbean and, more importantly to most of them, in strategic nuclear capability as well. Because of this, as Taylor later said, at some point Khrushchev had to back down.

These men had dealt with the Soviet Union as a difficult ally during World War II and as an enemy for fifteen Cold War years. They believed they understood the Soviets and how they would react to the basic realities of military power. In their view, Khrushchev would not risk incomparably greater devastation than the Soviet homeland had suffered in World War II in a cause in which the United States held all the trump cards.

On the other side of the deliberations, the side on which the President most often seemed to be found, were those who believed that any use of force might lead to an unwanted, uncontrollable escalation of violence that would cause one side or the other to feel compelled to employ nuclear weapons. Once the threshold of violence was crossed, this group believed, no one could predict the final outcome, but it would most likely lead to the devastation of both countries.

In their thinking, strategic nuclear balance was not a matter of the number of weapons on either side, of the relative ability of one side to attack and effectively disarm the other or of the numbers and types of weapons needed to retaliate effectively in the event of a first strike against it. In their view each superpower already had more than enough weapons to destroy the other. The capacity of those arsenals acted as a restraint on the exercise of military power, a limit on the intensity of confrontation, a factor in preserving balance.

McNamara was the most outspoken of this second group. In the evening of 16 October, at the second ExComm meeting, for example, he reported the Joint Chiefs' assertion that the MRBMs in Cuba changed the strategic balance "substantially." In his "personal view," he immediately added, the missiles did not change the strategic nuclear balance "at all."[42] The United States, he reasoned,

> had a great superiority, numerical superiority—superiority in strategic nuclear power before the Soviet moves into Cuba, but that superiority, numerical superiority, was not such that it could be translated into usable military power to support political objectives. Because before the missiles were placed in Cuba . . . the Soviets had enough strategic nuclear power to face us with the prospect of unacceptable damage if we used ours first against them, or if we used ours in any fashion against them."[43]

Bundy held essentially the same view, and in a later discussion he scored the widespread belief that U.S. superiority in strategic nuclear weapons had ensured the successful resolution of the Cuban crisis. Disagreeing with that analysis—as he said he did during the crisis itself—Bundy added that he was

> quite confident that the President believed, and his belief is decisive here, that nobody was going to make the hideous choice of using nuclear weapons if he could possibly avoid it, that—although indeed we had a certain superiority—it was not a useable superiority in the sense that we would ever want to go first, because if even one Soviet weapon landed on an American target, we would be the losers."[44]

McNamara's and Bundy's views carried great weight. In his 17 October list of "facts" agreed within the ExComm, Theodore Sorensen observed that there was general agreement that the missiles "do not significantly alter the balance of power—i.e., they do not significantly increase the potential megatonnage capable of being unleashed on American soil, even after a surprise American nuclear strike."[45] The "known presence" of the Soviet weapons ninety miles off U.S. shores was nonetheless unacceptable "if our courage and our commitments are ever to be believed by either allies or adversaries."[46]

Concern over the crisis leading to a nuclear war came up in the early minutes of the first ExComm meeting the morning of 16 October. Rusk stated that in his view, the United States had two alternatives: to conduct a quick strike or to consult with U.S. allies and then inform Khrushchev that he was creating a situation that could lead to a general nuclear war, hoping thereby to defuse the situation.[47] McNamara responded that any U.S. air strike should take place before the MRBMs became operational; otherwise the United States could not be assured that it could attack them before they were launched. And if they were launched, there would be "almost certain . . . chaos in part of the east coast. . . ."[48]

Rusk demurred, stating that he did not think it essential to strike the missiles before they became operational, because if the Soviets ever fired a missile from Cuba, "we are in general war." So the Soviet Union had an important decision to make.[49] McNamara responded by declaring that if he knew the missiles were operational and had nuclear warheads he would "strongly urge against an air strike . . . because of the danger to this country in relation to the gain that would accrue. . . ."[50]

In other words, McNamara did not believe the U.S. objectives in Cuba—even the removal of the missiles—were important enough to risk the use of nuclear weapons against the United States. He made that declaration very early in the deliberations of the ExComm, and although the ExComm members changed their minds on many aspects of the crisis and how to respond, there is nothing to indicate that McNamara then or later changed his view on this fundamental point.

Dillon, Nitze and the Joint Chiefs of Staff held a different view; they were doubtful that the crisis would lead to nuclear war and confident that the Soviets would eventually back down. They also believed that the strategic nuclear balance *did* make a difference, to both the United States and the Soviet Union. It was a significant and sometimes determining factor in Cold War decision-making.

They saw Khrushchev's effort to install the MRBMs and IRBMs in Cuba as a vivid illustration of the point. With the missiles there, the Soviet Union doubled the number of nuclear warheads it could fire against U.S. targets and made the centerpiece of U.S. strategic power—the Strategic Air Command's bomber force and bases—dramatically more vulnerable at the outset of war.[51] Such a shift in the apparent balance of power, they feared, could have a profound effect on U.S. resolve in a crisis.

These differing views about the significance of numbers of strategic nuclear weapons in determining relative advantage in East-West confrontations shaped more than just the tense debates of October 1962 in Washington. In many respects, the discussions in the ExComm reflected emerging public and private arguments that continued for nearly thirty years about the conduct of the Cold War. Did numerical strategic nuclear superiority mean anything? In building strategic nuclear forces, how much was enough?

More than any other episode in the "long, twilight struggle" against tyranny, poverty, disease and war that John Kennedy heralded in his inaugural address, the Cuban Missile Crisis focused the minds of U.S. policymakers on war, on the meaning of nuclear weapons and on the threat of nuclear annihilation. Facing this last danger firsthand, President Kennedy and his advisors were determined to resolve the crisis without force if at all possible. They did so, but they believed that in the process they had come far too close to the brink of nuclear war.

PART III

Afterwords

Thirty Years Later

by General Anatoli I. Gribkov

From March 1963 until mid-1991, my career in the Soviet armed forces took me away from Cuban affairs. I kept warm memories of my time on the island and of the civilian and military leaders who had been my hosts and comrades, but I followed events in the Caribbean only at a distance. The developments were sometimes worrisome.

Especially in the first few years after the crisis, foreign counterrevolutionaries tried hard to destabilize Castro's government, staging sixteen major attacks against industrial and administrative buildings on Cuba in 1963 alone. A scheme in 1964 reportedly involved a planned invasion by 10,000 troops massed in Nicaragua, Guatemala and Honduras with extensive air and naval support, but the plot was exposed in time. On the island, Cuban state security agencies have arrested hundreds of saboteurs over the years and frustrated many dangerous plots against the regime.

The continuous activity of the enemies of the Cuban revolution has forced both constant vigilance and a high degree of combat readiness to which the Soviet Union contributed for many years through both military training and supplies. Additionally, as a result of an unpublicized agreement, negotiated at Cuban insistence and signed in Moscow on 29 May 1963, a Soviet motorized rifle brigade was stationed on Cuba for thirty years as a sign of solidarity and a shield against aggression.

Although its purpose was more symbolic than military, the brigade became an issue in U.S.-Soviet relations. In fall 1979, under pressure from Washington and without advising Havana, the Brezhnev government renamed the unit a training center instead of a combat force. Again bowing to U.S. demands, Mikhail

Gorbachev unilaterally decided in 1990 to bring the brigade home. I was aware of these decisions but not a participant in them. They did stir feelings of indignation in me, however. Brezhnev and Gorbachev made decisions concerning Cuba without even informing the Cuban leadership, just as Khrushchev had done in 1962.

An invitation from the Cuban government to visit Havana in January 1992 helped to reawaken my interest in the past. I was asked to join a nine-member delegation from Moscow to take part in a conference of U.S., Soviet and Cuban crisis participants. For the first time, the conference would include Soviet military officers who had direct knowledge of Operation ANADYR: myself, Lt. Gen. Georgi Titov, who had headed the Group of Forces' Operations Directorate under Pliyev, and First Captain Igor Amosou, a former Soviet military attache in Havana. Oleg Troyanovsky, a senior diplomat who had been a junior foreign policy advisor to Khrushchev in 1962, headed the Soviet delegation to the three-day meeting. Among its other members were Aleksandr Alekseyev, Soviet ambassador in Havana during the crisis; Oleg Darusenkov, who had been Alekseyev's aide and later our ambassador to Mexico; Felix Kovalyov, also from the Foreign Ministry; and Sergei Khrushchev and Sergo Mikoyan, sons of Nikita Khrushchev and Anastas Mikoyan.

Our delegation did not meet as a group until we all reached Havana, to which my military colleagues and I flew only after I had pulled enough strings in Moscow to enable the General Staff to cover our airfare. Just as impecunious as thirty years before, the military representatives were each given a hard-currency allowance of five dollars a day to cover our expenses in Cuba, but the hospitality shown to us there by Raul Castro and other Cuban comrades made us feel welcome. Like his older brother Fidel, whose beard has gone gray, Raul remained as agile as ever, his tongue as witty as I remembered it. As for Fidel, who took a very active part in the meeting, his eyes were as youthful as in 1962, but their gaze was more intense. His expression and smile have remained kind and charming, and his step was quick and sure.

It was a great pleasure to renew acquaintance with these Cuban leaders and interesting to meet Americans like Robert McNamara, Arthur Schlesinger, Jr., Ray Cline of the CIA and Gen. William Y. Smith, who had played important roles in the crisis. The former Secretary of Defense impressed me as a logical thinker with an analytical mind. He was quick to react to the speeches of others and tactful in leading debates on a given issue. His speaking manner was simple, his dress was modest and the respect shown him by the other Americans was notable.

It was also reassuring to see that Havana, unlike Moscow, was a clean, well-kept, unpolluted city. Its people appeared to be bearing up well under difficult economic conditions. Cuba's leaders, Fidel in particular, also continued to show respect and gratitude to the Soviet military men who had stood alongside them, their people and their Revolutionary Armed Forces to defend the island's freedom and independence.

Unintended Sensation

Unlike the U.S. delegation, ours was ill-prepared for the conference. We had not consulted with one another beforehand about the content or order of our remarks, and, except for a solid speech by Oleg Darusenkov analyzing U.S. intentions toward Cuba and the international setting in October 1962, not a single member of our group said anything substantive. Sergo Mikoyan and Sergei Khrushchev, for example, mostly reminisced about their fathers. Troyanovsky, who made brief remarks at the opening session, asked me to make the first detailed presentation for our group.

After most of the journalists had left the meeting room, I took the floor. I thanked the Cuban leaders for their invitation, the hospitality they had shown us and for providing excellent conference arrangements. I introduced myself, described the part I had played in the events thirty years earlier and told the story of the work of the General Staff, specifically the Operations Directorate, which I headed at the time, in deploying Soviet troops and missiles to defend Cuba against possible U.S. attack.

I described the crisis as a clash of two great powers. On the one hand, the United States could not reconcile itself to the emergence so close to the American continent of a government which had chosen the socialist path of development. The Western press called Cuba a "Communist infestation." On the other hand, in a display of Communist solidarity, the Soviet Union wanted to help Cuba reinforce its socialist achievements and to protect the young state from possible U.S. hostilities.

I sensed that everyone was listening to my speech very intently. Since there was simultaneous interpretation into English and Spanish, I tried to talk slowly, but I noticed that McNamara seemed to be having trouble with the translation coming through his headset when I mentioned the "Luna" missiles and Pliyev's authority over them.

My disclosure that battlefield nuclear weapons had been part of the Soviet arsenal on Cuba in October 1962 caused a sensation among the conference participants and, later, in the Western press. I had no intention, however, of doing anything beyond filling in the historical record, and unfortunately, I did not get that record exactly right.

Although I had studied some documents in defense ministry archives in Moscow in preparation for the memoirs I was then writing, I did not remember every detail correctly. As a result, I accidentally spoke in Havana about six "Luna" launchers and nine missiles with nuclear warheads, when the actual number of warheads was twelve. Because I was not certain about what information was still to be kept secret, I did not mention the eighty small cruise missiles or the six atomic bombs for the Il-28s. Having no authority to breach the secrecy of coded telegrams, I also did not reveal Malinovsky's orders of 22 and 27 October that barred Pliyev from using any nuclear weapons without prior authorization.

My main goal was to convince the other participants, as I was and am convinced, that the purpose of Operation ANADYR was defensive. That was the gist of the specific articles I cited from the August 1962 Cuban-Soviet agreement, provisions that referred to the urgent necessity of taking measures to ensure mutual security against possible aggression against the Cuban Republic and the Soviet Union. As further proof, I described the way our forces had been based in Cuba, the emphasis in their deployment on defense against attack and the total absence of any Soviet intention to start a war.

The "Luna" missiles, with a range of only twenty-five miles, were no threat to the United States. Battlefield weapons only, they and the other tactical nuclear systems were installed to repel a direct landing of the enemy on the coast of Cuba. Conference participants were surprised to learn that the low-yield, short-range "Lunas" had been on Cuba when President Kennedy and his advisors were considering an attack on the island, but the truth is that any strike by U.S. forces against Cuba and its Soviet defenders would have heightened the risk of nuclear war, no matter whether the first response was with conventional or battlefield nuclear arms. That was the terrible danger that both John Kennedy and Nikita Khrushchev wisely recognized and acted to contain in 1962.

After my formal speech, I also requested that the American delegation describe Operation MONGOOSE, which had been directed against Cuba. We had known about it and about other activities that made the likelihood of an invasion of Cuba seem very real to Khrushchev and others in 1962. I wanted to hear directly from the high-ranking Americans at the conference about the threat to Cuba to which the Soviet Union had responded, but the answers that were given thirty years after the fact did not seem to me to be completely convincing. I believe the danger was real, and some response to it by the Soviet Union in the interests of socialism on Cuba was justified.

When Fidel Castro spoke to the conference with his customary vigor, I listened carefully and admired his courage. It grieves me that in comparison to the 1970s and 1980s, the Soviet Union, among other countries, has distanced itself so much from Cuba and its leadership. Moved by that feeling, I asked for the floor at the end of the meeting and proposed that the participants issue a written appeal to the leaders of the United States and Cuba to start negotiations on all controversial issues so as to bring an end to the Cold War in the Caribbean. It was time, I said, to give the Cuban and American peoples the opportunity to live in friendship, respecting each other's sovereignty.

To my great regret, however, the U.S. delegation did not accept my proposal, saying that their group was unofficial and nongovernmental. I replied that our delegation was also not governmental, but we were prepared to sign such an appeal. No one would reproach us for doing so. At a closing press conference, I raised the issue again, but only the Cubans supported me. Nonetheless, I think the time propitious to eliminate the U.S. Marine base in Guantánamo, its permanent garrison and the naval forces stationed there. The base is a destabilizing political and military factor in the Caribbean, and it should be closed.

Conclusions

From the many speeches of the American delegation and from conversations during the breaks, I came to understand that the United States is unlikely to use military force against Cuba. In that respect, Operation ANADYR achieved its goal; it made the Island of Freedom safe from overt attack. Although a harsh economic blockade and subversion both continue, Cuba has been able to preserve its freedom.

But to accomplish that end, was it necessary to put Soviet missiles on Cuba? Many Western authors and even some in my country have examined this question in terms of the 1962 balance of U.S. and Soviet missile forces capable of reaching one country or the other. Although Khrushchev worried a great deal that the ratio of strategic weapons—300 on the Soviet side to 5,000 in the U.S. arsenal—was heavily against the Soviet Union in 1962, the permanent stationing of 60 medium- and intermediate-range missiles in Cuba would have done almost nothing to change matters. If he wished to use the missile deployment to improve the correlation of strategic delivery systems, that aim was secondary to his main purpose: to help the young Cuban Republic defend the freedom it had won, to deter the U.S. aggression actively being planned against it.

It has also been argued that by installing Soviet missiles on Cuba, Khrushchev sought to answer the deployment of similar U.S. weapons in Turkey and other countries close to the USSR. We had every right to worry about the meaning of those missiles and the danger they posed to Soviet security, but Khrushchev did not raise the question of the missiles in Turkey with Kennedy until the very end of the crisis. They were far from being Khrushchev's first concern in deciding either to deploy our missiles or to withdraw them.

Because Khrushchev's initiative greatly increased the threat of nuclear disaster, I am profoundly convinced that the missiles should not have been brought to Cuba. The risk could have been avoided. Soviet, U.S. and Cuban leaders should have sat down at the negotiating table with the Secretary General of the United Nations to find an agreement that would leave Cuba in peace.

The secrecy that surrounded Operation ANADYR also contributed to the intensity of the crisis. Americans were understandably frightened by the sudden and covert appearance of missiles stationed so close to the United States that, despite their limited range, they took on strategic importance. Compounding the alarm was the fact that Soviet diplomats, when asked about the presence of Soviet missiles in Cuba, denied the truth up until the last minute.

Our ambassadors to the United States and the United Nations did not know the secret, but Khrushchev did, and he deliberately concealed it. His active disinformation campaign made Kennedy and his advisors suspect that the Soviet Union was preparing a sudden missile attack against the United States. That fear was misplaced, and a more open Soviet diplomatic and political course of action could have prevented it.

As the person who executed the main planning documents of Operation ANADYR, I assimilated one point very firmly: the missiles were deployed for the purpose of deterring U.S. aggression against Cuba. Khrushchev reiterated this message a number of times. He emphasized that the Soviet Union would never be an aggressor and would never be the first to use nuclear weapons. His statements became doctrine for our political, military, diplomatic and ideological officials.

Because of the secrecy of the missile deployment, however, Westerners doubted Khrushchev's sincerity. The 1962 crisis, with all its unpredictability, could have been avoided—or at least made less acute—if he had acted straightforwardly. Under public treaties and agreements with the Cuban government, the Soviet Union could have gradually and openly transferred weapons, hardware and military units. The United States would certainly have resisted those deployments fiercely, but the struggle would been a diplomatic and political one, not a military confrontation carrying the risk of nuclear war.

How great was the actual risk? Even thirty years later, I do not think it can be measured exactly. What is certain is that any battle for Cuba would have been long and bloody. The island's population in 1962 numbered over eight million. About 200,000 mobilized and highly motivated soldiers in the Cuban Army had modern weapons to resist any aggressor. In addition to the regular forces and the 40,000 well-armed Soviet soldiers who were ready to fight side by side with their Cuban comrades, ordinary Cubans would have risen up in great numbers to defend their island and their independence. At the Havana conference, a U.S. expert [Raymond Garthoff, a former State Department expert on Soviet affairs] disclosed estimates that even after prolonged air and sea bombardments, U.S.

invasion forces would have suffered as many as 18,500 casualties during the first ten days of combat.

Thus, President Kennedy's decision to refrain from aggression against Cuba was a wise one even though such an attack would probably not have been answered by a nuclear strike. Of the thirty-six medium-range missiles on Cuba, only half were ready to be fueled and mated with their warheads by 28 October. Not one had been programmed for flight. And at no time did the political or military leadership of the Soviet Union have any intention to permit an attack on the United States. That would have unleashed world-wide nuclear war and been tantamount to suicide.

Although the risk of global war is still difficult to define precisely, it is easier to pinpoint some of the military achievements and political faults of Operation ANADYR. In the first category, the performance of the Soviet Armed Forces was exemplary.

For the first time in its history, the Soviet Union transported an army of more than 40,000 with a large amount of weaponry and equipment across the ocean. All the tasks were completed on schedule, without any disruptions or emergencies. Our military personnel, from soldiers to generals, accomplished every assignment demanded of them. This was made possible by the thoroughly conceived and planned operation and also by the (mainly) successful camouflaging, counterintelligence and disinformation measures and other covert actions. The Soviet Group of Forces on Cuba was assembled literally under the nose of American intelligence.

On the other hand, I believe it was a major political mistake not to have Castro, as head of a sovereign state, take part in the negotiations between Khrushchev and Kennedy. That treatment greatly undermined the authority of the Cuban leadership. If from the very beginning Castro had joined the negotiations as a full-fledged third party, efforts to settle the conflict and remove the nuclear weapons would not have been so strained and at times humiliating for us.

That point has a broader application thirty years later. As a matter of principle and as the foundation for international order, the sovereign and human rights of small countries as well as large ones, of states that are close neighbors and of nations separated by great distances, must be fully respected. The peoples of the world have tired of hot and cold wars. They expect their government leaders to act firmly to guarantee the preservation of peace on the small planet we all have in common. I believe that my children, grandchildren and great-grandchildren will not have to suffer what my generation endured.

Looking Back

by General William Y. Smith

Until this point, I have based my analysis of Kennedy Administration decision-making during the 1962 crisis on what the United States knew at the time about Soviet and Cuban intentions, plans and actions. That body of knowledge has since been greatly expanded, in large measure as a result of a series of conferences held by participants in the crisis from the three countries. Observers now have a much-improved understanding of what each of the parties say they saw and thought at the time. To preface some concluding observations about the crisis and some of the misperceptions involved in it, it is useful to compare what we know about official U.S., Soviet and Cuban attitudes and perceptions at the time of the crisis on a variety of relevant points.

In estimating the likelihood of a U.S. attack on Cuba, for example, Moscow and Havana believed, from shortly after the failure of the Bay of Pigs invasion in 1961, that the United States intended to invade Cuba at some opportune time. To be sure, the Kennedy Administration felt frustrated by Castro and fervently wanted to see him removed from power. To this end in early 1962, it instituted a large-scale covert program, Operation MONGOOSE.

Despite a strong desire to see Castro overthrown and an inclination to act in pursuit of that goal, the Special Group (Augmented) that closely supervised Operation MONGOOSE never allowed consideration of the use of U.S. military force to proceed beyond the planning stage. On several occasions, moreover, it backed away from making a firm commitment to use military force in Cuba.

In preparing to defend Cuba, Soviets and Cubans mounted a loosely coordinated counter-invasion plan that was to rely heavily on mobilizing the Cuban population in defense of the island. U.S. plans called for a series of large air strikes to destroy the missiles and other Soviet and Cuban conventional and nuclear offensive and defensive military forces in Cuba and, if necessary, a follow-on invasion by Army and Marine troops.

Although not one nuclear weapon was seen on Cuba, the United States assumed that the Soviets had, or would have, such armament for their missiles once the latter reached a stage of operational readiness. Apparently that judgment was accurate. Russian delegates at the various conferences have stated that warheads were present for the thirty-six medium-range missiles that reached Cuba before the quarantine was imposed. On the issue of Soviet tactical nuclear weapons, the U.S. Joint Chiefs of Staff assumed that warheads for FROG ("Luna") rockets might be available and adopted contingency plans to respond to what they saw as the unlikely possibility that the Soviets would use such nuclear arms. The Chiefs did not know that the tactical nuclear arsenal on Cuba totalled ninety-eight weapons, as General Gribkov has stated.

Both sides knew that Soviet nuclear weapons had no locks or other impediments on them to prevent their use if authority to fire them was not granted from Moscow. U.S. planners did not, however, know—as General Gribkov has discussed—that in the early stages of the deployment, the Soviet field commander in Cuba had authority to use tactical nuclear weapons without recourse to Moscow if an extreme situation demanded. At the start of the October crisis, this latitude was revoked.

A final issue of importance was the connection, if any, between Soviet actions in the Caribbean and its aims in Europe. The United States saw the Berlin crisis and the Cuban crisis as two sides of the same coin; it expected a strong Soviet reaction in Berlin to any U.S. military action in Cuba. For their part, Soviet officials have stated that they viewed Cuba and Berlin as two separate and distinct issues with no close link between them.

The Cuban crisis underscored a number of significant lessons. Among the most important is that governments should closely examine the way their opponents may or do perceive their actions. The United States did badly on that count before the Cuban missile crisis. U. S. military exercises, covert actions, public statements—all had overtones of U.S. planning for an invasion of Cuba and the overthrow of Castro. In reality, top Kennedy Administration officials had no intent to invade, although some military and civilian officials expected that such harassment of Castro would compel him to think his hold on power was shaky. The hope was to force him to focus his attention on retaining power at home rather than subverting order in other Caribbean and Latin America countries.

The Cubans and the Soviets apparently saw U.S. actions far differently. They perceived U.S. conduct, both rhetorical and military, as visible evidence of serious preparation for an invasion. Those U.S. covert actions of which Moscow and Havana were aware fed those suspicions.

In connection with Europe, the Soviet Union misled the United States. Moscow undertook the missile deployment to Cuba when the United States felt seriously threatened by Soviet pressures on West Berlin, the symbol of U.S. strength in West Europe, the centerpiece of allied cohesion and the linchpin of West German participation in NATO. Khrushchev kept the pot boiling in Berlin throughout 1962, and although he stated that he would do nothing until after that year's congressional elections, he made clear his intentions to press hard on the city's status. In light of Khrushchev's focus on Berlin matters, the United States—until the missiles were discovered—viewed the Soviet build-up in Cuba that summer as a means of putting additional pressure on Berlin. Just how the pressure might be applied was not clear to officials who discussed the issue several times in August, but some feared Soviet moves that would perhaps irrevocably damage U.S. and allied vital interests in Europe.

The Soviets have said, however, that Berlin played no meaningful role in their assistance to Castro. Their objective was to improve their relative strategic nuclear power position and insure the survival of Castro.

Another important lesson from the crisis is that it demonstrates that the close relationship between domestic and foreign policies is a universal condition. Domestic considerations limited both Kennedy's and Khrushchev's freedom of action. Republican party leaders criticizing Kennedy for his "look-the-other-way" Cuba policy wanted to make Cuba a dominant issue in the fall congressional campaign. They nearly succeeded. Khrushchev's military reductions, his failing agricultural policies and the overall weakness in Soviet economic productivity caused him problems at home. Domestic pressures that required both leaders to handle the crisis with great circumspection made it more difficult for the two to find a satisfactory solution.

Calculating Nuclear Risks

By far the most important element of the crisis was the danger of its leading to the use of nuclear weapons by the world's two major powers. The Soviets have insisted in conferences that they never intended to go to war over Cuba. Gromyko in Moscow in 1989 baldly asserted that war was not imminent at any juncture during the crisis. When challenged by McNamara, Gromyko backed away from this blanket statement somewhat, but he consistently maintained that the Soviets intended no hostilities.[1] Georgi Kornienko, a former official in the Soviet embassy in Washington, has also reported that the Kremlin decision to remove the missiles was made on the night of 24/25 October. If correct, that claim would support Gromyko and help explain Khrushchev's rejection of Castro's 26 October call for direct Soviet military action to head off the invasion Castro feared was soon to occur. The recent reports, including those of General Gribkov, that Khrushchev withdrew authority to use tactical nuclear weapons in defense of Cuba further indicate Soviet reluctance to risk escalation. It appears that the Joint Chiefs of Staff and the CIA were correct in believing that the Soviets would not go to general nuclear war over Cuba.

Lending credence to that view is the fact that nothing that has been made public to date indicates that the Soviets and Cubans had sophisticated or well-coordinated plans for the defense of the island. Apparently, they planned to divide the island into sectors and allocate responsibilities accordingly. There is no evidence of a unified command structure, of detailed joint planning, of common logistics or, most importantly, of common command/control and communications structures. They did not even speak the same language. Under such circumstances, soldiers defending against well-planned U.S. landings, especially after days of air strikes, would have faced a daunting task, no matter how strongly they were motivated. The status of Soviet/Cuban planning shows that their forces were neither trained nor positioned as if they were in the early stages of a conflict that could lead to global war.

On the U.S. side, the invasion plans developed during 1962 did not contemplate the use of nuclear weapons. Since U.S. forces had the preponderance of conventional military power, atomic arms were not considered necessary. Once Soviet nuclear-capable FROG weapons were spotted on the island, U.S. plans were modified so that tactical or battlefield nuclear warheads in storage in the United States or afloat at sea could be released to U.S. forces if the Soviets used nuclear weapons and the President decided to respond in kind against airfields on Cuba and concentrations of military forces in the field.

The basic premise guiding U.S. military planning, however, remained the Joint Chiefs' advice to the President that only conventional arms would be used or needed in any clash on Cuba that pitted U.S. forces against the estimated 7,000 to 9,000 Soviet military personnel there. In the minds of those few U.S. analysts who gave the issue much thought, it surely seemed that the safety and survival of such a small Soviet force would not justify employing tactical nuclear weapons and running the accompanying risks of rapid nuclear escalation. At the very senior levels of the Administration, the possibility did not seem a real one. The question never arose, for instance, during the crucial 27 October ExComm discussions on how to respond to Khrushchev's contrasting messages.

The outcome of the crisis underscores that neither the Soviet Union nor the United States wanted war. Also, evidence to date indicates that neither side planned to use nuclear weapons if war came. Nonetheless, the question remains as to what might have happened if the United States had invaded Cuba in late

October 1962. Many would argue that such speculation serves no useful purpose. There is something to be said for that view, but the center of attention here is an historic event in which the leaders of the world's two major powers might have been faced with the most formidable decision of their lives. It therefore seems appropriate to pursue some of the "what if" possibilities a few steps down the path of logic.

With Soviet nuclear weapons on the island and no physical way for Moscow to prevent their being fired, the risks of nuclear escalation in defense of the island were not merely theoretical. The U.S. intent was to minimize those risks by destroying all Soviet nuclear-capable weapons in the early stages of a series of U.S. air strikes at the opening of hostilities. But no plan can be expected to be executed without flaw. Some weapons might have survived.

In this situation, three possibilities would arise. The first is that the Soviets would have decided that Cuba's fate was not worth a major war with the United States. They would have cut their losses and run. In this event, without using nuclear weapons, the United States would have invaded and captured Cuba notwithstanding fierce Soviet and Cuban determination to defend the island with conventional means and guerrilla tactics. The Soviets nevertheless would have been defeated in the field by U.S. forces, and the history of the Soviet Union, Cuba and the United States would have been greatly changed—whether for better or worse is beyond the scope of prudent speculation.

A second possibility is that one or more Soviet tactical nuclear weapons would have survived the air attacks. Moscow's withdrawal of sanction from the field commanders to use the weapons without explicit higher-level authority testifies to the considerable hesitation it had about how far it was willing to go in defending the island. If Gromyko is to be believed and there was no real danger of war, then Moscow would not have authorized use of any surviving nuclear weapons. But, suppose Moscow saw the situation changing to its great disadvantage, reassessed the global consequences, authorized use of tactical nuclear weapons and actually fired them. The United States would then have faced several alternatives. First, it could have decided that the damage inflicted was acceptable, that the likelihood of further successful attacks was small or nil because of the U.S. conventional armed response against the Soviet weapons that launched the initial attack, that U.S. forces were succeeding in their mission and that current operations should continue with conventional operations rather than risk unnecessary further escalation.

A second alternative would have been for the United States to use the attack as an excuse for a local escalation to end the operations in Cuba quickly. There probably would have been pressure for this course, probably from congressional critics of the Administration, and conceivably from the Joint Chiefs of Staff who were confident of U.S. nuclear capabilities. In this case the United States would have launched a punishing nuclear counterattack against Soviet and Cuban military targets in Cuba. This vigorous response might have led to a Soviet and Cuban capitulation or, conceivably, to escalation to a global nuclear war.

Experts like the late Llewellyn Thompson and Charles E. Bohlen believed that the overarching concern of Khrushchev and his fellow Politburo members was to remain in power and keep the Soviet Union intact. If such judgments proved correct, Khrushchev would have capitulated in order to bring the issue to a close without risking general nuclear war and the devastation of the Soviet Union. But one can by no means be certain; the risks of escalation in this situation would have been very real.

In a nuclear conflict limited to Cuba, in any case, the United States would almost certainly have been victorious, but at a very high cost in lives and property. Again, history would have been far different and far more dangerous. Nuclear weapons, having once been used in combat between the world's two major powers, might have proved easier to use again.

There was a third way the United States might have responded to an intentional Soviet first use of nuclear weapons. The President and his closest advisors had shown their deep and abiding concern about the dangers of any use of nuclear weapons—dangers for the world at large as well as for the Soviet Union and the United States. This very deep worry seemed to guide the recommendations of the President's closest advisors—Bundy, McNamara, Sorensen—and even the President himself.

It is therefore entirely possible that Soviet use of nuclear weapons on Cuba would have impelled the United States to seek alternatives other than further use of military force. The President might have sought a quick negotiated solution to the crisis. As a first step, for example, he could have called for an immediate ceasefire and standdown of the military forces on both sides, leaving open the question of whether Soviet missiles would be stationed in Cuba in the future, an issue to be settled through talks, not combat.

The Soviets might have been willing to accept such an offer. By that point, the series of massive U.S. air strikes would have severely hurt Soviet forces in Cuba. Moscow might well have decided that defending the island was a hopeless long-term task that was bringing the Soviet Union desperately close to grave nuclear risk. If the missile deployment were to have remained an open question, the Soviets would have scored a significant, if temporary, gain, and Khrushchev might have been tempted to seize it.

An even more attractive alternative was at hand for the President to consider. He could have informed Khrushchev that he accepted the terms of his second late-October message, the one received on the morning of 27 October. By choosing this course of action, the United States would have signified its willingness to agree not to invade Cuba and to remove its Jupiters from Turkey in exchange for removal of offensive weapons from Cuba.

Several considerations give this alternative the ring of a serious possibility. The President had made it clear in his discussions in the ExComm that he did not intend to go to war over the missiles in Turkey. Indeed, we now know that he had secret plans to have U Thant publicly intervene to suggest such a trade if all else failed. Further, some of the President's most trusted advisors, such as McNamara, have said that in no foreseeable circumstance would they have recommended use of force to settle the crisis. Rather than invade, McNamara has said, he would have recommended strengthening the quarantine or some other political action.[2]

For Khrushchev's part, he should have found acceptance of his terms fully satisfactory. To avoid further endangering the world, he might have said that both sides had gained something and given something. World history would be changed, but much less drastically than under the other two scenarios.

A number of alternative courses of action would have presented themselves in the unlikely event the Soviets had authorized the use of tactical nuclear weapons. What about *unauthorized* use of a nuclear weapon by one or more Soviet military personnel, men who were deeply dedicated to the defense of the island? Every military commander knows that he is entitled to use all feasible authorized weapons to insure survival of his unit. With Soviet field commanders normally having some latitude in making decisions on the use of tactical nuclear weapons, it cannot be ruled out that, if some tactical nuclear weapons survived the U.S. air strikes, a field commander could have decided to fire one or more—even without Moscow's approval—in the hope of repelling a U.S. invasion force.

What might have been the course of history if such a decision had been carried out? Since the weapon(s) would have been fired without Moscow's approval, Khrushchev most probably would have wanted to communicate that fact to President Kennedy as rapidly as possible. And he probably would want to initiate immediate actions that would prevent the United States from responding with nuclear weapons and thus raising the specter of global nuclear war.

Under this scenario Khrushchev would not have yet have replied to the President's 28 October message accepting the offer to remove the missiles from Cuba in exchange for a no-invasion pledge. Faced with a new and unwanted situation, Khrushchev might have decided that his best alternative was to accept the President's terms, no matter how unattractive they had first appeared. The crisis would have ended, with only the Soviets having used nuclear weapons, with the missiles being removed from Cuba and with no mention of the Jupiters in Turkey. Again, the course of world events would have been different.

Whether any of the above hypotheses—or some other—would have corresponded to the actual events had the United States decided to invade Cuba cannot be known. For that, we can be eternally grateful. One thing, however, is abundantly clear. President Kennedy and Premier Khrushchev made the wise, prudent and mutually satisfactory decision to end the crisis when they did. The two major world powers had been to the brink of nuclear war, looked over the precipice and decided that they must back away.

Early in the crisis, President Kennedy decided that his objective was to have the missiles removed from Cuba; he would deal with Castro separately. He never lost sight of that objective and kept his actions and decisions centered on it. The outcome thus was a success in his terms.

One final comment is required. Like the crisis itself, the hypothesizing about alternative outcomes graphically highlights a point Secretary McNamara has made: the major lesson of the Cuban Missile Crisis is not how to manage crises, but how to avoid them. October 1962 underscored that maxim in indelible terms.

Documents from Russian Archives

The documents reproduced on the following pages include four in the original Russian and three in translation. All were received by Gen. Anatoli I. Gribkov from the archives of the Russian (formerly Soviet) Ministry of Defense.

Of the Russian documents, the first two are the texts of top-secret telegrams sent from Moscow to Havana, from Defense Minister Malinovsky as "Director" to General Pliyev as "Pavlov" on 22 and 27 October, respectively. Both messages, cited in translation in Chapters 1 and 5, reassert Moscow's control over decisions to fire any Soviet nuclear weapons stationed on Cuba.

Document 3 is the text—as retyped by General Gribkov—of an unsent draft telegram addressed "To the Commander of the Group of Soviet Forces on Cuba" and dated 8 September 1962. The translation of the telegram, dealing with the dispatch of tactical nuclear weapons to Cuba and with emergency authority to use them, appears in Chapter 1. The unsent telegram was signed by Marshal Matvei Zakharov, chief of the General Staff of the Soviet Armed Forces, but not by Defense Minister Rodion Malinovsky. The original, one-page document showed that Zakharov's signature was witnessed by Lt. Gen. Semyon P. Ivanov, and, as the Russian notation indicates, had the following handwritten text on the back: "Completed in one copy. Completed by Major General G. Yeliseyev 08.09.62. Lieutenant General of Aviation Davidkov was advised of its contents on 10.09.62."

The fourth Russian-language document is an order, dated 8 September 1962, signed by both Malinovsky and Zakharov and confirmed by Lt. Gen. N. Yegorov of the engineering-technical service, to the chief of the 12th Main Directorate of the

Ministry of Defense. Copied to the chief of the Main Operations Directorate of the General Staff, the document refers to "directive No. 75272 of 13 June 1962" and orders the dispatch of twelve "901 A4" nuclear warheads for "Luna" rockets and six "407 N" atomic bombs. The text was retyped by General Gribkov.

The English translations of the three other documents are self-explanatory, but the paragraphing of the transcript of the Mikoyan-Castro conversation of 12 November 1962 has been altered to make the text easier to read. The few words missing from that transcript were also missing from the photocopied Russian original.

Document 1

СОВЕРШЕННО СЕКРЕТНО

ТРОСТНИК –

товарищу ПАВЛОВУ

в связи с возможным десантированием на о. Куба аме-
риканцев проводящих учение в Карибском море, примите
немедленные меры к повышению боевой готовности и к
отражению противника совместными силами кубинской
армии и всеми силами советских войск, исключая средства
СТАЦЕНКО и всех грузов БЕЛОБОРОДОВА.

ДИРЕКТОР

№ 4/389
22 октября 1962 г.
    23.30

Document 2

СОВЕРШЕННО СЕКРЕТНО

ТРОСТНИК – товарищу ПАВЛОВУ

На № 8/154

Категорически подтверждается, что применять ядерное оружие из ракет, ФКР, Луна и с самолетов без санкции из Москвы запрещается.

Получение подтвердить.

ДИРЕКТОР

№ 76639
27 октября 1962 г.
   16.30

Document 3

КОМАНДУЮЩЕМУ ГРУППОЙ СОВЕТСКИХ ВОЙСК НА о.КУБА

В целях усиления Группы советских войск на о. Куба и увеличения возможности борьбы с десантами противника, Вам направляются дополнительные средства:

– эскадрилья самолетов–носителей ИЛ–28 (6 самолетов и 6 атомных бомб – 407 Н) с ПРТБ

– три дивизиона "Луна" (всего 6 пусковых установок, 12 ракет–носителей, 12 специальных головных частей и 24 ракеты в обычном снаряжении) с ПТРБ

В случае высадки десантов противника на о. Куба и сосредоточения вражеских кораблей с десантом у побережья Куба в ее территориальных водах, когда уничтожение противника ведет к затяжке и нет возможности получить указания Министра обороны СССР, Вам разрешается лично принять решение и применить ядерные средства "Луна", ИЛ–28 или ФКР–1, как средства локальной войны, для уничтожения противника на суше и у побережья с целью полного разгрома десантов на территории Кубы и защиты Кубинской Республики.

Министр оборны СССР
Маршал Советского Союза /Р. Малиновский/

П. П.Начальник Генерального штаба
Маршал Советского Союза /М. Захаров/

8 сентября 1962 г.

Завизировано
С. П. Иванов

(На обороте директивы, написанной от руки: исполнено в одном экз. исполнил генерал–майор Г. Елисеев 08.09.62 г. Ознакомлен генерал–лейтенант авиации Давидков 10.09.62 г.)

Document 4

НАЧАЛЬНИКУ 12 ГЛАВНОГО УПРАВЛЕНИЯ МИНИСТЕРСТВА ОБОРОНЫ

Копия: НАЧАЛЬНИКУ ГЛАВНОГО ОПЕРАТИВНОГО УПРАВЛЕНИЯ ГЕНЕРАЛЬНОГО ШТАБА

В дополение к директиве № 75272 -ов от 13 июня 1962 года отправьте:
- специальные боевые части 901 А4 к ракете "Луна" - 12 шт.
- специальные авиационные бомбы 407 Н - 6 шт.

П.П. Министр обороны Союза ССР
Маршал Советского Союза

Р. Малиновский

П.П. Начальник Генерального штаба
Маршал Советского Союза

М. Захаров

8 сентября 1962 года

Верно: генерал-лейтенант
инженерно-технической службн

Н. Егоров

28.9.62

Document 5

TREATY
Between the Government of the Republic of Cuba and the Government of the Union of the Soviet Socialist Republics on Military Cooperation for the Defense of the National Territory of Cuba in Case of Aggression

The Government of the Republic of Cuba and the Government of the Union of Soviet Socialist Republics,

Guided by the principles and purposes of the Charter of the Organization of United Nations,

Affirming their desire to live in peace with all other states and peoples,

Full of determination to make all possible efforts in order to foster support for and strengthen the cause of peace throughout the world,

Moved by a wish to establish and reinforce friendship, cooperation and mutual aid among all peoples on the basis of respect for sovereignty and the independence of states, and also non-interference in their internal affairs,

Faithful to the principles of the policy of friendship and solidarity among peoples, defending a common cause, the chief purpose of which is the peaceful coexistence among states with various social systems, the right to defense in the face of aggression, the right of each people to have the form of government that they consider suitable for their welfare and progress, the right to a peaceful life that cannot be violated from without and to recognize the historical prerogative of any nation, when it so desires, to break off ties that would entail any form of economic domination or exploitation,

Imbued with determination to take the necessary steps for the joint defense of the legitimate rights of the peoples of Cuba and the Soviet Union,

Keeping, moreover, in mind the urgent necessity of taking measures to secure mutual security in the face of possible aggression against the Republic of Cuba and the USSR,

Wishing to reach agreement on all matters concerning the support that the Soviet Armed Forces will provide in the cause of defense of the national territory of Cuba in the event of aggression,

It has been agreed to sign the following Treaty:

Article 1
The Soviet Union will send to the Republic of Cuba its Armed Forces for the purpose of strengthening its defense capability in the face of danger of external aggression, thus fostering the support of peace throughout the world.

The types of Soviet Armed Forces and the sites of their deployment on the territory of the Republic of Cuba will be determined by the Representatives appointed in accordance with Article 11 of this Treaty.

Article 2

In the event of aggression against the Republic of Cuba or the Soviet Armed Forces deployed on the territory of the Republic of Cuba, the Government of the Republic of Cuba and the Government of the Union of Soviet Socialist Republics, enjoying the right to individual or collective defense stipulated by Article 51 of the Charter of the Organization of United Nations, will undertake all necessary measures to repel aggression.

All information about any act of aggression and actions undertaken to implement this Article will be presented to the Security Council in accordance with the provisions of the Charter of the Organization of United Nations.

Such actions will be interdicted as soon as the Security Council takes the measures necessary to restore and maintain international peace and security.

Article 3

The Soviet Armed Forces deployed on the territory of the Republic of Cuba will completely respect its sovereignty.

All persons belonging to the Soviet Armed Forces, and the members of their families, will show the same respect for the laws of the Republic of Cuba.

Article 4

The Government of the Union of Soviet Socialist Republics in accordance with this Treaty will bear all expenses for the maintenance of the Soviet Armed Forces deployed on the territory of the Republic of Cuba.

Article 5

In order not to impair the supplies of the Cuban population, foodstuffs, various materials, vehicles, machinery and other property intended for the Soviet Armed Forces will be delivered from the USSR.

Such goods, equipment and war materials intended for the Soviet Armed Forces and also ships used for their delivery will have free access to the territory of Cuba.

Article 6

The Government of the Republic of Cuba takes upon itself before the Government of the USSR the obligation to provide the Soviet Armed Forces any help in their deployment, deliveries and provision of communications.

The transfer of the personnel of the Soviet Armed Forces, the use of electric power and communications and also communal and other services provided to the Soviet Armed Forces will be reimbursed by them on the basis of the corresponding charges made to the Armed Forces of the Republic of Cuba.

The sites of bases for the deployment of the Soviet Armed Forces will be provided by the Republic of Cuba without any form of payment. The re-equipping and repair of the buildings will be at the expense of the Soviet Armed Forces.

Article 7

The construction of buildings, airports, highways, bridges, permanent structures for radio communications and other structures will be performed in the areas assigned to the Soviet Armed Forces through the efforts and means of the Soviet Armed Forces based on preliminary agreement about such matters with the appropriate agencies of the Republic of Cuba.

Article 8

Military garrisons, airports and other installations, including permanent structures which the Soviet Armed Forces cease to use will be transferred to the Government of the Republic of Cuba without any compensation.

Article 9

Matters of jurisdiction connected with the presence of the Soviet Armed Forces on the territory of the Republic of Cuba will be regulated by separate agreements on the basis of the principles outlined in Article 3 of this Treaty.

Article 10

Both sides have determined that the Armed Forces of each government will be under the command of their respective Governments, which will jointly resolve the matter of the deployment of their respective Armed Forces to repel external aggression and restore peace.

Article 11

For the purposes of resolving ongoing issues connected with the presence of the Soviet Armed Forces on the territory of the Republic of Cuba, the Government of the Republic of Cuba and the Government of the USSR appoint their respective Representatives.

Article 12

This Treaty is subject to ratification by the respective Governments and will enter into force starting on the day that documents of ratification are exchanged, which will take place on _____.

Article 13

This Treaty is to be in force for five years. Each side may nullify the treaty after having so informed the other side within a year of the expiration date of the Treaty.

In the event that the five-year period of the Treaty expires, and neither side has announced its nullification, the Treaty will remain in effect for another five years.

Article 14

When the Treaty ceases to be in force, the Soviet Armed Forces will leave the territory of the Republic of Cuba.

The Soviet side is granted the right to withdraw from the territory of the Republic of Cuba its materials, ammunition, equipment, vehicles, machinery, all military technology and other property belonging to the Soviet Armed Forces.

The Government of the Republic of Cuba will provide any assistance in evacuating the Soviet Armed Forces and their property from the territory of the Republic of Cuba.

This Treaty was drafted _____ 1962 in two copies; one is in the Spanish language and the other is in the Russian language, and both copies have equal force.

In affirming the above, the Heads of Governments of both States have affixed their seals and signed this Treaty.

Prime Minister of the Republic of Cuba	Chairman of the Council of Ministers of the USSR
Fidel Castro Ruz	N.S. Khrushchev

Document 6

To Comrade N.S. Khrushchev

COMMITTEE ON STATE SECURITY
OF THE COUNCIL OF MINISTERS OF THE USSR

Copying is   Must be Returned to   TOP SECRET
Categorically   Central Committee CPSU   (when filled in)
Prohibited   General Department Sector

No. 3397 13/XI 1962

INCOMING CODED TELEGRAM NO. 32918

Copy No. 1 Com. Khrushchev	Copy No. 3 Com. Kozlov	Copy No. 5
Copy No. 2 Com. Khrushchev	Copy No. 4 Dept. 8	Copy No. 6
From Havana Received: 12:20 a.m. November 13, 1962 Copy 1		

[Vertical notation along edge of original]
Must be returned to Dept. 8 of the Chief Directorate of the KGB of the
USSR Council of Ministers no later than 10 days from receipt

[Left margin heading]
For Resolutions and Notes

Central Committee of the CPSU

A meeting took place with Fidel Castro, [and] I fulfilled your assignment
(Your no. 1013 about everything connected to the "Il-28"), marshalling in
this conversation almost all the argumentation in Comrade Khrushchev's
letter to me.

In the middle of the conversation, he became agitated and almost blew up,
saying that instead of putting forth arguments, it should be just said outright
what the Soviet government wanted. Without losing my calm, I laid out our
proposal and cited our arguments. Fidel spoke very little.

In another telegram, I will report in full on everything concerning his
reaction.

Toward the end of the conversation he gradually began to calm down and
stated that he understood our arguments, that he was forming an opinion (he
did not say what it was) and that he would discuss this with his comrades, and
then a meeting would take place with us.

[Page 2 Copy 1]
[Continuation of Incoming Coded Telegram No. 32918]

In order to understand Fidel's mood the following facts are characteristic:
He asked if I was going to the university, where I was invited this evening,
and I asked, "Is it necessary?"

He replied that it would be good and useful. He himself returned to [the
subject of] tomorrow's trip to the province, and I expressed the opinion that
it might be better to use that time for discussion. He began to insist on the
trip, saying that a discussion would take place either tomorrow evening, after
I return from the trip, or on Wednesday.

We parted on friendly terms, bid farewell warmly, in a fraternal manner.

No. 864
12. XI. 62   A. Mikoyan

Typed: 12:50 a.m. 13.XI.   Typed 4 Copies

Released by [signature illegible]

Document 7

To the Central Committee Department and the International Department of the Central Committee of the CPSU
> Copy
> Top Secret

Transcription of Conversation
Between A.I. Mikoyan and Fidel Castro
November 12, 1962
Ambassador A.I. Alekseyev attended the discussion.

Fidel Castro reported that he seldom took time off and that he had spent the last few days on a trip around experimental plots in the provinces. He reported that in one of the villages an interesting new strain of bean had been discovered, or actually four different types of beans that had very much interested him. Castro told Mikoyan that this bean, which had vines like grapes, was a perennial. The farmer who had raised the bean said that it would keep growing back for four or five years. I brought some of these beans home, Castro continued, and was convinced that they were excellent for cooking and tasted fine.

A.I. Mikoyan noted that he had never heard of such a thing as a perennial bean.

F. Castro said that he, too, had never heard of the perennial bean. But the farmers had convinced him. He added that from just a few bean plants, which grew like grapes on a common vine, 25 beans had been gathered on one farm. The farmers who were growing these strains of beans could feed their families virtually entirely from the crop.
Castro continued: What did our country use to produce? Essentially only sugar and tobacco. In my opinion, using this type of bean could solve our food problem. I should note that this bean even withstood an eight-month drought, when most plantings in our country failed.

A.I. Mikoyan: I would like to discuss with you, Comrade Fidel, one of the important issues. We are interested in the most rapid resolution of the existing conflict in favor of Cuba. Our country has fulfilled its obligations, although the Americans have not removed the quarantine. They fear complications, are looking for catches, and are trying to find reasons not to keep the promises Kennedy gave to N.S. Khrushchev.

If the Soviet Union withdraws offensive weapons, they promise to guarantee non-intervention from the U.S. and restrain their allies. Then the situation in the Caribbean will normalize. Kennedy is being criticized in the U.S. for promising to provide a guarantee not to invade Cuba. This is happening because advocates of war are growing more active in the U.S. A number of American figures are advocating the use of force to resolve the situation. They are unhappy with the fact that the problem is being resolved in a peaceful fashion.

In our opinion, Kennedy wants to use the economic blockade and the bony hand of hunger to strangle Cuba. Such attempts were used against our country in the past. Of course, you have read about the economic blockade staged against the young Soviet republic by the imperialists and what advantages our enemies hoped to gain by using hunger against Russia. By trying to create economic difficulties, the Americans are hoping to undermine Cuba from within. Kennedy said outright that he would create conditions to weaken Cuba economically. Then the Soviet Union will not have the strength to aid Cuba, and the Cuban government will fall.

The military circles of the U.S., on the other hand, disagree with Kennedy and favor using force to resolve the crisis in the Caribbean Sea.

Without military pressure or a military blockade, the trade embargo by the Western countries will not hinder Cuba's development. The Soviet Union will provide all possible aid to revolutionary Cuba, so that Cuba will become a real model, a vivid example for all of Latin America. This is quite realistic. We deeply believe in this and can provide all the necessary conditions for this.

Kennedy and a number of other American political figures believe that the Soviet Union has not completely fulfilled its obligations. We believed that the agreement only referred to missiles, [but] in the opinion of the U.S.A., there is also the question of the Il-28 bombers. Kennedy spoke about the bombers in his letter [to Khrushchev] of October 22. He also spoke about the bombers in his public speech.

They believe that we have not completely fulfilled our obligations, meaning the Il-28 bombers. On formal, legal grounds, they are stating that we have not fulfilled our obligations and, proceeding from that, believe they are in the right to refuse to keep their promises to remove the quarantine and provide guarantees [against invasion].

We are refusing to remove the Il-28 bombers from Cuba and we can go on refusing. We do not think that war will break out over that. Of course, knowing the nature of these mad men, no one can guarantee that they will not take the route of a military confrontation. But, since formally we have not met Kennedy's demand to withdraw the bombers from Cuba, the U.S. will maintain the blockade against Cuba, will continue the quarantine for an indefinite time, will refuse to fulfill its obligations concerning non-intervention, and will keep up the tension in the Caribbean Sea in order to launch an attack on Cuba at some other time. That is one prospect.

Another prospect is possible. We agree to withdraw the Il-28 bombers with personnel and equipment if the Americans provide complete guarantees and a promise not to invade Cuba, and completely remove the quarantine and liquidate the tension in the Caribbean Sea. Of course, people can say: what are the American guarantees worth? Of course, they cannot be completely trusted. Imperialism and socialism are implacable enemies.

However, we cannot entirely dismiss the promises given by representatives of bourgeois countries. There are certain international proprieties, legal norms, laws, international public opinion. All these factors will force the imperialists to keep their word. But if the objective conditions change, they can forget their word and change their position drastically.

We need high vigilance. Nevertheless we cannot completely nullify the possibility of an agreement, since such a rejection would amount to denying the fact of the coexistence of two opposing social systems. After all, in the Party Program passed at the XXII Congress of the CPSU and the Declaration of the Conference of Representatives of Communist and Workers' Parties in 1957 and the Statement of 81 Fraternal Parties at the Conference in 1960, the fact is clearly determined that not war, but peaceful coexistence of two systems will decide the matter in favor of socialism. That means that all these most important documents talk about the peaceful coexistence of two systems, of the preservation, as it is said in law, of the *modus vivendi.*

We believe that UN approval of the documents that contain statements in support of Cuba would be an important diplomatic factor. These documents would restrain the imperialists, would tie their hands and would not allow aggression to be unleashed.

Socialism and capitalism are approximately equal. We cannot destroy imperialism. They cannot destroy socialism. Thus only one path lies before us, and that is the path of peaceful coexistence. We see how quickly the socialist countries are growing and gaining strength. And the forces advocating socialism in the capitalist countries are also growing stronger. The liberation movement in the colonial countries is growing. The number of neutral countries is increasing.

The question arises: is war possible? Yes, it is possible, but there is no fatal inevitability of war. War can be averted. Can the UN prevent a world war? That is quite unlikely. However the UN is one of the instruments of peace. True, there was once the League of Nations. When the contradictions between socialism and capitalism worsened, the League collapsed. The UN may also collapse. However at the present time, the UN can and should be used, since there are many representatives of neutral countries there. True, the representatives of neutral countries often let us down in difficult moments but inside the UN the correlation of forces is changing in our favor.

We must fight for peaceful coexistence and in that struggle use the representatives of peaceful countries.

At this juncture, it seems to me that we must be free from the power of all, even the most noble feelings and push to the side psychological considerations that are usually very important, and after soberly and calmly thinking through everything, take the decision that will be to Cuba's advantage.

We must analyze the positive and negative aspects of both prospects that you and I are discussing. We must soberly evaluate the significance of the Il-28 bomber and understand what we are losing if we agree to the removal from Cuba of this weapon.

Morally, of course, it is a loss. After all, it's a new concession. It causes you pain and distress. However, these planes have almost no real military value for Cuba.

F. Castro: Why are these arguments being cited? You should say outright what the Soviet government wants.

A.I. Mikoyan: We brought 42 Il-28 bombers here. Only two of them are assembled, and the rest remain in their containers. This was a good bomber, but it has grown quite outmoded. Our industry has taken it out of production.

A.I. Alekseyev: It has been removed from our arsenal.

A.I. Mikoyan: We believe that although the Il-28 is capable of long-distance flight, it has no importance for Cuba since its altitude is only 12,000 meters. It can be shot down by any type of antiaircraft weaponry. These planes can be used only along Cuba's coast. The Americans themselves understand that this plane is outmoded.

Cuba has the MiG-21. This is a modern aircraft whose tactical and technological capabilities considerably exceed the combat ability of the outmoded Il-28 bomber. It is important to note that the MiG-21 can carry bombs and missiles, can bomb and strafe infantry, destroy land and air targets and disable a ship. Moreover, the MiG-21 is capable of engaging in and maintaining aerial battle. There are 40 such planes in Cuba now. They will remain here in any event.

Kennedy knows that these planes are in Cuba. But he is not saying anything about them. From the military point of view, the Il-28 no longer has any significance. In the near future, we were intending to increase in Cuba the number of MiG-21s, which are the most modern combat aircraft.

If we resolve the matter of removing the Il-28s from Cuba, we will thus disarm the U.S. of the formal argument that it is trying to exploit. Although the U.S. is saying that these bombers are no threat to the United States itself, they claim, however, that the Il-28 bombers are terrifying to Latin America, because countries there do not have strong antiaircraft artillery. Having resolved the matter of removing these bombers and their service personnel and equipment from Cuba, which the Americans are calling offensive, we are forcing the U.S. to fulfill its obligations and normalize the situation in the Caribbean Sea region.

It is said that appetite grows during the meal. Of course, it is essential to put an end to appetites that have grown out of hand. However, it is difficult to argue about the Il-28. After all, it is a bomber, although only in the formal sense.

With regard to other means, we will give the Americans a complete and decisive rebuff. If we remove the bombers from Cuba, then we will gain support from the UN. In that case it will be easier to accept U Thant's plan and normalize the situation. I have many other arguments; however, I will not cite them here, but note that I am speaking with you, Comrade Castro, on behalf of the Central Committee of the CPSU. As Marxist-Leninists, we must resolve the question in order to rid Cuba of the blockade and force the U.S. to maintain its obligations.

We cannot guarantee escort of our ships en route to Cuba since the U.S. possesses the advantage in this region. If the blockade is continued, our forces will be undermined, and the plans of the imperialists will be carried out. If the Il-28 bombers are withdrawn, Cuba will cease to be under threat.

We urge you, Comrade Fidel, to understand us correctly. I am not asking you to answer now. Think about it and discuss this very important issue. Perhaps you will decide to meet with your comrades. This matters deserves the most profound study.

We trust you completely. You understand, of course, that we are not pursuing any other interests except the defense of the Cuban Revolution and the entire revolutionary movement, from imperialist predators.

We are not pursuing any commercial or national interests in Cuba. We are guided exclusively by the interests of internationalism.

We understand you completely. We admire very much the great spirit of the Cuban people. In the first years of the existence of our country, as you know, we were in very difficult circumstances, when the imperialists wanted to use a blockade to destroy us. We very much understand the high political meaning of your slogan "Motherland or Death." In the years of the [Russian] civil war and of foreign intervention, we were also guided by such a slogan. We recall how, going to the front in order to defend Soviet power, our patriots, who were so like Cuban patriots, sang: "And as one, we will die for the power of the Soviets."

Our people displayed great fortitude. We encountered great difficulties but we overcame them and grew very strong. V.I. Lenin, who led our country in those years, knew how to maneuver. He believed that maneuvering and flexibility were necessary to preserve the conquests of the revolution. All of our great experience of struggle for victory and preservation of the revolution tells us that a decision to withdraw the bombers would be correct. We are talking to you, outlining our considerations as brothers and comrades, and telling you all this from purely [text missing].

We will be together with you, we will always go shoulder to shoulder with you in our common struggle. You know that we sent our people to Cuba so that we could be with you constantly during these difficult moments. We gave the order to General Pavlov to defend Cuba along with you. Our only interest in this is to defend Cuba, to preserve the Cuban Revolution.

Some people believe that you can fight the imperialists by denouncing them. However, no matter how sharp the denunciation, the imperialists do not weaken because of it. We had a Comintern [Communist International] radio station at one time in our country. It resolutely scolded the imperialists in broadcasts in various languages. But it could not provide practical help to our friends abroad.

We are providing Cuba with military, economic and diplomatic aid. We have sent our military specialists here. We have done all of this to preserve Cuba as a revolutionary beacon on the American continent. We are with you, Comrade Fidel, as brothers and friends. True, there can be differences even among brothers. However, you must understand the sincerity of our intentions.

F. Castro: I think that this is a question of the torpedo carriers at the base in San Gallein.

A.I. Mikoyan: The Il-28 planes really can carry torpedoes.

I want to emphasize once again that Cuba has the MiG-21s. As the Cuban personnel are trained, we will transfer these planes to you. They can wage aerial combat and be used to attack land targets and destroy the enemy's paratroopers and perform as dive bombers. As for the Il-28s, we would have turned them into scrap metal if the Berlin crisis had not broken out and if Kennedy had not called up 150,000 reserves into the army.

We are not saying that the MiG-21 exceeds the Il-28 in its offensive tactical and technical capabilities. [Text missing] the artillery of the U.S. would be able to shoot it down without much difficulty. However, we must keep in mind the opinion of the Latin American public. In the documents known to you, Kennedy called the bombers as well as the missiles "offensive weapons."

F. Castro, without listening to the explanations of Mikoyan, asked the question: Will they later raise the issue of inspection of Cuban territory as well?

A.I. Mikoyan continued. Kennedy says that if the bombers are not withdrawn from Cuba, no guarantee of non-intervention with regard to Cuba can be given. Although these bombers are not so terrible for the Americans, the Il-28 is called a bomber. It was a good combat plane in its day. But for the defense of the country, the Il-28 is not needed, and the United States is not intending to invade

Cuba. The MiG-21 fighters, as we have already said, are very powerful fighting machines, although their range is a little less than the Il-28. These fighters can be used to perform combat missions against land targets and against enemy ships at sea.

These airplanes are so new that we do not even have very many of them. They completely meet the requirements for Cuba's defense. The MiG-21s can stay on Cuba the same as all other combat weapons.

As for the possibility of the U.S. raising the issue of inspecting Cuban territory and overseeing the withdrawal of the Il-28s bombers, I would like to say the following. We could agree to such inspection of the ships carrying the missiles out of Cuba. Of course, the Americans would like to carry out inspections on Cuban territory, but we respect the Cuban position and will never permit a unilateral inspection of Cuban territory. We could agree to a visual check at sea of the removal of the bombers.

We possess precise information. Kennedy is maneuvering. If he achieves his demands then he will be forced to keep his promises as well and give a guarantee that neither the U.S. nor its allies will invade Cuba, and he will have to lift the blockade. If Kennedy's demand is not met, then the U.S. will maintain the blockade and continue it, accusing us of not keeping our promises. In that case even the U.N. will not support us.

It is our informed judgment that, given the availability of such modern fighters as the MiG-21, the Il-28 bomber has no important significance for the defense of Cuba. We propose to meet Kennedy's demands, as long as the Americans remove the blockade and provide firm guarantees not to invade Cuba. If, on the other hand, we leave the bombers in Cuba, then we are thereby giving the U.S. grounds to withdraw the promise of guarantees and grounds to maintain the blockade. That would be bad both for you and for us.

Think this matter over several times, Comrade Castro. Think calmly and make a decision. If we stubbornly refuse to withdraw the Il-28 from Cuba, then the negotiations will be at a stalemate. That will give the U.S. the opportunity to keep up the blockade and achieve a worsening of the economic situation in Cuba. In that case, the example of Cuba will no longer inspire the peoples. Consequently, you will also suffer moral losses. A guarantee not to invade Cuba must be extracted from the U.S., using the Soviet Union's support and that of other socialist countries. Then Cuba may develop its economy rapidly and that is important for Latin America and for the whole world.

Predators are predators, but for the sake of achieving a great purpose, one often has to maneuver. We, Comrade Fidel, will also act in the interests of revolutionary Cuba. This statement reflects the determination of the entire Central Committee of the CPSU. We believe that the path described is the best path for Cuba. The defense capabilities of Cuba are quite great. Cuba is in the right.

Achieving an agreement in the U.S. will undermine all attempts to stifle Cuba using military force.

F. Castro: What position will the Soviet Union take if, despite the withdrawal of the bombers, the U.S. insists on inspections and using the excuse that Cuba did not agree to an inspection, does not remove the blockade?

A.I. Mikoyan: We will withdraw the bombers in the event that the U.S. fulfills its obligations. We will keep the bombers in Cuba until we attain an agreement with the Americans and a removal of the blockade. The practical question of the inspection was covered during my conversation in New York with [John] McCloy. We will tirelessly defend your position.

The procedure which could be used to oversee the removal of the planes from Cuba, as we see it, could be the same one that was used during the withdrawal of the missiles. This could be done at sea in order not to infringe Cuba's interests. That is the revolutionary government's wish, and thus the inspection of Cuban territory will not even be raised at the present time.

F. Castro: I would like to note, Comrade Mikoyan, that we will never permit an inspection. I ask you to convey to the Soviet government that this is our final decision and cannot be reviewed.

A.I. Mikoyan: I already informed the Soviet government about the determination of the Cuban government not to allow an inspection of its territory. This issue is not being raised. By allowing a visual inspection of our ships, we proved that we are fulfilling our obligations. No matter how much the American government insists, we will not yield.

It can be considered, continued A.I. Mikoyan, that you and we have never had any disagreements on this matter. We respect your sovereignty. I will report the opinion you have expressed to our government.

F. Castro: I will be meeting now with the rest of the members of the leadership in order to discuss this question, although I do not see any special reason to hurry.

A.I. Mikoyan: I would like to add as well that the withdrawal of the missiles has deprived you only of offensive weaponry. The missiles were a means to deter the enemy. But Cuba does not intend to invade the U.S. Thus you do not need the Il-28 bombers. As is known, they cannot be a means of deterrence. All the other combat weapons are the most modern means to defend the country.

Of course if the U.S. were to attack you with all its might, then even all these powerful means would not be enough to defend you. But if the governments of the Latin American countries tried to commit aggression against Cuba without the direct intervention of the U.S., they will suffer a harsh defeat. Cuba's fire power is very strong.

I think, continued Comrade Mikoyan, that not a single other socialist country, if we leave out the Soviet Union, possesses such modern powerful combat weapons as you have.

F. Castro: I would like to meet with my comrades now. I will remember all your arguments. I am already forming an opinion on this matter.

A. I. Mikoyan: I am prepared to meet with you or with all the leaders of the revolutionary government together at any time in order to provide additional explanations if they are needed.

I can cite other arguments if today's arguments have seemed unconvincing.

I ask you to convey warm greetings to your comrades.

F. Castro: Thank you. Tell me, Comrade Mikoyan, are you going to Havana University tonight, where you have been invited?

A.I. Mikoyan: Should I?

F. Castro: Of course you should. That would be good and useful. Are you going to Turiguano tomorrow?

A.I. Mikoyan: Perhaps it is better not to go to Turiguano, but to use that time for discussion?

F. Castro: No. I think that the trip will be interesting. I would very much recommend that you go. We can arrange to talk tomorrow evening when you return from the trip, or on Wednesday.

A.I. Mikoyan: All right. Good-bye, Comrade Fidel.

F. Castro: Thank you. Until we meet, Comrade Mikoyan.

Recorded by V. Tikhmenev
(Signature)

Documents from
U.S. Archives

The documents reproduced on the following pages are records of discussions and decisions of the Joint Chiefs of Staff during selected days of the Cuban Missile Crisis. The chronology, extracted from a more complete document that covers JCS decisions from 15 October through 28 November, was prepared in December 1962 and declassified in 1987. The extracts presented here cover fourteen days: October 16–22, 25 and 27– 29 and November 2, 16 and 21. Military censors have deleted short passages from many of the daily chronologies. But the key points—the issues confronted and the responses chosen—remain clear.

The notations (U) for unclassified, (S) for secret and (TS) for top secret have been left in the text alongside the passages to which they referred before the chronology was declassified. The copy used in this appendix was provided to General Smith by the National Security Archive, Washington, D.C.

The following glossary identifies various acronyms in the order in which they appear in the text.

Glossary

AA = Antiaircraft
AAA = Antiaircraft artillery
BLUE MOON = Reconnaissance mission over Cuba
BRASS KNOB = Reconnaissance mission over Cuba
C-119 and C-123 = Transport aircraft

CG = Commanding General
CG CONARC = Commanding General, Continental Army Command
CINCAFLANT = Commander in Chief, Air Force Forces, Atlantic Command
CINCARLANT = Commander in Chief, Army Forces, Atlantic Command
CINCLANT = Commander in Chief, Atlantic Command
CINCONAD = Commander in Chief, Continental Air Defense Command
CINCS = Commanders in Chief of U.S. Unified and Specified Commands
CINCSAC = Commander in Chief, Strategic Air Command
CINCSTRIKE = Commander in Chief, U.S. Strike Command
CJCS = Chairman of the Joint Chiefs of Staff
CJTF = Commander, Joint Task Force
CM = Chairman's Memorandum
CNO = Chief of Naval Operations
COMMATS = Commander, Military Air Transport Service
COMMSTS = Commander, Military Sea Transport Service
COMSOLANT = Commander, South Atlantic Command
COMTAC = Commander, Tactical Air Command
CONAD = Continental Air Defense Command
CONUS = Continental United States
CSA = Chief of Staff, Army
CSAF = Chief of Staff, Air Force
DC/S = Deputy Chief of Staff
DD = Destroyer
DEFCON = Defense Condition (state of military force readiness)
DIA = Defense Intelligence Agency
EUCOM = European Command
FAA = Federal Aviation Administration
GREY WOLF = Armed reconnaissance mission over Cuba
IADB = Inter-American Defense Board
J-3 = Operations Directorate, Joint Staff
J-5 = Policy and Planning Directorate, Joint Staff
JCS = Joint Chiefs of Staff
JRC = Joint Reconnaissance Center, Joint Staff
JS = Joint Staff (of the Joint Chiefs of Staff)
LANTCOM = Atlantic Command
LST = Landing Ship Tanks
MAG 14 = Marine Air Group 14
MATS = Military Air Transport Service
MEB = Marine Expeditionary Brigade
MEZ = Military Exclusion Zone, from which civilian planes were barred
MINIMIZE = Hold communication to lowest feasible level

MRBM, IRBM, ICBM = Respectively, medium-range, intermediate-range and intercontinental ballistic missile

NAS = Naval Air Station

NG = National Guard

n.m. = nautical miles

NORAD = North American Air Defense Command

NSC = National Security Council

OAS = Organization of American States

OPCON = Operational Control

OPLAN = Operations Plan

OpsDeps = Operations Deputies, Joint Chiefs of Staff

OSD = Office of the Secretary of Defense

PHIBRIGLEX = Amphibious Brigade exercise

P-Hour = Hour that President Kennedy made his speech on Cuba

SAC = Strategic Air Command

SACEUR = Supreme Allied Commander Europe

SACSA = Special Assistant to the Chairman, Special Activities

SAR = Search and Destroy

S-day = Day of President's speech on Cuba

SecDef = Secretary of Defense

STRAC = Strategic Army Command

STRICOM = U.S. Strike Command

UN/ICRC = United Nations/International Committee of the Red Cross

USCINCEUR = U.S. Commander in Chief, European Command

USEUCOM = U.S. European Command

The Joint Chiefs of Staff
Washington 25. D.C.

SM-1451-62

MEMORANDUM FOR: General Parker
　　　　　　　　　　　 Admiral Sharp
　　　　　　　　　　　 General Burchinal
　　　　　　　　　　　 General Hayes

Subject: Chronology of JCS Decisions Concerning the Cuban Crisis (U)

1.   Pursuant to your request during the Operations Deputies portion of the meeting of the Joint Chiefs of Staff on 28 December 1962, attached herewith as Enclosure A is a condensed version of the Chronological Summary of Actions Taken by the Joint Chiefs of Staff Reference the Cuban Crisis, which you examined on 27 December 1962.

2.   Subject chronology comprises the important decisions of the Joint Chiefs of Staff relating to Cuba taken during the period 15 October–28 November 1962, including summaries of pertinent intelligence data and implementation of decisions where considered appropriate and informative. It also contains as Appendices a list of high- and low-level reconnaissance flights over Cuba, and brief resumes of Service activities during the crisis.

3.   Not contained in subject chronology are the following:
　　a. Decisions taken by the Joint Chiefs of Staff during executive sessions.
　　b. Decisions and actions of, or guidance given by, higher authority, except in a few instances where inclusion was considered necessary to explain JCS actions.
　　c. Routine decisions, or decisions of so minor significance as not to warrant inclusion.

4.   Also attached (Enclosure B) is a draft report of the operational aspects of the Cuban Crisis prepared by J-3 for submission to OSD for use by the Secretary of Defense in Congressional meetings. It was based on the attached condensed version of the Chronology and a Cuban Chronology prepared by the Department of the Navy.

5.   It is requested that you review the attachments in order to discuss at an early meeting the terms of reference desired for the formulation of Congressional presentations for the members of the Joint Chiefs of Staff in connection with the Cuban Crisis. It is further requested that the attached documents be returned to the Secretary, Joint Chiefs of Staff, as soon as practicable.

[Signed]
R.C. Forbes
Colonel, USA
Deputy Secretary

Attachments

Chronology of JCS Decisions
Concerning the Cuban Crisis (U)

This Document Contains
Restricted Data Atomic Energy Act of 1954

Historical Division
Joint Secretariat
Joint Chiefs of Staff
21 December 1962

Copy 3 of 3 copies, pp 1–132
Series "A"

16 October

Further analysis by DIA of aerial photographs taken on 14 October confirmed the presence of a MRBM site and disclosed two other military encampments nearby, one of which contained missile trailers. The CJCS and later the entire membership of the JCS were briefed concerning the missiles. Photographic evidence of an aircraft fuselage, probably an IL-28, and 21 aircraft crates was presented. The Daily Intelligence Summary noted, among other things, the presence of 25 MIGs and 10 IL-28s in the Cuban air order of battle.   (S)

At a meeting (1630–1845) the JCS considered twelve questions posed by the Secretary of Defense and replied as follows: (TS)

1. Requirements for air attack on MRBMs?   (TS)
    a. Unsound. Selective MRBM strike dangerous—not eliminate total missile threat, Cubans may attack US and Guantánamo, high combat losses, loss of surprise.

    b. Should strike MRBMs, SAMs, airborne fighters, nuclear storage sites; defend Guantánamo.

    c. Air Strike ready 24 hours after approval.

2. Requirements for air attack on MRBMs and MIGs?   (TS)

    a. Unsound.

    b. Must strike air bases, air defenses of those bases and SAMs.

    c. Air strike ready 24 hours after approval.

3. Requirements for air attack on MRBMs, all combat aircraft, nuclear storage, and PT boats?   (TS)

    a. Unsound without naval blockade.

    b. Must also strike tanks and all other significant military targets—those which can affect US or its forces. Objectives—eliminate threat to US and liberate Cuba. [Five lines deleted by military censor.]

4. Requirements for (3) plus naval blockade?   (TS)

    a. Acceptable.

    b. Naval blockade initiated immediately; 10 days to complete.

5. Requirements for [Several lines deleted by military censor.]   (TS)

      Implementation—17 October, the J-3 requested DC/S, LANTCOM, by telephone to have OPLAN 316 [Four lines deleted by military censor.]   (TS)

CINCLANT reported to the JCS that the plan could be altered as desired by rescheduling the movements of the XVIII Airborne Corps.

6. Requirements for (4) plus 316-62?   (TS)

    a. Execute S+16 days.

7. Requirements for (4) plus 314-62?   (TS)

    a. Execute S+18.

8. How can air strike achieve maximum effect?   (TS)

    a. No low-level reconnaissance.

    b. Pilots must be provided target folders ASAP.

9. Should missiles be hit piecemeal when identified or wait until all or most are exposed?   (TS)

    a. As they appear.

10. What Soviet reaction may be anticipated? Which general war preparatory plans necessary?   (TS)

    a. Soviet reaction unknown. [Line deleted by military censor.]

    c. Disperse aircraft of SAC and NORAD with nuclear weapons. [Line deleted by military censor.]

    e. World-wide DEFCON 2—after S-Hour.

    f. Augment air defenses of SE-US.

11. What air defense measures should be taken?

a. Augment orbiting patrols of 75 vs 24 now available. [Six lines deleted by military censor.]

12. What degree of mobilization will be necessary and when? (TS)

    a. Up to 150,000.

    b. Consideration should be given to declaration of emergency.

The JCS also decided:

1. That the military danger of missiles in Cuba was sufficiently great to warrant attack even after the missiles were operational. (TS)

2. That CINCONAD was to be authorized to augment the air defense of southeastern U.S. (TS)

    Implementation—On 17 October, JCS directed CINCONAD to take necessary action without delay and to advise the JCS of his plan, its effective date and what aid was required. CINCLANT advised JCS on 17 October that he had alerted shore based Navy and Marine fighter squadrons to be ready to augment CONAD forces in the southeastern U.S. (TS)

17 October

At a meeting from 0930 to 1620, the JCS agreed or decided:

1. Soviet reaction to US action in Cuba could be additional pressure on us (Berlin, Quemoy, Iran, Turkey, Korea)—most likely place Berlin. (TS)

    Implementation—The JSSC produced a study, which the Chairman, JCS, took to a meeting of the "Inner Council" at 1600. The conclusions of the study were: that the USSR would not resort to general war in direct response to US military action against Cuba, that the most likely Soviet reactions would be at sea, against Iran, or by an ICBM "accident" on the Pacific Test Site (Johnston Island), and that sharp and strong encroaching actions at Berlin, short of direct seizure, could reasonably be expected. (TS)

2. Each Service Chief personally to be responsible for specific aspects of planning. (TS)

    a. CSA [Word or words deleted.]

    b. CNO—blockage and Guantánamo.

    c. CSAF—all defense of SE-US

3. Requirement exists for propaganda efforts in Cuba. (TS)

Implementation—SACSA assigned planning and monitoring responsibility.

4. Formally opposed attack on MRBM sites only.   (TS)

Implementation—In a memorandum for the Secretary of Defense, the JCS confirmed their views, presented orally the day before, advocating air attack against all missile sites, all combat aircraft and nuclear storage, combat ships, tanks, and other appropriate military targets in Cuba, in conjunction with a complete blockade; opposing a strike against IRBMs alone; and advising that the elimination of the Castro regime would require an invasion, preferably under OPLAN 314.   (TS)

18 October

Preliminary interpretation of 15 October high-altitude reconnaissance revealed: 1) two probable MR/IRBM fixed launch sites under construction; and 2) one MRBM field launch site confirmed and one evaluated as probable. The total launch sites identified to date were two confirmed and one probable MRBM sites and two MR/IRBM sites under construction; in 29 August photography, only the initial construction of one of the MR/IRBM sites had appeared.

In two meetings (0930–1150 and 1400–1740) the JCS agreed or decided:

1. If it was decided that only an air attack would be executed against missile sites, IL-28s should also be hit.   (TS)

Implementation—CJCS to present this view to State and Defense Departments.   (TS)

2. Exercise PHIBRIGLEX was to be delayed, and the troops were to be held aboard ships.   (TS)

Implementation—Decision overtaken by cancellation of Exercise 20 October.

[Two lines deleted by military censor.]   (TS)

Implementation—CINCLANT completed negotiation [Words deleted by military censor] on 22 October; [Words deleted by military censor] a staging and supply base.   (TS)

4. CG CONARC and COMTAC to be CINCARLANT and CINCAFLANT respectively.   (TS)

5. Of five courses of action under consideration the JCS favored the one that with modification, called for: (TS)
   a. No political preliminaries.
   b. Air strike against missile capability, nuclear storage sites, MIG and IL-28 airfields, additional airfields, and significant military installations (other than for invasion).
   c. Evacuation of dependents.
   d. Defense of Guantánamo.
   e. Readiness for invasion.
   f. Blockade of Cuba.

   [Word deleted by military censor] would be moved from the West Coast to Guantánamo by MATS, and the seaborne echelon [material deleted by military censor] would move to the CINCLANT area.

   Implementation—[Line deleted by military censor] airlift from El Toro and arrived in Guantánamo on 21–22 October [Two lines deleted by military censor] departed by sea on 27 October and arrived in area 12–13 November.   (TS)

7. a. Earliest feasible date for air attack was 21 October.
   b. Optimum date for air attack was 23 October.
   c. Earliest feasible date for initiation of OPLAN 316 was 28 October.
   d. Optimum date for initiation of OPLAN 316 was 30 October.

   Implementation—CJCS to present JCS view to White House and SecDef.

8. CINCLANT Command Organization was approved.   (TS)

9. Movement of CONAD aircraft was authorized for defense of Florida area.   (TS)

   Implementation—On 18 October [Three lines deleted by military censor] 21 October, following JCS authorization, [Extensive material deleted by military censor].

19 October

Analysis of 17 October photography revealed two more MRBM field launch sites, of which there had been *no* evidence as late as 5 September. The total MRBM field launch sites now numbered four confirmed and one probable, with a total of 16 MRBM launchers and an expectation of 8 more launchers soon to be deployed. Sixteen 1100 n.m. missiles were considered operationally ready, capable of being launched 18 hours after decision to launch. Additionally, the two MR/IRBM sites reported on 18 October were now evaluated as probable 2200 n.m. IRBM complexes, with a total of 8 launch pads and an estimated date for operational readiness of December 1962. Other significant intelligence estimates on forces in Cuba as of 19 October were: 1) one possible and three confirmed coastal defense cruise-missile sites; 2) 22 SA-2 sites; 3) not less than 8,000–9,000 Bloc military specialists; and 4) at least 35 and probably 39 MIG-21s.   (S)

In two meetings (0900–1052 and 1400–1713) the JCS agreed or decided:

1. Navy assigned responsibility for blockade planning.   (TS)
    Implementation—On 20 October Navy became engaged in preparation of position and policy papers, a scenario, and implementing instructions re limited blockade; position papers completed and provided to White House on same day.   (TS)
2. Only satisfactory solution to Cuban problem from the military point of view was: (TS)
    a. Notify Macmillan, and possibly Adenauer 2 hours in advance.
    b. Surprise attack on comprehensive targets.
    c. Reconnaissance surveillance.
    d. Complete blockade.
    e. Invasion—split (Army, Navy, Air Force for invasion; CJCS for being prepared to invade.)
    f. US must realize strain would be placed on US alliances and problems would arise with respect to Berlin.
        Implementation—JCS provided their individual and corporate views to the President at 1000 hours on 19 October.

[Five lines deleted by military censor.]   (TS)

[One line deleted by military censor]   (S)

4. SAC authorized to move aircraft [Words deleted by military censor].   (TS)
    Implementation—On 19 October CINCSAC directed movement of nonalert aircraft [Line deleted by military censor].   (TS)
5. Desired initial mobilization was:
    a. Army—units needed to round-out STRAC units [Two lines deleted by military censor].
    b. Navy—[Line deleted by military censor].
    c. Air Force—[Two lines deleted by military censor].
    d. Marine Corps—[Words deleted by military censor].
6. To approve a "Cuban Scenario," for White House use, which listed JCS actions taken and projected through 29 October.   (TS)

7. To approve a warning order to CINCs regarding the critical situation. (TS)

   Implementation—Warning order dispatched on 20 October.

8. To approve warning order to CINCSTRIKE regarding his Army and Air Force units passing to CINCLANT in event latter's OPLANS approved for implementation. (TS)

   Implementation—In accordance with JCS directive, appropriate STRICOM Army and Air Force units put under OPCON of CINCLANT on 21 October.

9. PHIBRIGLEX-62 should be cancelled. (TS)

   Implementation—After approval of SecDef PHIBRIGLEX cancelled on 20 October.

10. Air Defense posture of US should be verified. (TS)

    Implementation—In response to JCS query, CINCONAD on 20 October represented overall US posture as "not appreciably affected" by CONAD deployments; posture in SE-US "adequate," except for limitations of low-level radar and Key West communications. (TS)

21 October

Evaluation of 18 October high-altitude photography revealed one more possible IRBM site, and 19 October films showed one more confirmed MRBM site. A total of two confirmed and one possible fixed IRBM sites, and six field MRBM sites containing four launchers each, had been identified. The total SA-2 sites remained at 26, but the number operationally ready had increased from 16 on the previous day to 20.

At 1300 hours meeting, JCS informed President would speak evening of 22 October. (TS)

At 1715 hours meeting JCS were informed speech would call for quarantine rather than blockade. (TS)

In three meetings (1000–1215, 1300–1510, and 1715–1848 hours) the JCS agreed or decided:

1. Limited reconnaissance (U-2) should be flown tomorrow (22 October). (TS)

2. Authorization should be obtained from SecDef to:

    a. Disperse CONAD fighter aircraft prior to P-Hour.   (TS)

        Implementation—CONAD instructed [Words deleted by military censor] fighters dispersed [Words deleted by military censor] on 22 October.   (TS)

    b. Disperse SAC B-47 aircraft afternoon of 22 October.   (TS)

        Implementation—SAC instructed on 22 October; by 24 October [Words deleted by military censor] were dispersed.   (TS)

3. One Marine Air Group to move from Cherry Point, North Carolina, to Key West NAS by MATS.   (TS)

    Implementation—CINCLANT instructed on 21 October; MAG 14 arrived Key West 22 October, and its ground support element was in place on 24 October.   (TS)

4. A need existed for the development of a detailed and complete civil affairs directive for a military occupation of Cuba.   (TS)

    Implementation—CSA directed to establish civil affairs Special Planning Group on 21 October; CSA submitted directive to JCS on 16 November.   (TS)

5. [Five lines deleted by military censor]   (TS)

6. CG, Third Army, to be notified of possible requirement for execution of Joint Defense Plans for SE-US and Florida Keys. No action by CG, Third Army, prior to P-Hour.   (TS)

7. CINCLANT to prepare for protection of US shipping in Florida Straits, Windward Passage, and Yucatan Channel.   (TS)

    Implementation—CINCLANT instructed on 22 October; air and surface forces already assigned task on 21 October.   (TS)

8. Arrangements to be made discreetly to arrange with FAA for corridor reservations to Florida staging area as required by CINCLANT/ CINCONAD. Further, MEZ to be established at P-Hour.   (TS)

    Implementation—On 22 October Air Force and FAA representatives agreed to scope of MEZ, but MEZ never established; instead "Special Civil Air Regulation" issued by FAA on 24 October.   (S)

9. High-altitude photographic reconnaissance to continue.   (TS)

10. To approve a planning directive to CINCLANT for blockade of Cuba containing: (TS)

    a. Rules of engagement.

    b. Instructions for blockade of surface ships.

    c. Instructions for blockade of aircraft. (JCS unwilling to launch air blockade unless there was predetermination to shoot down aircraft which ignored blockade.)

    d. Concept of operations.

    e. Defense of Guantánamo.

   f. Control and protection of American shipping.

   g. Coordination with Allied or friendly forces.

> **Implementation**—With approval of SecDef, planning directive dispatched on 22 October; blockade directed 23 October for implementation on 24 October; on 24, 25, 26, 29, and 31 October amplifying and modifying instructions dispatched; although 22 October planning instruction encompassed aerial quarantine, the JCS advised CINCLANT on 24 October that the quarantine as invoked would not apply to aircraft.   (TS)

11.   To recommend the following actions:

   a. CINCSAC initiate force generation.   (TS)

   b. CONAD execute phased dispersal of nuclear-armed interceptors at P-Hour -12.   (TS)

   c. CINCSAC implement 1/8 airborne alert.   (TS)

12.   That it would be desirable to decode communications traffic between Russian diplomats in Latin American countries and their counterparts in other Latin American countries or at least delay the transmission of their messages. The purpose of this action was to forestall or delay communist anti-US activities in Latin America.   (TS)

22 October

On 22 October, there was no new information from photography, because poor weather had precluded photo-reconnaissance on 21 October. The operational readiness posture of missiles in Cuba as known on the morning of 22 October was therefore based essentially on photography through 19 October and was as follows: (S)

1.   San Cristobal MRBM Area.

Site No. 1: Fully operational capability (FOC) as of 19 October.
Site No. 2: Emergency operational capability (EOC) as of 17 October; FOC as of 22 October.
Site No. 3: EOC on 20 October; FOC on 25 October.
Site No. 4: EOC on 23 October; FOC on 28 October.

2.   Sagua La Grande MRBM Area.

Site No. 1: FOC on 22 October.
Site No. 2: FOC on 20 October.

3. Guanajay IRBM Area.

    Site No. 1: EOC on 15 November; FOC on 1 December.
    Site No. 2: EOC on 1 December; FOC on 15 December.

4. Remedios IRBM Area.

    One site: EOC on 1 December; FOC on 15 December.

5. SA-2 Sites.

    26 sites, 22 operationally ready.

There were "clear indications" available on 22 October that at least five Soviet missile regiments would become operational in Cuba, each regiment to have eight launchers and at least 16 missiles. This represented a first salvo potential of 40 missiles, with a refire capability of another 40. Finally, another possible nuclear weapons storage site was discovered, for a total of two identified to date.

In three meetings (0900–1157, 1330–1445, and 1620–1755) the JCS agreed or decided as follows:

1. CINCLANT to be authorized to reduce readiness to execute OPLAN 312 from six to twelve hours and thin out aircraft accordingly.   (TS)
    Implementation—CINCLANT instructed on 22 October, on same day CINCLANT entered reclama against "thin out"; still same day JCS made compliance of CINCLANT discretionary; on 24 October question reopened by higher authority.   (TS)
2. Chairman, JCS, to inform SACEUR of developments.   (TS)
    Implementation—SACEUR informed on 22 October.   (TS)
3. US military forces worldwide to go to DEFCON 3 at P-Hour, except for EUCOM.   (TS)
    Implementation—DEFCON 3 established worldwide effective 222300Z; USCINCEUR authorized to use his discretion in complying with directive in light of warning order of 21 October.   (TS)
4. CNO would take care of Latin American participation.   (TS)
    Implementation—CINCLANT prepared plan for combined US and Latin American quarantine; Latin American forces to take stations in Lesser Antilles and Caribbean approaches to Cuba under COMSOLANT; combined quarantine put into effect on 7 November. Latin American participation eventually involved: (S)
    a. Argentina—2DDs and 3 SAR aircraft.
    b. Dominican Republic—2 patrol frigates; naval and airport facilities.
    c. Venezuela—2 DDS.
    d. Costa Rica, Colombia, Ecuador, El Salvador, Guatemala, Haiti, Hon-

duras, Panama, Nicaragua, Trinidad-Tobago, and Jamaica—various measures of cooperation, including naval and airport facilities and pledges of full support if needed.

5. To approve MINIMIZE worldwide.   (TS)

    Implementation—MINIMIZE directed on 22 October.   (S)

6. To call up 21 C-119 squadrons and 5 interceptor squadrons.   (TS)

    Implementation—Disapproved by SecDef on same day, but subsequently on 28 October 21 C-119, 3 C-123 troop carriers, and 6 aerial port squadrons mobilized; call-up totaled 14,214 men.   (TS)

7. To hold up announcement of extension of enlistments until reserves called up.   (TS)

    Implementation—Reserves not called up, except for Air Force units indicated above, but tours of duty of Navy and Marine Corps personnel extended indefinitely on 23 October.   (S)

8. To authorize Services to move support units and fillers; this to be left to CSA.   (TS)

    Implementation—On 22 October CSA lifted restrictions from movement of "detachments, small units and fillers."   (TS)

9. Chairman, JCS to take up with SecDef the following: (TS)

    a. Aircraft problem in Florida; JCS taking action.

    b. Air defense situation critical; CSAF checking.

    c. Security code word category to be eliminated unless SecDef feels it should be retained.

    d. Submarine incident and 23 Soviet ships on way over.

    e. Time of blockade; that CNO wants it at P+24 hours.

    f. Services will forward requests on reserve call-up.

    g. Move of 5th MEB (-).

    h. SAC generation.

    i. Declaration of DEFCON 3 worldwide.

10. USCINCEUR to be instructed to destroy or make inoperable JUPITERs if any attempt made to fire them without specific authorization of President.   (TS)

    Implementation—USCINCEUR instructed on 22 October, and directed to inform US custodians and their commanders of instructions.   (TS)

11. Latin American and NATO attaches and NATO Military Committee (Standing Group) to be briefed prior to the President's speech.   (TS)

12. Loading of combat command from 1st Armored Division was OK.   (TS)

    Implementation—Task Force CHARLIE began departing Fort Hood on 23 October, closed Fort Stewart on 29 October.   (TS)

13. CINCLANT to be requested to modify his message (201716Z) concerning command set-up for CINCLANT OPLAN 314.   (TS)

    Implementation—Change accomplished on 22 October; CG XVIII Airborne Corps would, subsequent to initial assault, become CJTF Cuba vice CINC-ARLANT.

14. JCS answer to President's question concerning action in event Soviet build-up in Cuba continues to be that blockade should be stepped up and decision on general attack reviewed, either well in advance of IRBM operational date or Khrushchev's next estimated political move against Berlin.   (TS)

15. To send message to Chairman, US Delegation IADB, requesting him and Lt. Gen. Burns to use influence with IADB members in support of President's desire for OAS participation, including provision of naval forces.   (TS)

16. SAC to initiate 1/8 airborne alert beginning 1200 local time, 22 October. To be done quietly and gradually, in full effect by afternoon 23 October.   (TS)

    Implementation—SAC so instructed on 22 October; 1/8 airborne alert, involving 66 B-52s, was initiated within 1/2 hour of dispatch of JCS directive.   (TS)

17. SAC, at discretion, to implement dispersal plans for B-47 forces beginning 1200 hours, 22 October.   (TS)

    Implementation—See para. 2b., 21 October.

18. CONAD to implement plan for dispersal of CONUS fighter interceptor force on quiet basis.   (TS)

    Implementation—See para. 2a., 21 October.

19. If SecDef approved, SAC to generate its forces toward maximum readiness posture beginning 1200 hours, 22 October, to be at maximum by 1200 hours, 23 October.   (TS)

    Implementation—see para. 6, 23 October.

25 October

Three of the Soviet ships suspected as possible missile carriers enroute to Cuba were reportedly altering their courses. All of the Soviet dry cargo ships seemed to be pulling back from the quarantine line, but Soviet tankers were continuing toward Cuba.   (S)

All of the 24 occupied SA-2 sites were now estimated to be operational.

In two meetings (0900–1238 and 1400–1655) the JCS agreed or decided:

1. To approve, as amended, a draft memorandum to SecDef on "Timing Factors"; paper listed timing from receipt of implementation orders to initiation of action on or over Cuba: (TS)
    a. Low-level reconnaissance—2 hours.
    b. Reprisal strike on one SA-2 site—2 hours.
    c. Air strike on all SA-2 sites—2 hours (contingent on maintaining present posture).
    d. Full air strike—12 hours.
    e. Implement 316—Initial Assault, Decision Day+7.
2. CSAF to answer offer of support from Argentine Air Force by responding that IADB will be kept informed.   (TS)
3. In event of mobilization, CSA to move available AA units to Florida, and CINCONAD to be queried on effects of IL-28s on his plans, and on priorities he had indicated on 24 October.   (TS)

    Implementation—CINCONAD queried on 25 October; CINCONAD responded on 26 October by requesting additional AA units, but JCS decided on 3 November that additional AA deployments to SE-US not necessary "at this time."   (TS)
4. To approve the proposal of CSA to increase troop list for OPLAN 316.   (TS)

    Implementation—On 26 October JCS informed CINCLANT that a revised Army Task Organization for CINCLANT OPLAN 316-61 was approved; the revised Task Organization increased the combat power [Material deleted by military censor]   (TS)

27 October

The previously reported rapid pace of construction of Cuban missile sites was confirmed by analysis of 25 and 26 October low-level reconnaissance. There continued to be no evidence of any intention to halt construction or dismantle or move the sites. Five of the six MRBM sites were now considered fully operational and the sixth would probably achieve this status on 28 October. At that time, the capability would exist to launch 24 1100 n.m. missiles within six to eight hours of a decision to launch, and to refire with 24 additional missiles within another four to six hours.   (S)

Photography of 25 October had confirmed the presence in Cuba of FROG tactical missiles, unguided rockets with a range of 20 to 25 n.m. A probable FROG launcher had been detected in a large camp and vehicle park, in company with 31 probable T-54 medium tanks and at least 31 other armored vehicles.   (S)

Possible nuclear warhead storage sites had been identified at five of the launch sites, as of 25 October.   (S)

Four long-range conventionally powered Soviet torpedo attack submarines had been observed near quarantine area in recent days.   (S)

Latin American reaction to US moves continued favorable.   (S)

In a memorandum to the Chairman, JCS, DIA concluded that the Soviets had staged their buildup in Cuba probably because 1) they desired to improve their nuclear attack capabilities against the US, and 2) they estimated that the US could not prevent the advance of Soviet offensive power into the Western hemisphere.   (TS)

At two meetings (0900–1245, 1330–1953), the JCS agreed or decided:

1. That, on further considering responsibility for reconnaissance missions, the JCS would assign missions through the Joint Reconnaissance Center, CINCLANT would conduct operational planning and exercise operational direction, and the DOD would obtain approval for missions. (TS)
2. In response to an inquiry raised by higher authority on 22 October, to forward an outline operation plan for an air quarantine of Cuba to the SecDef.   (TS)
    Implementation—Plan submitted to SecDef for approval on 29 October; copies forwarded to CINCSAC, CINCLANT and CINCONAD for development of supporting plans.   (TS)
3. In view of latest intelligence data, to recommend that OPLAN 312 be executed no later than 29 October unless irrefutable evidence of the dismantling of the offensive weapons in Cuba were obtained in the meantime.   (TS)
    Implementation—A memorandum including the foregoing, coupled with a recommendation that an invasion [material deleted by military censor] follow the air strike [material deleted by military censor] by seven days, was presented to the President and the NSC Executive Committee on this day by the Chairman, JCS. In an accompanying memorandum for the SecDef, the Chairman recommended against "taking the decision to execute now," but to maintain the existing

        condition of readiness to execute OPLAN 312 (12-hour notice). (TS)

4. In connection with above decision to instruct CINCLANT and CINCAFLANT to hold up on dispersal. (TS)

5. To seek approval to drop six million leaflets over Cuba explaining the cause, purpose, and scope of the quarantine. (TS)

        Implementation—Program for project submitted to SecDef on same day, but on 29 October project cancelled and on 7 November CINCLANT authorized to destroy leaflets. (TS)

6. To bring back from the Mediterranean for possible use in Cuban operations the amphibious command ship USS POCONO. (TS)

7. That, if the pattern of actions elsewhere in the NORAD/CONAD system indicated the existence of a Cuban and Sino-Soviet attack, nuclear weapons could be used to destroy hostile aircraft. (TS)

        Implementation—By a message the next day, 28 October, the JCS advised CINCONAD to the above effect, emphasizing that CINCONAD's authority under his "Rules for Engagement" (NORAD Regulation 55–6) had not been changed by the Cuban contingency plans. This message, the JCS further advised, did not change the rules of engagement in the contingency plans, prescribing non-nuclear armaments. (TS)

8. In response to a SecDef request, to approve a memorandum setting forth order of magnitude of sortie requirements for four concepts of attack on offensive weapons in Cuba. Concepts were: (TS)

    a. Limited attack against MRBMs only.

    b. Same as a, above, but assure all MRBMs inoperable.

    c. Rendering inoperable all SAM sites.

    d. The 312/62 concept of allout attack on all offensive weapons.

        The JCS recommended rejection of all except the last, approval of which they recommended.

        Implementation—Memo provided Chairman for use as he saw fit. (TS)

9. To send to CINCLANT "Timing Factors" paper (see item 1 of 25 October) with information that basic paper had been sent to President. (TS)

28 October

As of this date, all 24 MRBM launchers in Cuba were estimated to be operational, capable of salvo of 24×1100-n.m. missiles within 6–8 hours of decision.

At the three IRBM sites, moreover, construction continued at a rapid pace and some missile support equipment was being moved into vicinity of Guanajay sites, although no IRBMs had yet been observed. Camouflage, concealment, and dispersal measures were more extensive at the missile sites, and AAA positions were now evident at many MRBM sites. One US low-level reconnaissance mission of the 27th had been fired upon by these weapons.　(S)

Regarding IL-28s, there were now five partially assembled, one fuselage uncrated, and 21 aircraft crates at San Julian airfield.　(S)

At a meeting (0900–1104) the JCS agreed or decided:

1. In view of recent intelligence data on Soviet equipment in Cuba, to request recommendations from CINCLANT on any changes necessary [material deleted by military censor] particularly whether US invasion and supporting forces should be equipped with tactical nuclear weapons.　(TS)

   Implementation—Message dispatched the same day; CINCLANT replied that he considered it prudent that US air and ground forces earmarked for Cuban operations have an atomic delivery capability and that he intended to modify his plans accordingly.　(TS)

2. Tentatively to schedule four low-level reconnaissance flights for late afternoon, one of which would cover eastern Cuba, and that they would fly through any fire encountered.　(TS)

3. That Chairman should recommend that announcement should be made that reconnaissance over Cuba would continue until UN observers arrived and that the US would strike any missile sites that fired on US planes.　(TS)

4. To draw to the attention of the CINCs operational commanders the latest Khrushchev message, which the JCS thought might be an insincere proposal intended to gain time.　(TS)

5. To inform CINCSTRIKE, COMMATS, and COMMSTS, that forces planned for the reinforcement of Europe, except one Marine Div/Wing team, were available over and above the requirements of OPLANS 312, 314, and 316, and further to direct them to maintain in readiness their plans for reinforcing USEUCOM.　(TS)

6. That in response to CINCLANT's request for use of Key West International Airport as a staging field for Army aircraft, it was not necessary at this time to obtain the airport.　(TS)

   Implementation—On 31 October, the JCS decided to authorize CINCLANT to commence negotiations with local authorities for the use of the airport. By a message on 3 November, CINCLANT was given discretion to preposition logistical support and to make ready the operational facilities at the airfield, after he had completed the necessary arrangements with County officials, but that no aircraft were to be moved to the field.   (TS)

29 October

Continuing analysis of 27 October low-level reconnaissance indicated that construction and concealment activities were continuing at all missile sites, and that the status of the IL-28s remained basically as indicated on 28 October. Camouflage and other concealment measures were becoming more effective. At San Julian one IL-28 was in final stage of construction, four in varying stages of assembly, one fuselage uncrated, 21 shipping crates present.   (S)

On 29 October the Daily Intelligence Summary stated that:

1. Khrushchev's 28 October message to the President ordering dismantlement of Soviet bases in Cuba appeared to be an attempt to ward off any contemplated US action that might destroy the bases.
2. There was no proof that the Soviets had begun dismantling missile sites or IL-28s. The latest photography, taken prior to the Soviet statement, showed that construction was proceeding rapidly.   (S)

In a study distributed to the Chairman, JCS, Director, JS, and others, DIA concluded that: the Soviets attempted to establish an offensive base in Cuba which, if unhampered, would add substantially to their total nuclear capability against the US, and would, in their estimate, demonstrate that the US was no longer able to prevent the advance of Soviet power into the Western Hemisphere; further, that the Soviets miscalculated the rapidity with which the US became aware of this attempt, as well as underestimated the degree of world support for the US.   (TS)

At two meetings (0900–1107, 1400–1737), the JCS agreed or decided:

1. To conduct aerial reconnaissance of Cuba during this day, but without UN observers in aircraft, and that the UN should be so informed.   (TS)
2. To forward to the Secretary of Defense an outline plan for the UN to use in connection with inspection for offensive weapons. The plan provided for aerial, ground, and port inspection by technically qualified UN personnel. The JCS recommended that the US fleet remain deployed as it was,

that US reconnaissance flights be continued, and that the existing covert intelligence efforts continue.

3. That if the UN undertook photo-reconnaisance flights over Cuba in C-130's with Indonesian crews, the US should insist for reasons of safety, on having a US pilot aboard the aircraft, and also a US photographer, if possible.　　(TS)

4. That suspension of US air reconnaissance for two days (30–31 October) would be acceptable, but resumption on third day would be necessary.　　(TS)

5. To [approve] CINCONAD's rotation and reduction in dispersal of aircraft necessary to maintain combat-ready posture in view of maintenance needs of aircraft and weapons, short of complete cessation of dispersal.　　(TS)

6. That the Services should continue the current level of activity in exploiting training benefits of Cuban contingency force movements, without starting new projects.　　(TS)

7. That CG, CONARC (CINCARLANT) should be instructed to plan but not to implement a scheme for deploying the School Brigade from Ft. Benning to southern Florida as a Cuban contingency move.　　(TS)

2 November

The DIA reported as follows on information derived from low-level photography on 1 November:　　(S)

1. *It was concluded that the Soviets were abandoning the known MRBM and IRBM sites. The missiles, basic launching equipment, and camouflage had been removed. In addition, the launch sites had been partially destroyed, apparently by bulldozers.*

2. The present location of the removed equipment was unknown.

3. Construction on the probable nuclear bunkers had apparently ceased.

4. Assembly of the IL-28s at San Julian airfield was continuing.

The Daily Intelligence Summary reported that:　　(S)

1. All known MRBM sites in Cuba were now being or had been dismantled according to photography of 1 November. Launch pads had been destroyed and missiles and launch equipment removed. Their present loca-

tion was not known and alternate deployment sites were possible, though unlikely.

2. Construction activity at IRBM sites had stopped and installations had been partially destroyed.

3. Five of the six probable nuclear warhead bunker sites showed no construction activity.

4. None of the Soviet dry cargo ships in Cuba was capable of carrying MRBMs or IRBMs below deck. The seven suspected missile carriers could return to Cuba by 16–25 November. Loading of missiles could take as much as a week longer.

5. IL-28 bombers were being worked on, as of 1 November. One was observed taxiing. Another appeared completely assembled; five were partially assembled; 21 were still in crates.   (S)

Director, DIA, on request of Director J-5, forwarded a memorandum on "Evaluation of Next Actions by USSR in Respect to the Cuban Situation." This study concluded that military actions related to Cuba would probably be viewed by the Soviets as too dangerous, while military actions not related to Cuba would probably depend on local issues.

At two meetings (0900–1055, 1400–1833), the JCS agreed or decided:

1. To approve a draft memorandum to the President, assessing the effect of modern Soviet weapons in Cuba [material deleted by military censor] The JCS concluded that since there were nuclear-capable delivery systems in Cuba the possibility of enemy use of nuclear weapons to repel invasion had to be accepted, although US could respond with overwhelming nuclear force against military targets. In more likely case that no nuclear weapons would be used, present plan of invasion was adequate and feasible, despite increase in Cuban conventional capability. Medical plans drawn up to accommodate 18,500 casualties in first ten days assuming nuclear weapons not used, although it was not expected that this figure would be reached.   (TS)

2. To refer to OpsDeps for further consideration an "Outline Inspection and Surveillance Plan for Cuba," which had grown out of discussions on 31 October and 1 November of "Minimum Acceptable Actions in Support of Measures Necessary to Meet US Interests in Cuban-Soviet Negotiations."   (TS)

> **Implementation**—Later in the day, a memorandum embodying the outline plan was approved by the OpsDeps and presented to the Secretary of Defense as a negotiating objective for the US delegation at the UN. It contained the minimum requirements for verifying the

withdrawal of Soviet offensive weapons in three phases. The plan called for US aerial reconnaissance in all Phases, UN aerial reconnaissance in at least the first two Phases, UN systematic ground inspection in Phase II, UN periodic ground inspection during Phase III, UN/ICRC inspection parties at nine ports, three international airports and, as necessary, at sea, and UN spot checks of suspicious activities during Phase II and, if possible, Phase I. Participation of US personnel in the UN Inspection Organization was considered essential. In connection with the plan the JCS advised that the threat from Cuban-based offensive weapons could not be entirely eliminated until a friendly government controlled the island, for the weapons in question could easily be hidden.   (S)

3. That the deployment of additional air defense artillery units to the southeastern US was not necessary at this time, but that, if circumstances changed, up to three HAWK battalions would be made available to augment CINCONAD forces.   (TS)

   Implementation—A message to the above effect was dispatched to CINCONAD on 3 November.   (TS)

4. To approve CINCLANT's request that authority be obtained to use Key West International Airport to stage Army aircraft during execution [material deleted by military censor].

16 November

DIA reported that the following information had been derived from high- and low-level photography on 15 November: (S)

1. There was no change in the IL-28 situation; assembly was continuing at San Julian.
2. At the Mayari-Arriba military installation, shipping crates and equipment had been identified which appeared to be associated with the coastal-defense cruise missiles. The installation was possibly a support base for these missiles.

On 16 November the Daily Intelligence Summary reported that photos of 14 November showed no evidence of uncrating of the IL-28 crates at Holguin. At San Julian on 13 November camouflage netting had been placed over most of the IL-28s and several of the crates, but apparently no additional fuselages had been uncrated. Seven aircraft had been assembled or were in the final stages of assembly. (TS)

At a meeting from 0900 to 1026, the JCS agreed or decided:

1. To send to commanders concerned with reconnaissance the text of Castro letter to U Thant vowing to fire on US reconnaissance aircraft. (TS)

2. After being informed of higher-level decision to cancel low-level flights for 16 November in view of Castro threat, to recommend low-level reconnaissance flights for 17 November, the number and routes to be based on CINCLANT's recommendation, after CINCLANT was advised to expect hostile reaction, to omit the most hotly defended targets, and to ready GREY WOLF mission. (TS)

3. To advise the President that the Armed Forces were at optimum posture to execute OPLANs 312 and 316, that the study requested by the President had resulted in earmarking additional forces as ready reserve for OPLAN 316, with additional shipping requirements and cost, that the current status of alert could be maintained for about 30 more days without adverse effect on capabilities, that thereafter a reaction capability of twelve hours for OPLAN 312 and seven days for OPLAN 316 could be maintained if in DEFCON 3, or of two days and ten to twelve days respectively if in DEFCON 5, and further that they recommended maintaining the present posture for the immediate future. (TS)

    Implementation—Based on J-5 paper "Military Aspects of the Cuban Situation," the JCS dispatched a memorandum to the President on 16 November to the above effect, under the title "Status of Readiness for the Cuban Operation." A copy also was sent to the SecDef. (TS)

4. For purposes of the discussion with the President later on 16 November, to recommend that IL-28's be removed from Cuba, preferably by negotiation, otherwise by blockade and, if need be, by military action, that the US make withdrawal of Soviet personnel an immediate negotiating objective, that any assurance given Castro be made dependent on his good behavior and acceptance of air reconnaissance and not contravene US obligations under the Rio Pact, and that the US seek the essential goal of long-term verification and inspection by means other than the current proposals for reciprocal UN inspection in the Caribbean and for a nuclear-free zone in Latin America. (TS)

    Implementation—Copy of "Chairman's Talking Paper for Meeting with the President" sent to SecDef as enclosure to a CM. (TS)

5. To recommend to SecDef that existing force levels of OPLAN 316 be accepted as probably adequate, but that the 5th Infantry Division and a

Combat Command of 2d Armored Division be earmarked as ready reserve, without movement until directed, and that National Guard divisions not be called up to reconstitute strategic reserve until needed, but that two NG divisions for occupation duty be alerted on S-day of OPLAN 312. Further, to advise the SecDef that they considered the existing Guantánamo Defense Force, with carrier aviation and naval gun fire support, adequate for defense of the present perimeter, but that there was an immediate requirement for activation of 11 LST's, a cost estimate of which was included. (TS)

>   **Implementation**—A memorandum to the above effect was dispatched to the SecDef on 20 November.   (TS)

21 November

DIA reported the following information derived from high-altitude photography of 20 November.   (S)

1. There was no photographic evidence to substantiate a report of a Soviet submarine base being located at Cayo Largo.
2. There was no photographic evidence to substantiate a report of unusual military activity in Las Villas Province.
3. The nine shipping crates at Holguin airfield remained unopened.

The Daily Intelligence Summary reported that further study of photographs of the Holguin military camp had resulted in identification of some 350 Soviet military vehicles, including 31 T-54 tanks, 4–5 PT-76 amphibious tanks, nine SU-100 assault guns, and 56 squad and 44 pyramidal tents. At least 1000 Soviet troops were probably located there.

At two meetings (0900–1030, 1400–1551) the JCS agreed or decided:

1. That, in view of the President's announcement of 20 November lifting the quarantine, they should submit recommendations as soon as possible on relaxing the readiness posture and returning forces to their normal stations, and in this connection, to ask CINCLANT, CINCONAD and CINCSAC for recommendations as follows: (TS)
    a. CINCLANT (and CINCSAC as involved):—on the DEFCON and return of units, assuming relaxed reaction times as follows:
        (1) U-2 flights—an average of no more than two per day in any 10-day period and no more than 5 in one day.

      (2)   Low-level reconnaissance—four aircraft on 12-hour alert, eight on 24-hour alert, similar readiness for all supporting aircraft.

      (3)   Local reprisal strike aircraft—same readiness as BRASS KNOB and BLUE MOON missions plus two hours.

      (4)   Attack on SAM sites, IL-28's, and/or all Cuban defenses—48 hours.

      (5)   [Line deleted by military censor.]

      (6)   [Line deleted by military censor.]

   b.   CINCONAD:—on the permanent augmentation of air defenses in southeastern US following termination of Cuban incident, and on the phasedown of the current reinforcements of the area, assuming normal status by 20 December.

   c.   CINCSAC:—on the level of readiness for SAC during the next 30 days, excluding U-2's.

   d.   All three commanders:—on intelligence objectives requiring aerial reconnaissance during the next 30 days.

2.   In response to CINCLANT's recommendation of 16 November for immediate reinforcement of Guantánamo, that such reinforcement was unnecessary at this time in view of the recent announcement on the removal of offensive weapons from Cuba, and that CINCLANT should plan for reinforcement, in the event it became necessary later, with forces other than the 5th MEB, which would best be used in amphibious operations in Western Cuba.   (TS)

     Implementation—Joint Staff was instructed to prepare a reply to the above effect, and on 24 November a message conforming to the above was dispatched to CINCLANT.   (TS)

3.   That a draft message to Stevenson and McCloy, "Next Steps in New York Negotiations," should be amended to make the language more specific, particularly to insure that the right of overflight surveillance was not affected by noninvasion assurances, and to avoid the implication that the US was interested in the departure of only those Soviet personnel charged with defending weapons systems.   (TS)

4.   That a report by SACSA on "Cuba Planning" had been overtaken by events.   (TS)

Notes

Chapter 1

1. David L. Larson, ed. *The "Cuban Crisis" of 1962, Selected Documents and Chronology* (Boston: Houghton Mifflin, 1963), 41–46.
2. Ibid.
3. Dino A. Brugioni, *Eyeball to Eyeball: The Inside Story of the Cuban Missile Crisis* (New York: Random House, 1990, 1991), 173.
4. See Appendix I for Russian text.
5. Nikita S. Khrushchev, *Khrushchev Remembers*, trans. and ed. Strobe Talbott (New York: Little Brown, 1971), 493.
6. Michael R. Beschloss, *The Crisis Years: Kennedy and Khrushchev, 1960–1963* (New York: Harper Collins, 1991), 388–89.
7. Ibid., 551.
8. Ibid., 200.
9. Yu. Sigov, "Uroki karibskogo krizisa," interview with Aleksandr I. Alekseyev, *Argumenty i fakty*, No. 10, 11–17 March 1989, 4–5.
10. Ibid., 5.
11. Copied by the author from the classified original document in the Ministry of Defense archives in Moscow.

Chapter 2

1. Michael R. Beschloss and Strobe Talbott, *At the Highest Levels: The Inside Story of the End of the Cold War* (Boston: Little Brown, 1993), 123.

2. Copied by the author from the classified original document in the Ministry of Defense archives in Moscow.
3. Beschloss, 398–99.
4. Vassili G. Bakayev, unpublished memoirs, made available to the author in Moscow.
5. Copied by the author from the classified original document in the Ministry of Defense archives in Moscow.
6. Copied by the author from the classified original document in the Ministry of Defense archives in Moscow.
7. Ibid.

Chapter 3

1. Copied by the author from the classified original document in the Ministry of Defense archives in Moscow.

Chapter 5

1. Nikita S. Khrushchev, Message of October 23, 1962, "Kennedy-Khrushchev Correspondence," *Problems of Communism*, Spring 1992, Vol. XLI, 32.
2. See Appendix I for Russian text.
3. See Appendix I for Russian text.
4. Raymond Garthoff, in James G. Blight, Bruce J. Allyn and David A. Welch, *Cuba on the Brink: Castro, the Missile Crisis, and the Soviet Collapse* (New York: Pantheon, 1993), 163.
5. Pavlov (Pliyev) to the Director, "Incoming telegram No. 109366, transmitted at 2150 hours 26.10.62, received (in Moscow) at 0923 hours, 27.10.62," photoreproduction illustrating V. Badurkin interview with Gen. Dmitri A. Volkogonov, "Operatsiya Anadyr," *Trud*, 27 October 1992; also quoted in Lt. Col. Anatoli Dokuchayev, "Operatsiya Anadyr," *Krasnaya Zvezda*, 21 October 1992.
6. Copied by the author from the classified original document in the Ministry of Defense archives in Moscow.
7. Nikita S. Khrushchev, Letter to Fidel Castro, 28 October 1962, as translated from text released to author by Russian Ministry of Foreign Affairs, January, 1992.
8. Nikita S. Khrushchev, Letter to Fidel Castro, 30 October 1962, as translated from text released to author by Russian Ministry of Foreign Affairs, January, 1992.
9. Robert McNamara, in Blight, Allyn and Welch, 254.
10. Ibid.
11. Fidel Castro, in Blight, Allyn and Welch, 250.

12. Castro to Khrushchev, 26 October 1962, in Blight, Allyn and Welch, 478.
13. Ibid.
14. Khrushchev letter to Castro, 28 October 1962, op. cit.
15. Ibid.
16. Carlos Franqui, *Family Portrait with Fidel: A Memoir*, translated from the Spanish by Alfred MacAdam (New York: Random House, 1984), 194.
17. Castro to Khrushchev, 31 October 1962, in Blight, Allyn and Welch, 486.

Chapter 6
1. Arthur M. Schlesinger, Jr., *A Thousand Days: John F. Kennedy in the White House* (Boston: Houghton Mifflin, 1965), 303.
2. Larson, ed., *"Cuban Crisis" of 1962*, 298.
3. Stephen E. Ambrose, *Eisenhower the President* (New York: Simon & Schuster, 1984), 557.
4. Maxwell D. Taylor, "Narrative of the Anti-Castro Cuban Operation Zapata," Report to the President, 13 June 1961, in the Washington, D.C. National Security Archive files on the Cuban Missile Crisis 1962, hereafter, *Missile Crisis Files—NSA.*
5. Ibid., 4–5.
6. Ibid., Memorandum No. 4, Recommendation No. 2, 4–5.
7. Laurence Chang, ed., *Chronology of the Cuban Missile Crisis* January 20, 1989 Draft (Washington: The National Security Archive, 1989), 14.
8. Beschloss, 131.
9. Brugioni, *Eyeball to Eyeball*, 42.
10. Schlesinger, 295.
11. Brugioni, 60.
12. Schlesinger, 319.
13. *The New York Times*, "US Missile Lead Claimed in Study," 19 November 1961, 1.
14. Theodore C. Sorensen, *Kennedy* (New York: Harper & Row, 1965), 305, 347.
15. Maxwell D. Taylor, *Swords and Plowshares* (New York: W.W. Norton, 1972), 180.
16. Schlesinger, 338.
17. Taylor, "Narrative . . . ," Recommendation No. 5, Memorandum No. 4, 7.
18. Schlesinger, 384.
19. U.S. Congress, Senate Select Committee to Study Government Operations with Respect to Intelligence Activities, *Alleged Assassination Plots Involving Foreign Leaders*, 94th Cong., lst sess., [1975], 158–59.
20. Brugioni, 69.

21. James G. Hershberg, "Before 'The Missiles in October': Did Kennedy Plan a Military Strike Against Cuba?" in James A. Nathan, ed., *The Cuban Missile Crisis Revisited* (New York: St. Martin's Press, 1992), 243.

22. "Minutes of First Operation MONGOOSE Meeting with Attorney General Robert Kennedy, December 1, 1961," Laurence Chang and Peter Kornbluh, eds., *The Cuban Missile Crisis, 1962: A National Security Archive Documents Reader* (New York: The New Press, 1992), 20.

23. Sorensen, 630.

24. Memorandum to G - Mr. [U. Alexis] Johnson from CMA/[Robert A.] Hurwitch, *Missile Crisis Files—NSA.*

25. For a summary of these exercises, see Raymond L. Garthoff, *Reflections on the Cuban Missile Crisis* (Washington, D.C.: The Brookings Institution, 1989), 6.

26. Chang and Kornbluh, eds., Brig. Gen. Edward Lansdale, "The Cuba Project," February 20, 1962, 23.

27. Ibid., 24.

28. Ibid.

29. Chang and Kornbluh, eds., "Special Group Augmented, 'Guidelines for Operation MONGOOSE,' March 14, 1962," ibid., 38.

30. Ibid.

31. Hershberg, 246.

32. Chang and Kornbluh, eds., Brig. Gen. Edward Lansdale, "Review of Operation MONGOOSE, Phase One," July 25, 1962, 42.

33. Ibid., 45.

34. Ibid.

35. Ibid., 46.

36. Ibid., 47.

37. John A. McCone, "Memorandum of Discussion with Mr. McGeorge Bundy, Friday, October 5, 1962, 5:15 P.M.," in Mary S. McAuliffe, ed., *CIA Documents on the Cuban Missile Crisis, 1962* (Washington, D.C.: Central Intelligence Agency, 1992), 116; hereafter, *CIA Documents.*

38. Chang and Kornbluh, eds., "Transcript of the Executive Committee meeting, October 27, 1962," 203.

39. Sorensen, 630.

40. "Timetable of Soviet Military Buildup in Cuba, July–October 1962," *CIA Documents,* 7.

Chapter 7

1. Memorandum to G, *Missile Crisis Files—NSA.*

2. John A. McCone, Memorandum, "Soviet MRBMs in Cuba," 31 October 1962, *CIA Documents,* 13.

3. Brugioni, *Eyeball to Eyeball*, 88.

4. McCone, "Soviet MRBMs in Cuba," 13.

5. McCone, Memorandum for the File, "Discussion in Secretary Rusk's Office at 12 o'clock, 21 August 1962," *CIA Documents*, 21.

6. Ibid., 22.

7. McCone, "Memorandum of Meeting with the President at 6:00 P.M. on August 22, 1962," *CIA Documents*, 26.

8. McCone, "Memorandum of Meeting with the President," 23 August 1962, *CIA Documents*, 27–29.

9. Chang and Kornbluh, eds., "National Security Action Memorandum No. 181," 23 August 1962, 62.

10. McCone, "Memorandum . . . ," 23 August 1962, 28.

11. Ibid., 29.

12. J. A. M. [McCone] Memorandum, "Proposed Plan of Action for Cuba," 21 August 1962, *CIA Documents*, 32.

13. Sorensen, 670.

14. Brugioni, 111.

15. Ibid., 113–114.

16. Ibid., 102.

17. Ibid., 105.

18. Ibid., 114.

19. McGeorge Bundy, *Danger and Survival* (New York: Random House, 1988), 415.

20. James G. Blight and David A. Welch, *On the Brink: Americans and Soviets Reexamine the Cuban Missile Crisis*, 2nd ed. (New York: Noonday Press, 1990), 177.

21. Ibid., 140.

22. Ray S. Cline, Memorandum for Acting Director of Central Intelligence, "Recent Soviet Military Actions in Cuba," 3 September 1962, *CIA Documents*, 37.

23. *Alleged Assassination Plots . . .* , 142.

24. [Richard Lehman], Excerpt from Memorandum for Director of Central Intelligence, "CIA Handling of the Soviet Buildup in Cuba," 14 November 1962, *CIA Documents*, 99–102, esp. 100.

25. Bruce J. Allyn, James G. Blight and David A. Welch, *Back to the Brink: Proceedings of the Moscow Conference on the Cuban Missile Crisis, January 27–28, 1989* (Lanham, Maryland: University Press of America, Inc., 1992), 53.

26. National Intelligence Estimate 85-2-62, "The Situation and Prospects in Cuba," 1 August 1962 (Excerpt), *CIA Documents*, 10–11.

27. Ibid., 11.

28. Ibid.
29. Chang and Kornbluh, eds., CIA Intelligence Memorandum, "Recent Soviet Military Aid to Cuba," August 22, 1962, 59.
30. Ibid., 60.
31. Ibid., Defense Department/Joint Chiefs of Staff, "Projection of Consequences of U.S. Military Intervention in Cuba," prepared for Special Group Augmented, August 8, 1962, 50–51.
32. Ibid., 51.
33. McCone, "Proposed Plan of Action for Cuba," 31.
34. Ibid., 32.
35. McCone, Memorandum for the File, "Discussion in Secretary Rusk's Office at 12 o'clock, 21 August 1962," *CIA Documents*, 23.
36. Chang and Kornbluh, eds., "National Security Action Memorandum No. 181," 61–62.
37. Hershberg, 252.
38. Chang and Kornbluh, eds., W. W. Rostow, "Memorandum to the President," September 3, 1962, 66–68.
39. *The New York Times*, August 8, 1962, 11; August 9, 1962, 10.
40. *The New York Times*, August 30, 1962, 8.
41. *Congressional Record*, August 31, 1962, 18360.
42. Ibid.
43. Ibid., 18361.
44. The most serious effort to date has been made by Thomas G. Paterson, "The Historian as Detective: Senator Kenneth Keating, the Missiles in Cuba, and His Mysterious Sources," in *Diplomatic History*, vol. 11, no. 1 (Winter 1987), 67–70.
45. *Congressional Record*, September 6, 1962, 18729.
46. Robert F. Kennedy, *Thirteen Days: A Memoir of the Cuban Missile Crisis* (New York: W.W. Norton & Company, 1969), 25–26.
47. Sorensen, 667.
48. *The New York Times*, September 12, 1962, 1.
49. McCone to Carter, "Cable, 7 September 1962," *CIA Documents*, 51–52.
50. Lyman B. Kirkpatrick, Memorandum to the Director, "Action Generated by DCI Cables Concerning Cuban Low-Level Photography and Offensive Weapons," (no date), *CIA Documents*, 41.
51. Beschloss, *Crisis Years*, 564.
52. *Public Papers of the Presidents of the United States: John F. Kennedy, 1962* (Washington, D.C.: U.S. Government Printing Office, 1963), 674.
53. McCone to Carter, "Cable, with attached note from MSC [Carter]," 16 September 1962, *CIA Documents*, 77–79.

54. Special National Intelligence Estimate 85–3-62, "The Military Buildup in Cuba," *Missile Crisis Files—NSA.*
55. Ibid., 2.
56. Ibid.
57. Ibid., 8.
58. Ibid., 9.

Chapter 8

1. "CINCLANT Historical Account of the Cuban Missile Crisis—1963," 29 April 1963, 41, *Missile Crisis Files—NSA.*
2. Ibid.
3. McCone, "Memorandum of Discussion with Mr. McGeorge Bundy, Friday, October 5, 1962, 5:15 P.M.," *CIA Documents,* 115.
4. Ibid.
5. Sherman Kent, "Memorandum for the Director . . ." *CIA Documents,* 119–122.
6. Memorandum, "U-2 Overflights of Cuba, 29 August through 14 October 1962," 27 February 1963, *CIA Documents,* 127–137, esp. 136.
7. Brugioni, *Eyeball to Eyeball,* 135–140, 159–160.
8. Ibid., 155.
9. Ibid., 151–152.
10. *Congressional Record,* October 9, 1962, 22888–90.
11. Ibid., October 10, 1962, 22957.
12. McCone, "Memorandum on Donovan Project," 11 October 1962, *CIA Documents,* 123–125, esp. 123.
13. Ibid.
14. McCone, "Memorandum of MONGOOSE Meeting Held on Thursday, October 4, 1962," *CIA Documents,* 111–113, esp. 111.
15. Ibid., 111.
16. Ibid., 112.
17. John McCone, "Memorandum of Discussion with Mr. McGeorge Bundy, Friday, October 5, 1962, 5:15 P.M.," *CIA Documents,* 115.
18. Ibid., 116.
19. Richard Helms, Memorandum for the Record, "MONGOOSE Meeting with the Attorney General," 16 October 1962, *CIA Documents,* 153.
20. Ibid., 153–154.
21. Ibid., 154.
22. MSC [Carter], Memorandum for the Director, "MONGOOSE Operations and General Lansdale's Problems," 25 October 1962, *CIA Documents,* 311; McCone, "Memorandum of MONGOOSE Meeting in the

JCS Operations Room, October 26, 1962, at 2:30 P.M.," 29 October 1962, *CIA Documents,* 319–320.

23. Chang, *Chronology,* 42, 113; CINCLANT, *Historical Account,* 6.

24. U.S. Air Force Historical Division Liaison Office, Headquarters, U.S. Air Force, "The Air Force Response to the Cuban Missile Crisis," 21, *Missile Crisis Files—NSA.*

25. Historical Division, Joint Secretariat, Joint Chiefs of Staff, "Chronology of JCS Decisions Concerning the Cuban Crisis," 21 December 1962, 7, *Missile Crisis Files—NSA,* hereafter *JCS Chronology.*

26. CIA Memorandum, "Probable Soviet MRBM Sites in Cuba," 16 October 1962, *CIA Documents,* 140.

27. Kennedy, *Thirteen Days,* 27, 31.

28. Ibid., 31.

29. Chang and Kornbluh, eds., "Transcript of the first Executive Committee Meeting, October 16, 1962, 11:50 A.M.–12:57 P.M.," 88.

30. Ibid.

31. Ibid., 96.

32. Ibid., 91.

33. Ibid., 90.

34. Ibid., 91.

35. *JCS Chronology,* 11–12.

Chapter 9

1. Beschloss, *Crisis Years,* 469.

2. *JCS Chronology,* 14.

3. Kennedy, *Thirteen Days,* 36.

4. Arthur M. Schlesinger, Jr., *Robert Kennedy and His Times* (Boston: Houghton Mifflin, 1978), 511.

5. Bundy, *Danger and Survival,* 397–98.

6. Ibid., 416.

7. *JCS Chronology,* 15.

8. McCone, "Memorandum for the File, 'Memorandum of Meeting October 17th at 8:30 A.M. and again at 4:00 P.M.,' " 19 October 1962, *CIA Documents,* 170.

9. Kennedy, 34.

10. McCone memorandum, "Brief Discussion with the President—9:30 A.M.—17 October 1962," *CIA Documents,* 165.

11. McCone, "Memorandum of Meeting, Wednesday, October 17th," 170; Kennedy, 37.

12. McCone, "Memorandum to USIB Members," 19 October 1962, *CIA Documents,* 193–94.

13. *JCS Chronology*, 16–17.
14. Ibid., 17–18
15. "Joint Evaluation of Soviet Missile Threat in Cuba," 18 October 1962 (Excerpt), *CIA Documents*, 187–191, esp. 188.
16. Ibid., 189.
17. Ibid., 190.
18. Special National Intelligence Estimate 11-18-62, "Soviet Reactions to Certain US Courses of Action on Cuba," 19 October 1962 (Excerpt), *CIA Documents*, 197.
19. Ibid., 198–99.
20. Ibid., 199, 201–202.
21. *JCS Chronology*, 19.
22. Ibid., 20.
23. Beschloss, 479.
24. Brugioni, *Eyeball to Eyeball*, 352.
25. Elie Abel, *The Missile Crisis* (Philadelphia and New York: J.B. Lippincott Company, 1966), 91.
26. Chang, *Chronology*, 147.
27. Blight and Welch, *On the Brink*, 63–64.
28. Chang, *Chronology*, 201.
29. Ibid., 209.
30. Graham T. Allison, *Essence of Decision: Explaining the Cuban Missile Crisis* (Boston: Little, Brown, 1971), 168.
31. Kennedy, 119.
32. Kennedy, 54.
33. *JCS Chronology*, 25.
34. Air Force Response, 6, *Missile Crisis Files—NSA*.
35. *JCS Chronology*, 32–33.
36. *JCS Chronology*, 34–35; Chang, *Chronology*, 162–63.
37. Intelligence Memorandum, "Evaluation of Offensive Threat in Cuba," 21 October 1962, *CIA Documents*, 238.
38. MSC [Carter], Memorandum for the Director, "MONGOOSE Operations and General Lansdale's Problems," 25 October 1962, *CIA Documents*, 311–12.
39. "Supplement 7, to Joint Evaluation of Soviet Missile Threat in Cuba," 27 October 1962, (Excerpt) *CIA Documents*, 325.
40. Ibid., 324.
41. *JCS Chronology*, 52.
42. Chang and Kornbluh, eds., "CINCLANT's request to have tactical nuclear weapons available for U.S. invasion force," December 29, 1962, 176.
43. *JCS Chronology*, 64–65.

44. Abel, 134.
45. Central Intelligence Agency Memorandum, "The Crisis, USSR/Cuba," 24 October 1962, *CIA Documents*, 296.
46. Chang and Kornbluh, eds., " 'Cuba Fact Sheet,' U.S. military preparedness information provided to President Kennedy," October 27, 1962, 193.
47. Ibid., 191–92.
48. [McCone], "Memorandum of Meeting attended in Secretary Ball's Conference Room . . . at 0830, 17 October," *CIA Documents*, 160.
49. Chang and Kornbluh, eds., "Transcript of Executive Committee meeting, October 27, 1962," 209.
50. Chang and Kornbluh, eds., McGeorge Bundy, "Executive Committee Minutes, October 23, 1962," 157.
51. Beschloss, 531.
52. Kennedy, 98.
53. Walter S. Poole, "How Well Did the JCS Work?," *Naval History*, Winter 1992, 20–21.
54. Chang and Kornbluh, eds., "Transcript of the Executive Committee meeting, October 27, 1962," 215.
55. Khrushchev Message of October 26, 1962, "Kennedy–Khrushchev Correspondence," *Problems of Communism*, Spring 1992, Vol. XLI, 43.
56. *JCS Chronology*, 48.
57. *JCS Chronology*, 49.
58. Chang and Kornbluh, eds., "Transcript of the Executive Committee meeting, October 27, 1962," 209.
59. Beschloss, 530.

Chapter 10

1. Chang and Kornbluh, eds., "Transcript of the Executive Committee meeting, October 27, 1962," 205.
2. "Khrushchev Message of October 28, 1962," *Problems of Communism*, Spring 1992, Vol. XLI, 52–54.
3. *JCS Chronology*, 53.
4. Beschloss, *Crisis Years*, 544.
5. Schlesinger, *Robert Kennedy*, 524.
6. Memorandum to the Director, "Your Briefings of the NSC Executive Committee," 3 November 1962, *CIA Documents*, 354–55.
7. *JCS Chronology*, 57.
8. Ibid., 61.
9. Ibid., 64.
10. "Kennedy Message of October 27, 1962," *Problems of Communism*, 50.

11. Larson, ed., *"Cuban Crisis" of 1962*, "Department of Defense Statement on Removal of Missiles," November 8, 1962, 179.
12. *JCS Chronology*, 53, 55, 60, 64.
13. "Khrushchev Oral Message of November 11, 1962," *Problems of Communism*, 85.
14. Chang and Kornbluh, eds., General Maxwell Taylor, "Chairman's Talking Paper for Meeting with the President," November 16, 1962, 280.
15. *JCS Chronology*, 72.
16. Ibid., 76.
17. Ibid., 81.
18. Ibid., 89.
19. Ibid., 98.
20. Chang, *Chronology*, 314.
21. Ibid., 333–34.
22. Ibid.
23. Ibid., 348–349
24. McCone, "Memorandum of Discussion with Mr. McGeorge Bundy, Friday, October 5, 1962, 5:15 P.M.," *CIA Documents*, 115–16.
25. "Khrushchev Oral Message of November 11, 1962," *Problems of Communism*, 87.
26. Chang and Kornbluh, eds., "Transcript of the first Executive Committee Meeting, October 16, 1962," 88–94.
27. Bundy, *Danger and Survival*, 457.
28. Blight and Welch, *On the Brink*, 144–45.
29. Bundy, 456.
30. Schlesinger, *A Thousand Days*, op. cit., 831.
31. Benjamin C. Bradlee, *Conversations with Kennedy* (New York: W.W. Norton & Company, 1975), 122.
32. Blight and Welch, 80.
33. Ibid., 79.
34. Chang and Kornbluh, eds., Taylor, "Talking Points . . . ," 280.
35. Ibid., 281.
36. Ibid., 280–81.
37. Ibid., 281.
38. Schlesinger, 912.
39. Ibid., 910.
40. Ibid., 912.
41. Beschloss, 633.
42. Chang and Kornbluh, eds., "Transcript of the second Executive Committee meeting, October 16, 1962, 6:30 P.M.–7:55 P.M.," 103.

43. "A transcript of a Discussion about the Cuban Missile Crisis," 1983, *Missile Crisis Files—NSA*, no. 3307.

44. "Retrospective on the Cuban Missile Crisis," 22 January 1983, *Missile Crisis Files—NSA*, no. 3308.

45. Chang and Kornbluh, eds., Sorensen, "Summary of Agreed Facts . . . ," 114.

46. Ibid.

47. Chang and Kornbluh, eds., "Transcript of the first Executive Committee meeting . . . ," 88–89.

48. Ibid., 90.

49. Ibid., 91–92.

50. Ibid., 92.

51. For views of Dillon see Blight and Welch, 158–161; for Nitze's, ibid., 147–151.

Chapter 12

1. Allyn, Blight and Welch, *Back to the Brink*, 50; 65–66.

2. Ibid., 98–100.

Index

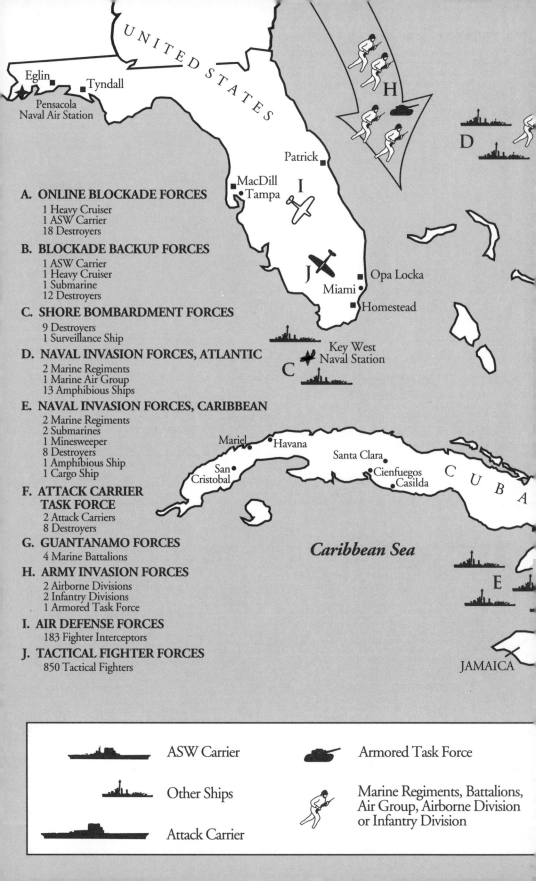

A. ONLINE BLOCKADE FORCES

1 Heavy Cruiser
1 ASW Carrier
18 Destroyers

B. BLOCKADE BACKUP FORCES

1 ASW Carrier
1 Heavy Cruiser
1 Submarine
12 Destroyers

C. SHORE BOMBARDMENT FORCES

9 Destroyers
1 Surveillance Ship

D. NAVAL INVASION FORCES, ATLANTIC

2 Marine Regiments
1 Marine Air Group
13 Amphibious Ships

E. NAVAL INVASION FORCES, CARIBBEAN

2 Marine Regiments
2 Submarines
1 Minesweeper
8 Destroyers
1 Amphibious Ship
1 Cargo Ship

F. ATTACK CARRIER TASK FORCE

2 Attack Carriers
8 Destroyers

G. GUANTANAMO FORCES

4 Marine Battalions

H. ARMY INVASION FORCES

2 Airborne Divisions
2 Infantry Divisions
1 Armored Task Force

I. AIR DEFENSE FORCES

183 Fighter Interceptors

J. TACTICAL FIGHTER FORCES

850 Tactical Fighters

UNITED STATES

Eglin · Tyndall
Pensacola
Naval Air Station

Patrick

MacDill
Tampa

I

J

Opa Locka
Miami
Homestead

Key West
Naval Station

H

D

Mariel · Havana

San
Cristobal

Santa Clara
Cienfuegos
Casilda

C U B A

Caribbean Sea

E

JAMAICA

ASW Carrier

Other Ships

Attack Carrier

Armored Task Force

Marine Regiments, Battalions,
Air Group, Airborne Division
or Infantry Division